SECRETS

BETTY LOWREY

ISBN 979-8-9906818-5-9 (paperback)
ISBN 979-8-9906818-4-2 (eBook)

Printed in the United States of America

Chapter One

Something was bothering him, had bothered him all day. The old expression came to his mind of waiting for the axe to fall. He tried to pray. He was a Minister, for heaven's sakes, but nothing was working. Acid flowed through his stomach pressing up to his esophagus. He was miserable.

God help me. Fear ran icy cold through his veins. I signed on to follow you all my life. Why am I feeling this darkness of the soul? Why is it, Lord, even when I'm trying, sometimes I feel something is hanging over my head? What do we that follow you do? Press down our own personal fears until our personalities become weak and the only thing we know, is, our soul belongs to you but our minds run rampant. We become as helpless as the sinner who doesn't know you. He felt the chafing, enough to let him know he was a child of God. He did have a heavenly Father. He was just weak today.

He would check on the ladies of the church at their weekly meeting, always doing something to help the community. It was their way of witnessing to those who neither wanted to attend the church or felt a stigma between class of people in the small community. New Haven had its cliques, too.

New Haven Women's Society of the Shining Light Church was hard at work, making lap pads for the shut ins down at Lost Creek Residential Care. Pastor Markel stopped on his way to the sanctuary, to glance in and perhaps say hello to the ladies. They never knew he was there, so busy were they talking and sewing. Hannah Noyes was at the machine, her foot on the pedal, electricity feeding the machine exactly as Hannah drove. Full speed. Kathleen Tanner stood at the ironing board, a pile of lap pads to the right of her, listening.

"I don't know about asking that pastor from Christ Church to do our revival," Hannah Noyes, paused, threading a needle, her mouth puckered and eyes squinted as she tried to push the thread through the hole of the needle. It appeared she wasn't having any luck. "You know city folks do things differently, than we do."

"If he's preaching the word, what harm can come of it?" Kathleen asked. "I didn't expect that from you, Hannah, what with you being younger than the rest of us."

"Well, I was speaking to Vivien Langly and she knows him. She said her son attends his church."

"Really," Mabel Hisaw stopped to pick up the lap pads that were ready and watched as Hannah sewed the end of another, finished and stared back at her. "What would Vivien know? She hasn't darkened the door to this church in years."

"Her husband has been sick." Hannah pulled the thread through and began the tacking on the pad.

"Don't pull that one on me. Vivien didn't come when Bill was well and he wanted to."

"How would you know?" Kathleen's laughter popped through the air, raucous and hearty. "I forgot, you were struck on him when we were young. Just clear forgot that." She slapped her knees. "But Old Vivien stole him away, didn't she?"

Mabel visibly smarted. A retort was on the tip of her tongue, but she reigned it in. "I declare you haven't changed one bit since we were teenagers. You need to grow up."

"Sixty years old and I can still do you in," Kathleen chortled. "Ain't that something? Everybody listen up." Her voice changed to an authoritive commanding level. "We got to clean this mess up, good.

The hall will be filled with people who come in to eat on Wednesday night and who knows what else might come out of this revival if he's as different as Hannah seems to think." Laughter started up behind her words.

"Me? I could use a good shake up here at New Haven. I am tired of the molly-coddling of some folks." She glanced around. "Do you see those holier than thou folks here making lowly lap pads for lowly folks at the nursing home?"

"Special care units," Hannah corrected.

Kathleen's eyes narrowed. "You call it what you want. It's a glorified nursing home with sick folks, folks who got no home due to mean relatives who take everything for themselves and leave nothing for the ones who made the means to have something in the first place." She paused for breath. "As I said, we need to stop this sewing, store everything properly and clean up this hall."

"Sorry, I have to leave. Sally James apologized. I have to take Jeremy for a dentist appointment."

"You still keeping your boy's little one?" Kathleen nodded approval.

Three ladies from the cutting room entered. "We could hear you all the way down the hall. What's going on that's got you excited?"

"Revival," Kathleen boomed. "You ready for it, Margaret? Hannah can't wait to meet the evangelist."

Levi Markel walked on down the hall. So, they couldn't wait, could they? His spirit smarted some at the honesty of the three in conversation. Had he walked in, they would've clammed up. He sighed, heavily, wondering who they meant were the molly-coddled ones. There was no way he could keep everyone happy. No need even trying. And he was tired. Coaching the church team, visiting the shut-in's, not to mention he had a book about ready from the publishers and he had no idea how it would be received. Levi Markel was tired. For all the times he prayed for others, dispensed scripture and advice, used his own car and gas to deliver folks to the doctor, sometimes it hit home, he was underpaid and unappreciated.

Clapping her hands, Suze Norman got their attention. "We did hear what you were saying and so did our pastor. Brother Levi was standing just outside the door." Her eyes wore a troubled expression. "I don't think anything was said to hurt him, but you know he's been pretty tied down lately, with his mother here. With Mrs. Markel being ill, the same old schedule going on at New Haven that has for years, it has to be pretty trying for him, and he is coaching the boy's church team." She tilted her head to one side. "Let's pray for our pastor, how about it?"

"You pray, Suze," Kathleen said. "I've been properly chastised and to top it off, I have to apologize to Mabel." She glanced around the room, landing on Mabel. "I got a bit carried away, like a school girl. I'm truly sorry. I hit you with the teasin' pretty hard. Will you forgive me?" Mabel nodded and Suze prayed.

"Father, God," Suze hand was reaching toward heaven. "We ask you to hear our prayer. Lord, hear us as we thank you for every blessing you bestow upon us; that we can gather In your name to do simple little honors for those in nursing homes who have few to love and care for them. Let us thank you for the life you have given us through your son, Jesus, dying on the cross for our sins. Heavenly Father, we are so unworthy. But we love you and ask you to bless our church, our leader and the people. Dear God, forgive us our iniquities, for we fail you often and we need your forgiveness. Bless this church and the leadership as we encounter Revival. Help us to fall in line and do our part...... Let us remember not to be found standing idly by when the fields are ripe to harvest. Now, Lord we ask a double portion of your love on our pastor. Strengthen him as he leads us. Let him feel the encouragement he needs and make his sermons the lamp we need unto our feet. We love you, praise you and covet your presence wherever we go, Heavenly Father. It is in your name we ask. Amen.

Mabel lingered a moment as the others were finished with the putting away. She touched Suze on the arm, for her attention. "Suze, I wouldn't hurt our pastor for anything. I was a bit angry with Kathleen, did I say anything I shouldn't?"

Suze sweet smile crossed her face. "I'm not even certain he would want us to know he heard." She sighed. "I live too close not to see the lights on in the middle of the night, at their house, Mabel. I think Mrs. Markel's state of health is declining to the point they don't get much rest."

Mabel searched Suze face. Sadness had a way of flitting across Suze like a shadow one couldn't put down. "And why are you up in the middle of the night, Suze? Is it not getting any better?"

Suze shoulders slumped, as her hands came to her breast in a folded position. "No, I miss him more each day. It's been three months since he died and I keep expecting him to walk through the door and call my name."

Mabel pulled her friend into her arms, for a moment's hug, then stepped away to look into Suze face as she said, "It's too soon, dear. When you've lived that many years with one you loved and that one is taken home by God, for whatever the reason, it takes time. Grieving is a hard task."

"I keep telling myself I'll get through this but I do miss him so." Suze wiped the tears from her cheeks. "Seems like I feel ashamed my faith isn't strong enough to ward off this heavy sadness. I know I'm supposed to trust fully in the Lord, but the transition of looking to Wade to help me with things to relying on the Lord, now, isn't that easy. I'm just so inadequate."

Levi settled into his chair, glancing out the window. In the distance he could see the bright yellow shirts of the Crusaders. He had to chuckle. Tom Hanson said sometimes it pressed his patience sorely that not one could hit the ball. "But they're only six and seven year olds." He'd shaken his head.

"Going on twenty," Levi spoke out loud. Reaching for the phone he dialed Joe's number at the Cape, waiting for Joe to pick up. A smile broadened on his face as Joe answered. "How are you, Father Joe?" It was their joke, he called Joe, Father and Joe called him Padre'. Seminary was a number of years back but the comradery remained. They had formed a bond that lasted and often said how fortunate they were their calling to churches was in close enough proximity to visit if needed, and there was always the phone.

"Well, Padre', we buried a dear soul this last week an we're all trying to let her absence sink in."

"Not just a church member, I take it a friend, too."

"Yes, she was. She was part of that group I told you I could always count on. What's up?"

Levi scratched his head, moving about in the squeaking chair, "I hate to ask this, but would you have a person capable of leading the music through revival and it looks like we've lost our piano player, too." Levi's head dropped to stare at the floor, wondering that God would allow that to happen just as the Revival week was upon them and the husband wife team that covered that area of worship was being called out of town due to the wife's mother possibly dying in a hospital in Tennessee. He understood the situation with his own mother's demanding illness but it had put a nick in the Revival's success. He explained the circumstance to Joe. "You know a Revival goes a lot better if there's good singing."

"Let me think on this, Padre'." Joe's first thoughts were of Daniel and Ellen, part of the circle of friends he could count on but asking them to drive sixty miles every night for a week was another thing.

With two sets of twins nothing they did was taken lightly. Those boys were all over the place."

They talked a few minutes longer, verifying the Revival's schedule. Their conversation ended, left both pastors staring out the windows. Their calling was about the good times, weddings, births, celebrations, but it was also ladened with sickness, tragedies and death. A man could question the calling, those times when his own life was burdened with his own set of problems. Levi felt a pain of apprehension course through his body that left a gnawing ache in his stomach. How could he bear the pain if Leah left him?

A timid knock at the door, brought Joe away from the window. "I knew it would be you. Come in, Sweetheart." Leah stepped inside and closed the door firmly behind her. While she gathered her thoughts, Levi studied his wife. Frail, he thought. She's frail and he knew her nerves were on edge. "Are you upset, my love?" He asked, gently for these days Leah's emotions swarmed at a moment's notice.

"I can't do it, Levi." Leah twisted her hands together as her head bowed and her hair curtained around her face. "Your mother is spitting up blood." She sighed, sinking into the chair opposite her husband's desk. "I know they said this would happen and I'm sorry. Your mother can't help it but I've got to get away, Levi. I feel as though I'm going to split apart, just lose it all. I've got to go."

He stifled the anxiety he felt. He'd known this was coming. "Where will you go, to your mothers?" The Revival is next week. What will the members of Newhaven think? How will I explain my wife's absence during Revival? The questions hit like balls on the window when Little League triumphed and someone hit a home run that made the distance to the church. But he didn't remind her of Revival. His eyes never left her face, this woman he loved dearly was under attack and most of it was his fault bringing his mother to live with them, the daily care had grown, tantamount, full time. Leah's time.

"I can't go there but I've spoken to my sister. There's no one living with her presently. The children are out on summer sabbaticals of their own and she goes to work every day. I'll be alone most of the time."

Levi's sadness dulled his eyes. "Is that what you want, to be alone?"

"It's what I need. I'm so tired, Levi. I have a lot to think over."

"Are you leaving me, Leah?" Though it pained him, he had to ask. "Are you considering divorcing me?"

"I don't know." A whimper escaped as Leah pressed a hand to her mouth. "It's got to be so much, Levi; If it were any one thing, but it isn't. There's something happening every night and the responsibility I feel I must take in every…" She paused, the words pushing farther, worrying between them. "I loved you, Levi, but lately I'm so tired I don't know how to care for anyone or do any one job effectively."

He arose from the chair. "I'll miss you," he said, gently. "May I hold you?"

She walked into his open arms, laid her head against his chest and listened to the beat of his heart. "I never meant to hurt you, Levi." Her voice sounded as drained as it was. "What will the people think?"

"I don't know."

"Will you lose the church?" Her voice was dim but then responsibility reared its head. "I've called a nursing service to check on your mother each day and they will send someone to stay with her if needed. I'll be going in the morning, Levi."

He could tell her mind was made up. Levi pulled Leah tighter into his arms. "I'll miss you," he said, while his heart whispered, take me with you, but he didn't say it out loud. God, how can I bear this? She is my life. How can you let her go? Didn't I promise I would serve you? Haven't I tried? Why are you doing this?

Chapter Two

Newhaven lay along the river; The Mississippi river. Sixty miles from the Arkansas line one way and ten the other. It was a rural area; farming country. Most of Levi's congregation made their living from the land, and then there were the business's that supported the whole agricultural framework. Most of the members contributed as harvest rolled around, it was then they were assured their bank accounts could stand the offering.

Levi stared through the doorway where Leah was busy packing a suitcase. He saw her place a swimming suit in a Ziplock bag and press it into the corner pocket. Where would she be swimming? For a moment a ludicrous thought entered his mind to which the imaginary angel on his left shoulder scoffed and made faces, no doubt at the red horned entity on his right shoulder.

It was difficult, trying to behave like a pastor when in truth his husband heart was riddled with doubt and animosity that the wife of his youth was leaving him at a most undesirable time, Revival. The ringing of the phone brought him out of the negative thoughts. "Hello," he said into the receiver. Leah paused to listen. "It's Joe," Levi explained. "Well, I'm happy to hear that. Is there anything the Gates will need?"

She had finished packing, closed the closet doors and was trying to carry her suitcase through the rooms. "That conversation," Levi said, taking her suitcase, "Was Joe from Christ Church saying the

Gates couple will lead in worship with music for the Revival. Thank God, with the Hutchen's going out of town, I was wondering how we would handle that situation…you can't have a good Revival without good music." Sitting the suitcase down by the front door, he reached for Leah's hand. "I'm really sorry it has come to this, what with the Revival and strangers coming, it is going to be a bit difficult. You did know Jake and Laurie were going to Tennessee, didn't you?"

"Yes," she mumbled, "to be with Laurie's mother." Rising on tiptoe she planted a light kiss on his lips. "I'll check in with you occasionally."

"Daily?" His grip on her hands tightened. "I feel like I'm falling apart, Leah. Will you call, daily?"

"No. I don't think that is necessary." Her head was down, she did not look up. "Occasionally."

"How long will you be away?"

"I don't know, Levi. We've discussed this."

"No, we haven't. We've danced all around the subject." His voice dropped from Minister status to wounded husband. "You say everything has closed in on you. My mother's presence or her escalating illness has imprisoned you, and the schedule we've always kept is no longer tolerable." He stepped directly in front of her, placing one finger beneath her chin, "Look at me, Leah. Am I no longer tolerable?" He waited, not removing his hand, but she tried shrugging away. "I asked you before, are you leaving me or will you return? What am I to tell our congregation?" He felt his body tremble. "Don't you owe that to me? Seven years down the drain, is that what I'm supposed to think?"

She sighed, slipping out of his reach now, noticing his slumped shoulders, his anger receding to be replaced with despair. "At this point, I'm so tired of it all; I don't know what you should tell them. For your sake, not mine. I've had all I can take, either I leave or explode, and what if I said something to one of your dear parishioners that caused an unamendable rift?"

"My parishioners?" The body trembling turned into a huge shudder. "What could I have done differently?"

"I don't know. Maybe if we could have had children. Seven years without our own to hold in our arms and saying all the right words when couples bring their babies before the congregation to be blessed, expecting us to glow happily in their good fortune…I don't know if that disappointment is part of it or not." She sighed, picking up her purse. "Thank you for letting me drive the good car. I've got to go."

Without a word, Levi picked up her suitcase, walked to the car and placed it in the trunk. Silent, he turned back to the house. He had pled his case and lost. How could he dwell on personal problems when it was time for Revival? His thoughts and prayers must be on the community and its people. Then why id his heart ache and feel as though it had dropped to the bottom of his stomach? He hurried inside, made it to the bathroom and threw up until there was nothing left.

Leah couldn't describe her feelings. Was she sad, filled with remorse or relieved? There was a slight sting that she was letting him down. Of all times, when Revival was planned, but she had wanted to leave before and couldn't. Levi was a dear soul. Once she loved him but life had become so fraught, she needed to blame someone and he was the one responsible for every day's schedule. Their world revolved around the church curriculum. That wasn't fair. She was the one neglected but maybe Levi was too.

Levi didn't look back. Leah was backing from the parsonage drive when Larry Smith pulled into the curb and got out, waiting for her. She rolled down the window and smiled up at one of Levi's deacons. "Hey," Larry stooped to peer into the car. "Where you headed?" He patted her hand on the steering wheel, "Figured you and Levi would be finding a few minutes to breathe before the Revival begins."

She hesitated, and then decided to break the news. Larry would circulate it more fairly than most and she hoped without speculation. "I won't be here, Larry. I'm going to spend a week with my sister." She sighed, "Maybe longer."

"Everything all right?" Larry's eyes were in that squinted stage of wanting to ask more but deciding not to. "I mean, Leah, Levi won't know what to do without you, will he?" Larry scratched his head. "We men need you ladies to keep us on the straight and narrow, find things, fix things." He laughed. "Protect us."

Her voice was firm. "Levi will do just fine, Larry. He has this couple coming to take charge of the music. You're his friend, you will be there."

"Yeah?" Larry's expression was dubious. "Whatever you say, you just be safe and don't forget to come back." He watched as she cleared the curb and went on her way. He almost forgot why he'd come to see Levi. With a deep sigh and for some reason a restless feeling he stepped on to the front door to see Levi.

"Hey, buddy, you don't look so good. Are you sick?" Larry stood just inside the door studying Levi.

"Heart sick." Levi motioned him inside. "Larry, I know you are my friend or you wouldn't be here." He pointed to a chair as he slid into the one opposite. "I need to tell you confidentially, before everyone starts jumping to conclusions. All right?" Those sad eyes locked on to Larry's face. "Can you handle it?"

"I'll give it my best." His mind went into a spin. "Is Leah sick, or you? She just told me she's going away a few days." Levi was shaking his head. "I'll shut up and let you tell me."

"It seems my wife, the love of my life, is leaving me. She doesn't know if it is forever or awhile."

"What?" Disbelief shone on Larry's face. "You two are the ultimate example of what a marriage…"

"That's just it, we're not," Levi interrupted. "I don't know if it's having mother with us, the condition of her disease is escalating and going into a Nursing facility is probably in the future, though we were trying to avoid that procedure." Levi slumped, his body easing into a position with his head bowed, his arms on his knees as he stared at the floor. "The timing, Man, the timing couldn't be more wrong with Revival."

"You want to cancel the Revival?" Wheels were spinning in Larry's head. "We can, but there'll be talk."

"For my sake that would be wonderful," Levi sighed, raising his head to meet Larry's stare, "But all the plans have been made. It's not my Revival, it's for the Church." He cringed within his spirit, thinking, "If I just didn't have to explain any of this…if Leah comes back…its better if the church doesn't know the circumstances."

"What are the circumstances?"

"She's tired, tired of our weekly schedule of something going on every night and we have to be there; tired of caring for mother, I guess. It's not that mother complains, there's just things she can't do for herself and Leah has been doing them." He rubbed a hand over his face. He felt as though cobwebs had wrapped around his body, he was stiff on the inside and tied up on the outer. "I don't know, Lar, maybe part of it has to do with our being childless."

Larry whistled. "The Barnes just had that new baby girl and you performed the dedication last Sunday." He shook his head slowly as the scene unrolled in his memory. "I saw tears in Leah's eyes but she was smiling so I thought she was just happy for them. Old Jimmy seems to roll one kid out a year."

"We don't begrudge any of our couples having children, Larry. It's just that Jim and Caroline have five kids in seven years of marriage and we can't even have one." The fact tried Levi, sorely. "We've been to the doctors, tried whatever they suggest but nothing helps. I have my work, Leah doesn't."

"How long have you guys been married?"

"Seven."

Studying that fact a moment, suddenly Larry's face lit up like sunshine. "Seven's a perfect number, brother, just stop worrying and trust in the Lord. He's got your back."

Levi grinned. "I think I was supposed to say that to you." Pushing up from the chair, he reached across to give Larry a hand shake but Larry grabbed him, giving him a bear hug that lifted him off the floor.

"Let's go get the ladder, Bro. Where is it, in the Narnia closet that you walk into and no one may ever see you again?" Larry was pulling him down the hall. "That bill board won't require our finagling's if we install one of those electronic ones you operate from a center inside the church."

"The members of Shining Light Church will never spend ten thousand dollars on such."

"Bro, never say never." Larry was pulling the ladder out of the far corner. "Get the door, Bro." His mind on a dozen things he had planned for the day, were set aside. Levi needed diversion. It was Saturday. He hadn't been fishing in weeks. "You got Sunday's sermon ready to go?"

"It's Revival, Lar." Levi pointed to the magnetized letters Larry was straightening on the metal. "Joe will be bringing the message. He will be here all week." A desolate sigh slipped unbidden from Levi, "Man, I didn't ask for this. God works in mysterious ways, but I just don't need this. My spirit is sorely chaffed."

"Who's the preacher guy got filling in for him?" Lar was climbing down.

"I asked that. He said he's got a lawyer that used to be as wild as a boar, speaking."

"So there's nothing to hold you here. Go lock up. We're going fishing."

"I don't know where Leah put my fishing gear."

"Quit." Larry held up his hand, palm forward. "Stop that. You're procrastinating." All of a sudden, he rushed up the steps, reached the porch, opened the door and turned the lock. "There, that takes care of that. Come on, I've got two poles...they'll be enough."

"I hope you have clothes to fit me if we can't get back in."

Larry laughed. "Do I actually know something you don't know?" His grin was infectious. "Your dear little secretary has a key to your house in the drawer of her desk and it's like pulling hens teeth to make Miss Tully turn loose of it. I know, because that time, when you were away, I had to fix the water leak."

Chapter Three

"Are we about ready?" Daniel scrutinized the twins. "I don't know about this," he voiced his concern out loud and Ruthie heard. He found Ellen in their bedroom. She finished buttoning her blouse, zipped the skirt and handed him the pearls he liked her to wear. "Don't they make these little do-jiggies any larger, love? If they do, let's send these pearls in to the shop and change the clasp. My fingers must be getting thicker or the clasp smaller."

"What were you meaning when you said you didn't know about this?" Ellen flipped her hair, reached for her purse and a stack of music and was ready but she waited for his reply.

"I was questioning whether we are smart taking the twins with us. Sixty miles in the back seat, they'll go to sleep and when we arrive they will be fresh as daisies and Lord help us in the midst of Revival."

"You are leading, I am playing the piano and Ruthie is riding shot gun on the boys. Harriet volunteered to keep the wee ones, but we may have to take them a few. I can't expect Harriet keeping them every night." For a moment Ellen's face crumbled as she went willingly into Dan's arms. "It's hard, Dan, Bitty was always here. She was like a second mother to Ruthie and more like a sister than a friend to me, helping with the children…and now she's gone."

"I know," he patted her shoulders. "I worry about you." He drew her close. "What if this is too much for you? You've not had time to recover from the radiation, much less the surgery or Bitty's death."

Ellen smiled through tears. "I'm fine. Sixty miles is a bit of a push, but at least school hasn't started and the children can sleep late mornings to catch up. I'm almost excited to be playing in service for Joe's friend's revival…and Joe preaching it." She grinned. "So, you got your list and the special for tonight?"

"In your book, I was afraid I'd lose them." He followed her from the room, flipping off the light switch. "All right, Buckaroos," he eyed the boys sitting on the sofa watching cartoon. "Let's roll."

Newhaven

Levi was on the lawn pacing. He'd been ready since five o'clock hoping Joe would arrive early to go over the order of service. The members had opted for six thirty but in view of the song leader and evangelist having to travel sixty miles he's held out for starting at seven. That concerned him, too. Just knowing they had an hour's drive once the service was over didn't seem fair. The days of staying in homes were a thing of the past. Traveling evangelist and those who did Revivals needed more rest than one received staying in the member's homes and there were other unmentioned problems with that, too. Usually, the church rented rooms from the local hotel but the Gates fellow, according to Joe had five children to put to bed each night and the father was a working man. He was only filling the spot to lead singing because the Hutchenson's had to go out of town. Bad timing. Yes, bad timing, just like Leah's leaving and not being present for the Revival. That chaffed his spirit, too, she hadn't called. He was a ship without a sail.

Mabel Hisaw came swishing up the sidewalk carrying a large covered dish and it smelled good. Levi's stomach growled, reminding him he hadn't eaten since the tuna sandwich at lunch.

"Brought something for you, Pastor. Just in case there's reason to chat with someone after service, I'll just sit this in the kitchen. And if it's all right with you I'm going to lay out a few silverware and stack those small plates on the side. Napkins are handy and glasses will be cooling in the frig because I'm going to go ahead and put ice in them so you won't have to do a thing. How does that sound?"

"That sounds wonderful, Mabel. I don't know what I'd do without you."

"Is that your stomach rumbling? Didn't Leah feed you?"

He just as well get it over with. "Leah's out of town, Mabel. She won't be here for the Revival. And no, I haven't eaten."

Mabel didn't bat an eye. "You follow me. There were a few sandwiches left from our lap pad session the other day. I forgot to take them home with me and they'll be just fine for you to eat. Now, come on."

A few minutes later Suze Norman ushered Joe in to find Levi finishing a huge slice of the cake Mabel had brought. "Well, well, well, Father Joe I see you've met Suze and over there is Mabel Hisaw. She's always busy, but she'll get around to you. You want a piece of cake?" Levi was hugging his friend, all the while brandishing a fork in his hand. "We have time and we can nail the schedule while you're at it."

Laughing, Joe accepted the plate Suze was offering. "Nothing more," he said as she asked about a sandwich or a drink. "You've heard of a drum being too tight to play? Well, I have to keep that in mind." There was the sound of piano and Joe smiled. "That means the Gates arrived."

"Would they like a piece of cake?"

“Mercy no, Padre’, those twins would have it all over their face and behind their ears. Ellen would skin me alive.”

There was an understatement of unrest in the congregation. Dan noticed it took the third song to loosen up Shining Light Church voices. He felt reluctance in the people to meld together. What could be problem? There was prayer, an offering taken and Ellen’s piano playing all the while. A sinner would know God is in this place, Daniel was thinking and then it was time for his solo. Ellen gave the introduction. “This is one I wrote, folks,” he said. “I hope you will listen to the words and apply them to your life.” He smiled at Ellen and began. “In the quietness of the night when my heart is troubled sore and I cannot sleep nor rest… and each hour brings me more… when I try to handle all that brings sadness to my soul…you speak to my mind and say I’m blessed. Though I travel down life’s road and my burdens weigh me down, my mind is on me and mine and I ignore those around me who have needs you speak and remind me I am blessed…who has sorrow let him come to the well of comfort and peace, to the one who has secrets hidden let him get down on his knees…for the Father knows the way, salvation is here today…don’t let your burdens weigh you down when the Lord can turn things around… in the assurance of His love, in the quiet of the night…let the Father have your troubles…accept his comfort and his peace…”

Joe reached out to the people, asking them to commit themselves the whole week, to go out into the community and bring the people in. “For the harvest is truly ready,” he said. “When people will not come on their own, then it is our job to ask them and take the opportunity to tell them what the Lord has done for us.”

Before loading up to go home, Daniel and Joe spoke briefly. "That was a good message, Pastor," Daniel was trying to decide whether to speak what was on his mind when Ruthie spoke up.

"Daddy, why is Pastor Levi sad? Did he lose his wife like my Bitty when she died?"

"I don't know, Ruthie. Do you think the congregation is sad?" He and Joe wore guarded expressions.

"He is very sad, Daddy but the people don't know why. They are confused."

Joe mumbled under his breath, so only Daniel could hear. "He told me his wife, Leah, is out of town but I get the feeling there's more."

"She didn't want to be here for the revival," Ruthie said. "She has gone away to think."

"When did you receive that revelation, Ruthie," Daniel stared hard at this child he had adopted. "She's usually right, Pastor Joe." The two men nodded agreement.

"Jesus just told me. That's why Mr. Levi is sad, because she doesn't know if she is coming back."

"How can we go beyond this, Pastor?" Daniel drew a deep breath, waiting. "I couldn't get anyone to open up into real worship, during the song service. It's going to take every prayer we can muster to go beyond this problem."

Pastor Joe shook his head. "You feel the undercurrent don't you? Padre' is saying nothing and the congregation, though in the dark, are shielding him." The long hours of the day were catching up with him. "We've got sixty miles to think on this as we travel home. We can't solve it tonight."

It was later, when the younger twins were retrieved from Harriet's house; the older ones in bed and Ruthie in with Holly and Noel, one on each side of her, Ellen turned out the light and joined Daniel.

"Did you notice the attractive lady in the bright blue dress, Dan?" Ellen slid down beside him on the sofa. "I saw that grin, just now. You did, didn't you? But did you recognize her?"

"Well, in my defense, she was the only pretty one sitting back there and the color of that dress did stand out." He pulled her to his side. "Who is she?"

"That is the woman who wrote Marigold a letter saying she wanted Matt if Marigold was through with him. She is Matt's childhood friend and his mother's choice for daughter in law, in spite of her son being married."

"Are you kidding me?" Daniel leaned forward to stare at Ellen. "What's going on here? First, the pastor's wife has left him. Now you tell me the center of attention to our friend's marriage nearly falling apart is sitting out there in a pew at revival? Is this coincidence, or what? We drive sixty miles to find the devil stirring up another congregation?" He shook his head, wearily pondering this information. "Where does blue dress live?"

"From what Marigold explained to me, she has quite a large farm, left to her when her parents were killed in an accident, that stretches along that same highway the church community is on, possibly she doesn't attend the church of her youth because of a past scandal when she was involved with a married man but I did notice the people from the congregation seemed to know her."

"All we need now is for Marigold's mother-in-law to join us during Revival. Something is quenching the spirit and until the obstacle is removed our efforts are in vain." He sighed. "I feel sorry for Brother Joe. There was hardly any response from the people tonight. They just sit there and stared."

"You, remember to stay away from the owner of the blue dress, Buster."

Daniel settled back pulling her into his arms. Kissing Ellen, he said, "Who looks for hamburger when they have steak?" Yawning, as he kissed the top of her hair, he counted his blessings. "It is time for you to go to bed, my love. We're pushing it as it is. I have to remember your health."

Mabel and Suze were wiping down the back of the pews. Kathleen left early to pick up a grandson.

"How many years have we been doing this, straightening up after every night of Revival?"

Suze stopped, the dust cloth hanging limp in her hand to pick up a can of furniture spray, used it and set it back down as she gazed out the window toward the street where she lived. "It's been many," she replied. "Wade and I were married in nineteen seventy. He brought me home to this little town and that first year we joined Shining Light." She giggled like a girl. "They needed someone to clean up each night and I felt every eye was on me, so I volunteered." A drop of Suze features followed the giggle. Next thing she knew tears were running down her cheeks. "Excuse me," she said, turning toward the rest room. "I thought I was getting better, but sometimes...things catch me off guard."

Mabel laid a hand on Suze as she caught her on the way. "Suze. Come here." Mabel folded Suze to her bosom. "You don't have to apologize. You have lost the love of your life. It is fitting you honor his memory with tears." Suze allowed Mabel to hold her. To Mabel, that was a sign of direct need. She tightened her grip on her friend. "Now, when you want to talk, you call me, I'll listen."

"I'm so ashamed," Suze words came in a torrent of apology between trying to control the sobs that had burst forth, with Mabel's kindness. "Sometimes I don't know what gets into me, I wail." Her chest heaving, Suze glanced around making sure no one else was in listening distance. "You've read how they said the Indians mourned their loss, well…I do that." She slumped down on the nearest pew. "Do you think I'm going crazy?" And she was a bit amazed the usual boisterous Mabel seemed sincere.

"If you are, there's a bunch more out there in the same fix."

Suze gave a half sob, half snort, observing Mabel's troubled expression. "You really care, don't you, or is it that you went through this yourself?"

"I don't think me and Earl had the marriage you and Wade Wade did, Suze. Earl, with all his drinking nearly killed us, financially and our bond of matrimony. By the time he settled down, it was nearly too late, his lungs were bad. We didn't have many years after that."

"But you know the pain of losing someone you love?" Suze persisted. "You couldn't understand, otherwise."

"I'm ten years older than you, Suze. I lost two babies by miscarriage before you and Wade Wade even came to New Haven… then burying a husband…yes, I believe I understand a part of your sadness."

"I wondered that you have no children." Suze turned toward the door. "You know Pastor and Leah," she sighed, searching for words. "They have about given up on having a child…I wonder if that's why Leah's not with us through this Revival. You know the Tally's will be here and they have that new baby."

Mabel sit down beside her. "It looks bad on the part of our pastor, doesn't it?" Mabel picked a hymnal up off the cushion beside her. The pages fell open to What a Friend We Have in Jesus. She studied the words for a moment and then read aloud, "Oh, what peace we often forfeit, Oh, what needless pain we bear all because we do not carry everything to God in prayer." Patting Suze's hand she arose. "That about says it all, doesn't it? I think you and I should hurry on home to get ready for tonight's service."

"If it isn't more receptive tonight than last night, Mabel, I don't see much use to continue."

"That's not our decision," Mabel replied, softly. "Our lot is to pray for whatever is quenching the spirit to leave."

"We have no idea what that is. Do we?" Suze was puzzled. "Am I missing something?"

Mabel walked the three blocks to her home. Retired. No children. No husband. No ties, except she was loyal to the church, there for any service, when the doors were open. It hurt, knowing what she knew. She had told no one to this point and was praying faithfully she wouldn't have to. She found Leah leaving town a confoundment. The whole thing had put a damper on her usual buoyant self. She thought the girl loved her husband enough not to humiliate his leadership during the revival.

Last night tongues were wagging; different ones making up their own stories about the church problem. And there sit Britany, wide eyed and innocent appearing, although her sins were many. Who knew if Britany had repented of her affair with a married man? Then there was the tale going around she tried to disrupt Matt Langley's marriage and of course Vivien was right there in the mix; his own mother. That boy would've been better off if he hadn't come back to help steer the farm through harvest.

Matt was a good boy. She'd like to meet his wife. Rumor had it, his wife had a prosperous shop in the Cape and Matt had won awards for his paintings. She wondered how Nate felt about that. Her troubled heart mellowed considering Nate's interest in the boy. He'd managed through all the childhood years.

She had time for a glass of iced tea and maybe a salad before returning to church. Mabel sank wearily into the old club chair she'd had recovered in material of red yellow and sage stripes. It had been Earl's chair and she'd never sit in it until he died, then for all the misery the man had brought into her life, she sat there and missed him. Misery does love company, she thought and her mind strayed to the other couple who had left town and she said a silent prayer that God would drive sense into that man's head.

Awakening, Mabel had the terrible notion she had slept through the night and missed Revival all together. But the hands on the clock revealed thirty minutes until the second night's service began. How were the two ministers going to pull this one off? She questioned their ability as it mixed in with her prayer that they could.

Seated at the piano, Ellen began to play a reverie of the old hymns. She smiled at her children as they sat on the front row. Ruthie had the babies, one on each side of her and the other two coloring wild strokes of color on the books she'd brought for them. What would I do without her, Ellen wondered. And her heart skipped a beat as she remembered Bitty giving Ruthie all the instructions, she had used herself in loving Ellen's children. Bitty gone, Ellen felt the wave of sadness wash over her as her fingers tripped on the keys missing a note and she brought her mind back to the Revival ready to begin. Pastor Levi introduced Brother Joe from Christ Church in the Cape and opened with prayer.

"I think," Daniel was saying to the congregation, "We will begin this service with Ellen and I singing a duet and when we arrive at the chorus, I want you all to join in. Let's just praise the Lord and let Him come into our hearts." He smiled at Ellen. "Now, someone was kind enough to print off the order of service and if you need a page number, it's there, but we are going to sing through a few hymns and let the Lord bless us and open our spirit to receive his word tonight."

Daniel felt an ease of hearts and minds as the music swelled into the last hymn, To God be the glory, great things He hath done. His own spirit had progressed from concern to thankfulness. Thank you, Jesus, he was thinking. Thank you, Father. Come Holy Spirit come. He listened to Pastor Levi's prayer.

"Lord, we welcome you. Father, we need your forgiveness for our sins. We ask your divine presence to dwell in our midst, to erase the problems of the day that we might think on you, that our hearts are pure, our thoughts clear and your word the lamp unto our feet that you have promised. Lord, wipe us clean that we listen; that if one, Lord, one person is here that does not know you…that one will not rest until they come to you. Now, Lord, feed your servant, anoint him with words we understand through the work of the Holy Spirit. Bless him with boldness to declare the word we must hear. Thank you, Lord Jesus. Amen.

"Everyone said amen." Joe studied the congregation, a few he had met, but most he did not know. "All we like sheep have gone astray," he began, "We have turned each to his own way and the Lord has laid upon Him the iniquity of us all. Isaiah 53:6. What does it mean? The message tonight is this. Jesus took our sins upon himself when he died on the cross. His father laid our sins on his sinless son at Calvary and Jesus paid full ransom for us. How could that be, that the son of God would die for one as worthless as me?" Joe paused and looked beyond the people. His vision was locked on the door that emptied into the vestibule, he stared so long, the people turned to stare at the door as if expecting someone to enter." Who among us has not sinned? In Matthew 7:14," Joe continued, his voice going out to the corners of the room, to ears that strained to hear, caught up in the wonderment of the state of man's heart. "Strait is the gate and narrow is the way which leadeth unto life and few there be that find it. Now wait a minute, what does the preceding verse say? Enter ye in at the straight gate, for wide is the gate and broad is the way that leadeth to destruction and many there be which go in. Going the wrong way is easy but the right way has confinements. Straight is the gate and narrow is the way which leadeth unto life…and few there be that find it. Shouldn't that be our chWadege, instead of being disagreeable and showing the world we can do what we want? Why is it, we don't want anyone to tell us we can't?"

"We are a contrary people. Someone gives us instruction, we don't want it, we want to find our own way. Warn a child not to do something…what do they do?" Joe smiled. "But, you say, I'm an adult I have the right…do you? Do I? Have we given our life for anyone? If we are Christians, do we owe it to our Savior to follow the scripture? If we are unsaved, do we realize the consequence?"

"This is where the message gets serious." Brother Joe leaned across the pulpit. "Now we know, in the Bible we can read of those in New Testament times who died and were brought back to life, for instance Lazarus. I encourage you to read about Lazarus when you return to your home. But the majorities of us are going to die and stay dead, and then comes judgement. Unlike Lazarus, Hebrews 9:27 reads, "It is appointed unto man, once to die, but after this, the judgement."

"My question to you, is, if you walk out of this building and die tonight, where will you spend eternity? Is it time to turn your life around, quit going your own way, doing your own thing, hurting yourself and others? Is it time to realize Jesus paid the price for my sin, your sins…but unless we bow down before him, confess those sins and ask forgiveness, we will lose the gift he gave us. What is that gift? You know. When he died on that cross, Jesus gave us the gift of eternal life."

"I'm going to ask you, as Ellen plays, to bow your heads now and do business with the Lord. You are the only one knows what you need to do. God is present and the Holy Spirit is speaking to hearts."

Mabel felt the Vanduser kid squirming, as he stood next to her. She glanced down to see his hands clenched tightly to the bench in front, as if it were his life line and she smiled to herself, in fact letting go and going forward was his lifeline. She'd had Billy Joe in youth class long enough to know while he was a good boy, he was also a rascal of sorts, meaning where there was action Billy would be there. No telling what he'd been up t, but those were her own private thoughts and thinking these days was causing problems. She gave a quick peek down the aisle to the other side and sure enough there stood Britany. Now there's one needs repentance. She almost sighed out loud except she heard the pastor closing the Revival. Well, maybe tomorrow Billy and Britany would wise up and go forward. Tonight was better.

"Two nights down and three to go," Daniel said, as he and Ellen each slipped pajamas on their own little ward. Already Ruthie, Daniel and Samuel were sound asleep. "What do you think? How are you holding up?" He couldn't help but worry over Ellen's fatigue. Radiation had its side effects.

Yawning, Ellen nodded. "I'm tired but so are these two sleeping right through clothes change." She smiled. "I felt better about the services tonight. It was so obvious something was amiss, last night," her eyes met his. "Do you think it was the congregation having to come to grips with their pastor's wife being gone?"

"In a small town, like Newhaven, word travels fast and assumptions are made. By now, in the community's view, I'd say the majority believe she has left him, divorce is imminent and there's no turning back."

"He really is a basket case." Ellen was gathering Holly and Noel's soiled clothes. "He is trying hard not to let his congregation see, but a pastor whose church is holding revival needs the support of his wife."

"They're no different than us, are they?" He took the clothes from her arms. "Spend a few minutes on yourself. I'll take care of these." Still, he waited. "Are they any different, El?"

"No. But a congregation never sees it that way. Those called to ministry have problems just like anyone else. But she was part of the deal when Levi signed contract to lead the people, it must weigh on her heavily. We know it does Levi."

"We just met the people and already we're concerned for them." Daniel set two little pair of shoes on the bedside table lamp. "I saw the girl you pointed out as Marigold's contention was there again."

"May the Lord help us that Marigold and Britany never run into each other. I can't imagine how that would go." Ellen was in the adjoining bath room, removing her make-up, viewing Daniel from the mirror.

"I don't believe Matt ever did anything wrong. He loves Marigold too much." He grinned, mischievously, waiting a moment for Ellen's response to his next words. "That girl is a looker."

"Just remember, daddy of two sets of twins, look but no touch." A wet wash cloth hit him on the shoulder. "You, the song boy. Me, piano girl. Looker no exists in our world." She turned to face him, one finger wagging in the air. "I got you babe."

"Yeah, maybe we could do that song for the opening of Revival tomorrow night. Hmm. Sonny and Cher. Who woulda thought it, but you?" He left as she ran water over a second washcloth.

Ellen felt the tiredness but she was happy. Men like Daniel Gates were hard to find. For a moment she considered why the contender to Matt's affection, as Daniel called her, was there in Shining Light Church and if she was there what was the likely hood in the next three nights of Vivien Langly making an appearance? Then Pastor Levi's troubled countenance crossed her mind and she was resolved it was time to pray and put to rest any supposition on her part…but what about the absent Leah, whom she had not met?

Chapter Four

Leah heard the doorbell ring, to her sister's home. She hadn't told Levi that Candace was away for the week, on her own private brand of vacation which had no appeal whatsoever to Leah, and was the reason she'd turned down the invitation and then asked if she could use her sister's home a few days.

"You're on your own," Candace had quipped. "I'll be snorkeling while you hole up here, sure you don't want to go?"

Now, Jake was waiting on the steps; a smile wreathe his face as she opened door, pausing, as he ask am I late?" He stepped into the room, aware for a moment all the plans they'd made so hastily were suddenly like a knife stabbing him in the chest. But they'd agreed only to talk, nothing wrong with that.

"Laurie's not with you?" Leah peeked to the outer curb before closing the door and leading him into the living room. "I've had second thoughts on this, Jake, I don't know if it's a good idea or not."

He halted behind her. "I can leave right now." But his hand was on her arm, turning her to face him. "We agreed; we need to talk. What we are experiencing at church under two hundred sets of eyes is a bit sobering. We are having these feelings and we aren't sure what to do about them."

Leah's eyes brimmed with tears. "I wonder if we should have separately sought counsel on this, Jake."

"Why bring a third party into it," Jake's voice was serious, soft and inviting. "Why don't we sit?"

"Where's Laurie?"

"In the hotel room, all comfy, reading her favorite writer's latest offering. Lauri's fine."

"I don't know how she does it. I think that's what has drawn us to each other. Laurie can't have a baby and I can't…"

"Laurie doesn't want a child and never has." For a moment there was a sharp edge to Jake's words. "You do and I understand the frustration. I'm a doctor, for heaven's sakes, Leah, its part of my…"

"But," she interrupted, "there's no way we can help each other. That day when I was sick and came to your office, I never meant to discuss my and Levi's disappointment that I have never conceived. It just slipped out. I was vulnerable to your kindness."

"I could tell it made you uncomfortable under the scrutiny of my nurse. That's why I found a way at church to ask if you would like to meet." His head tilted, eyes a serious match to her own, he was aware of her indecision, that she had revealed insecurity in her marriage much as he felt in his own. "I tell you what, why don't we leave here, go out and have a bit of fun and let the conversation flow naturally?"

"What about Laurie? What if we meet someone we know? What would they think?"

"Laurie's settled in for the night. I told her I was making a house call on a patient and that it might take a while. I do this, Leah. You don't have to worry and we are a hundred miles from home." He smiled. "Is that good enough?" He was rising, holding out his hand. "I felt you needed confidentiality, for whatever was on your mind."

It was almost a flash of warning, but Leah decided it was truth surfacing, she was ready to close the door on her insecurities and whatever she was inviting into her life she was completely aware if there were consequences to confiding in someone from the church she trust, then she would face them. What about your husband? The question popped into her mind like a lit up billboard on the highway. Wrinkling her nose in defiance, she heard his laugh. "What?" She stared up at him, holding her hand.

"Evidently you aren't aware, I've stood here watching the expressions on your face. It's as though some world event is playing out in your mind."

"It is."

"Have you eaten?"

"No. I forgot."

His laughter was like gentle rain on her soul. "Come on, then. I'll treat you to the best taco in town."

It was good to smile again. Retrieving her keys and a light jacket from the table where she'd laid them earlier, Leah followed the good doctor.

An hour later, sitting across the table from Jake, listening to the old fashioned juke box playing Patsy Cline's I'm Sorry, they had exhausted themselves with stories from teenage years, firsts of marriage and now it was time to leave. Jake would resume his stay with Laurie. Leah would return to her sisters.

"So how is your wife's mother? Isn't that why you are here?"

Jake rubbed the end of day stubble on his chin. 'Yeah, she's not doing well, not going to make it, I'd say but there's always hope. Isn't there?" His eyes settled on Leah. "We are staying at the hotel because the whole family is in and you can hardly stir them with a stick." He sighed. "But, let's talk about hope. There is still hope to correct whatever's going on in your marriage." He asked it as a question.

Leah unconsciously went into a protective stance, her shoulders rounded. "I'm not sure what's going to happen." Moving the salt and pepper shakers to the far end of the table, she asked, "And you, how's your marriage?"

"Truth?" His hands met hers, stilled the movement on the table and held both. "There's a part of me loves Laurie, to the last breath so to speak, but we've somehow gotten this barrier and we sometimes tiptoe around certain subjects…just to ward off disfavor. Simply put, we are tired of the discord."

"Over the matter of children?"

"Yes." A sadness flit across his face. "There will be none."

"Then, how can you possibly understand my situation?"

"Because, like me, you want a child, Laurie doesn't." Jake shook his head. "I need to clear the cobwebs out of my brain. I'm a doctor stuck in a one horse town, going nowhere and my marriage is too."

Leah removed her hands. "Did you speak to Levi about this?"

"No." Jake sat up straighter "I'd be too embarrassed. Not being able to have a child would be one thing but your wife not wanting children, period, that's another." He closed his eyes tight. "She only wants us." Now he stared at her. "I feel disloyal to Laurie but it feels good to get it out of my system with you."

Leah started to rise. "I don't know what I was thinking, accepting seeing you…like this…but when you said there was something you wanted to talk over and would I see you this weekend…I didn't even tell Levi, because I already had this trip to my sister's planned."

"Why, Leah? Why would you do that when Revival is in progress and you know Levi needs you there?"

"I wonder, myself." Leah was quiet for a moment, then drawing a deep breath, replied. "We have lost what we once had. The disappointment of not having a child bears heavily on me these days. I don't know why but I felt if I didn't get away I would explode. Men don't understand. No one does."

There was sadness in his smile. "Do you really believe that?" He collected the jacket she'd hung on the back of her chair and placed it around her shoulders, noticing the thinness; she was almost frail.

"I'll walk you to your door," he said as they pulled into her sister's drive. "And I do thank you for your time. There's really not anyone I feel free to…" He was removing the keys from the ignition.

"Don't." She opened the door and slid out quickly. "It was nice, Jake, but may be a mistake."

"I'd like to see you again, Leah." For a moment she felt stricken. What had she been thinking? She shook her head and turned toward the house. She fumbled the key in the door and then it caught. She was relieved to hear the car leave.

Pulling a pair of pajamas out of her sister's drawer, she undressed and slipped into bed needing the creature comfort that her sister kept there for her. But what would she say if she knew about tonight? Doesn't matter, it's over. She yawned, turned to where the Bible lay on the bedside table and as was the habit she and Levi shared found the scripture reading for the month. They were in Philippians and tonight's reading was verses one through five. 'If there be therefore any consolation in Christ, if any comfort of love, if any fellowship of the Spirit, if any bowels and mercies, Fulfill ye my joy, that ye be like minded, having the same love, being of one accord of one mind. Let nothing be done through strife or vainglory, but in lowliness of mind let each esteem other better than themselves. Look not every man on his own things, but every man also on the things of other. Let this mind be in you, which was also in Christ Jesus.'

She had done nothing wrong. Still, she felt wary, that she a married woman had sit at table with a married man and they had discussed intimate subjects when they both felt the emptiness, and unfulfilled need. Now the first verse questioned. Did she have comfort in fellowship of the spirit, where was her heart these days? She had abandoned Levi and the congregation in time of Revival; at a time when she thought she could no longer face the monotony of expectation on their life, day after day. She tossed and turned until near daylight when she fell into troubled sleep to dream a doctor was chasing her down the hall and all the doors to the rooms were locked. There was no escape.

A few days later she read Laurie's mother's obituary in the newspaper and wondered if she should attend the funeral. The same day Levi called. "I miss you, Leah. Please come home." She heard the break in his voice. "The Revival ended. There were two came by faith and three joined by letter." He sounded wounded in the spirit when he should be rejoicing. "I'm grateful for those, Leah, but I've too much time on my hands now. I think only of you." She placed the phone back on the cradle, whispering words he did not hear.

Monday morning Daniel helped Ellen unpack the diaper bags and as Ruthie called Daniel and Samuel's bag the Go Bag, containing whatever Ruthie had deemed necessary to keep the older twins quiet through the evening message but he wasn't certain the potato he found in it was considered acceptable. He placed it on the bedside table. Surely the boys weren't into raw potatoes for snacks.

"Well, love, the Revival could not bring forth a great harvest when the church people were tied up in whether their pastor's wife had left him or not, and why the beautiful Britany had returned to their midst, could it?" He felt the thud of an item hit his back and turned to Ellen, the twinkle in his eyes revealing the fact his words had been planned for effect. "What?"

"Don't play innocent with me, Buddy. I see that smile. You are trying to get a rise out of me." She snorted. "Beautiful, huh?" She stood in the center of the room surveying the children's bags, a pile of laundry waiting for the washer, her own clothes on hangers in various spots around the room. "Why, may I ask, was this mother of five playing the piano in a small town Revival when they had an accomplished person such as her there all the time? Why didn't they ask her?"

"Hmm. Could it be they still remember she had an affair with a married man and maybe, just maybe she has yet to confess her sins and rectify her status in the community... she is from that community, isn't she?" He came up behind her, pulled her into his arms and backed down into the nearest chair. "Are you worn out?"

She smiled, her arms going around his neck. "For my answer, could I just sit her all day?"

He pulled her comfortably into his lap, pressing her head on his shoulder. "Yes. If four of the five children don't interrupt." He kissed her on the neck. "Ruthie never bothers...but your other four..."

Daniel ran into the room, followed by Samuel. It was clear one had something the other wanted.

"Whoa. Whoa. Whoa." Daniel's voice rose with each word. "What's going on?"

"Daddy, Daniel got my potato. He lost his." Samuel opened his hand to display miniature body parts.

Ellen was disembarking from pure comfort. "Daddys got to go to work. Momma's got laundry to do." She stooped down to draw the boys, one into each arm. "Do you suppose we could find another potato and the two of you do your very best to build a body for Mr. Potato and tonight," she glanced to Daniel still sitting in the chair, "maybe tonight Daddy will bring home a surprise and we'll have a look at what you have built. Can you do that?"

"I don't know where my potato is," Daniel whimpered. "I lost it."

"How about that potato over there, by the lamp?" Daniel pointed, eyebrows raised comically as he glanced at Ellen.

"Daddy. Daddy," Daniel's expression changed instantly. "That's my potato."

The boys were running from the room. “Good, Daddy.” Ellen smirked, leaning to give him a smooch on the lips. “How’d you know that potato was Daniel’s?” He was pulling her back onto his lap.

“A good daddy knows everything.” He was nibbling at her neck, trailing up to her lips. “I know I’d be lost without you.”

“Then help me up. You can’t imagine what those two will do next and you can’t see their finished Mr. Potato Head until tonight.” She sighed, content. “Or, you could stay home and help with laundry, but then there’s the surprise.” He groaned and she laughed. “There’s no place like home, Bud. Dorothy’s right.”

Newhaven’s finest were on the street early. Suze waved as they drove past. She tried to walk in the early morning hours before the humidity rose to its throat choking stage. One thing for certain, the weather with its high heat index had taken control of their lives.

Revival had ended. The Sunday night crowd had paid honor to the evangelist and the song leader and his wife by attending and staying for the ice cream social though she knew most of them had rather be home watching the Cardinals play on television.

Their pastor’s wife had not attended any service and this concerned all. Bereft, that described him; as bereaved and mourning as if she had died and maybe she had died to this community. Death. Suze counted the days since Wade went to his Creator. One hundred ninety three days since she’d laid him to rest, except she hadn’t found rest herself. Why she could walk at three in the morning if she so desired. Sleep had become an elusive thing. On her bureau were endless pictures of Wade. When she couldn’t sleep she studied those pictures that represented their life together.

Now, as she finished the walk and entered her house, the quietness was deafening. Tears streamed down her cheeks. She was a believer and berated herself for her depth of grief. "Wade." She whispered, then, "Jesus, help me." She always thought of Mabel, who had lost her husband and an only son. Mabel seemed strong, "but I'm not," Mabel had whispered once when she was trying to console Suze. "I didn't have the sweet loyalty from my husband you did, Suze. That might make a difference." Still, out of the women at Shining Light Church, Mabel was the one understood her pain. "Give it time," she'd say. Suze couldn't help but remember in their younger days Mabel's name had been coupled with Nate Watson's. Being five years younger changed the nature of things, but ten, nearly impossible to make connections and now widowhood made them equal.

The ringing of the phone brought her around to the present. "Hello." She listened. Laurie Hutchenson's mother had passed. The funeral would be in the city where she lived but there was some sort of tribute the church would pay to Laurie on Sunday next. "Then, there's this thing with our pastor." Mabel's voice went on, "He is so down in the dumps. I don't know what we can do to bring him out of them." Mabel paused to breathe deep. "This humidity is going to kill us all. Oh, yes, and the other thing is, Pastor is going to the city to attend funeral today. So we should say a pray for him and as Kathleen said, "That wife of his, too." Mabel laughed. "Only Kathleen can coin a phrase."

Suze held her tongue, though she wanted to mention seeing Jake Hutcheson speaking with their pastor's wife. Fact was, she believed Mabel overheard the conversation and to Suze it sounded like making a date rather than an appointment by the town's only physician. Suze shuddered. Could Shining Light stand another embarrassment? The last one involving Britany James and Kirk Stanfield was bad. The Stanfield's had moved away to prevent any encounter with the third party of the affair and that party had showed up in the week's Revival as though taunting the members to do something about it.

She had to admit, Kirk Stanfield was eye candy for women who needed that kind of titillation. He was an outgoing man of such physical attraction even Tully, the church secretary smiled when he came around. "Kirk grew up here," she'd say in that down home southern drawl. "He's been away up Not'h, married a little Northern girl. She's Methodist." Tully related the last as though it were heaven's sin. "We never see her, word has it she bides time between Newhaven and wherever it is her Momma lives." Tully would sigh as if Kirk were her own. "Our boy gets a little restless, sometimes."

The main problem with Britany James, Suze reflected, was being spoiled by elderly parents. The girl was straight as a board, wore clothes like a model and always had the dime to spend on anyone. Maybe someone should have stepped in and told Britany that Kirk Stanfield was married and that it was said his little dark eyed bride from up North possessed a quick temper. She just might come bearing arms. And she did a baseball bat! Come to find out there were children. "Didn't he keep that well-hidden?" Tully quipped, as though he'd won the Oscar for best actor. "Well, you're right," she conceded. "He needs to straighten up." On the other hand, the community's gossip grapevine labeled Britany a harlot.

Staring at Wade's picture, Suze shook her head. "What a mess." She kissed his picture. "I miss you."

Chapter Five

Sunday morning, Levi awakened to the sound of the fire alarm; jumping up to run to the window as it sounded unreasonably close. If it could, his hair stood on end. A stream of water was directed through one of the windows of Shining Light Church. What was happening? Hastily, he donned clothing. Oh, Lord, Please, Lord, don't let them break that stained glass window the Hopkins bought. I'll never hear the last of it. Please Lord, please. He prayed as he ran toward the sanctuary with parking lot in between.

"We've about got it, Reverend," Jerry Caulley called as Levi approached. "Were you planning a baptism, maybe, this morning?" Levi nodded. "Well, that's where it started up around the baptistery." He saw Levi's shaken state, his body hadn't quite caught up with the fact the church truly was on fire. "Well, we believe that little ole heater you use to warm the water, just might have a short in it. Anyway, it's gone now." Jerry was trying to keep up with Levi, crossing the parking lot, headed toward entry. "We probably caused a bit of damage ourselves, Reverend. The carpet is pretty much saturated." He reached to grab one of the doors. "We already opened up." With those words the door sprang open and gallons of water rushed down the steps, swishing past their feet to well up before it hit the circle drive.

"Oh, my word." Levi clutched his sides. "Everything's ruined. Songbooks. Piano. Carpet, all for one little malfunctioning heater?"

Fear claimed his heart, tears streamed down his face. This was his church. How dare they? But he couldn't cast blame, could he? He was the one placed the heater in the water, as he had many times before. "What will the members think," he asked, instead. "And today is Sunday." All the while his mind was in a fizz. He'd lost so much sleep, last night he'd taken a sleeping pill and slept.

On Monday Levi called Joe. "I guess you heard?"

"Heard what?"

"It's in the papers."

"They're not out, yet."

"We have damage to Shining Light. We couldn't meet yesterday. We just stood in the yard. Fire and water."

"Much damage?"

"Enough. Seems like a lot to us. Carpet. Piano. Books. One stained glass window fell apart."

"What can we do? What can I do Padre?"

"The committee's meeting. Do you know a reputable designer? Someone who can take ashes and make our sanctuary beautiful? They'll be working with two cranky old women, two crabby old men and me." He heard Joe's stifled laughter. "I'm serious. This may the worst I've encountered. I may not last."

"I know just who you need. I'll send her down."

"Five o'clock, sharp, this evening Father Joe."

Marigold crossed out an advertisement in Cape's Herald. Lay the receiver back in the cradle and stared at Harriet coming through the door. "That," she said, with emphasis, "was a very strange call." Harriet waited, eyebrows arched. "Brother Joe." Marigold glanced at the clock. "Not even ten and he tells me I need to drive down to

Newhaven and help some people out." She laughed. "He would but he says he doesn't have the talent and I do."|

"That's sixty miles away," Harriet offered. "What is it he needs? Or someone, he knows needs?"

"Remember Dan and Ellen drove down to lead singing at a little rural church, where one of Joe's friends pastors? You kept the twins. The babies."

"Go on."

"Well, that church suffered a fire and water damage to the extreme everything has to be replaced."

"They need a designer?" Harriet's frown over the church problem eased into a smile. "You can do it."

"I have…"

"You have me," Harriet glowed. "I can take care of M.J. and the shop and you can take Haley or Cindy and help these poor people."

"That's just it; they may be poor…what he mentioned needing replacing cost money. Lots of it."

The two stood staring at each other, until finally Marigold asked, "Are you sure?" She glanced around taking inventory of the shop. "I really don't have stock on hand for their needs. And I never overspend my budget. I want this shop to stand on its; own, not look to Dan to keep going."

"It's a church." Harriet patted her purse. "I'll fund your expense if you won't mention my involvement. Then, you can bill the church accordingly. Let's not make profit…can you do that this one time? Take out the expense for your travel, pay yourself hourly but no profit on the supplies."

Marigold grinned. "As Ellen says, God does work in mysterious ways, doesn't he? His miracles to perform." For a moment she remembered first meeting Ellen. "What Ellen said, way back then was a bit foreign to me at the time, that God sets up a plan for our life, knows every twist and turn, who we will meet, what we will do…" Marigold grinned. "Who knew that rigid rich lady I moved two doors down from would become my Mom?"

"I've softened a bit, haven't I?" Harriet reached for Marigold to give her a hug. "And I'm lovin' it." For a second she pulled back. "No glass bells or tassels, though, only serenity. O.K?"

Newhaven

Marigold arrived with only minutes to spare and was examining the ruins when Joe came to meet her.

"I'm Joe's friend, Levi Markel. Thank you for coming on such short notice."

"Marigold Langley," she replied, extending her hand. "My pleasure."

"I hope it is," he replied. "Come meet the committee with a thousand questions and twenty cents."

Marigold laughed. "Sounds interesting."

"You look a bit haggard." Harriet was closing the blinds to the shop; placing the closed sign on the door and ready to kick off her shoes for a spell. "How did it go?"

"Joe's description per his friend were right on. He said I'd be working with two crabby old women, two cranky old men and the minister, who is indecisive, seems to have his mind on a hundred things at once and…"

"Don't we all?" Harriet interrupted. "So what's the color scheme?"

"The one called Talulah wants blue carpet. Blue pads on the benches and striped drapes in shades of blue, green and beige and the walls must be beige." Marigold sank opposite her mother in the last set for the summer of rattan furniture. "I'm so glad we have a left over. At this point I think I'll use it daily."

"Go on, what do the others want?"

"It's not amusing, Harriet." Marigold sounded a bit carpy. "The two men agree, it should be brown carpet, that way soil won't show. The pew cushions should be a solid beige and the walls a slightly lighter shade. As long as it reflects brown as stated I can do what I want." She yawned. "Of course they all have to agree."

"And your opinion?"

"This minister, Levi Markel with the troubled eyes and his mind on only God knows what," she yawned again, patting her stomach. She was beginning to feel as tight as a drum. "I don't know, maybe the timing isn't the best for baby and church remodeling to come together. I'm surprised you agreed."

Harriet grinned. "You've been so restless lately, I thought it might be good for you, with Matt still helping his parents on the farm. Him down there, you here, maybe the two of you, twain could meet."

"Oh, I hadn't reached that point of the equation, yet." She considered a moment. "Hmmm."

"Finish about the pastor with the troubled eyes. I'm intrigued."

"He was wearing this light green shirt, it matched his eyes and I can't get that combination out of my head. It's a little country church, very well done, architecturally…" Enthusiasm eased into her words. "The wood work was painted white, those wide baseboard, the window trim, country but upscale…and pale shades of green that bear a hint of blue kept coming to my mind as I listened to the committee."

"So, you have a plan." Harriet leaned over to touch Marigold's leg and move her foot into her lap where she began to massage it. "When do you return?" She glanced up. "What's the plan?"

"I told them to do their best to clear all debris; start cleaning the woodwork and I'd be there Friday with my samples. I've got to collect those samples and have them on the boards in four days. And I do have a backup color in mind if they don't accept this one...but it is on the cool side, not as warming."

"Isn't it exciting?" Harriet glowed. "I'm so proud of you and Hattie and I will do our part."

"Just let me lay here a minute." Marigold's voice became hazy. "What was your plan for Matt and me?" She had left the shop and Harriet and the little church at New Haven as she curled into comfort.

"I'll work on that," Harriet whispered because Marigold was asleep. She moved toward the phone.

Her second call was to Matt. "Hello, Ma," he said and she replied. "I'm not your ma." After they both laughed she said, "I know Marigold has filled you in on her latest project. How would you feel about meeting her Friday evening around six o'clock at the church, the two of you go out for a nice dinner and there's a bed and breakfast on the South end of town for the night...wouldn't that allow you to spend time with her and still be close enough to the farm if they called, or if your parents needed you?"

"We're into the last watering," he said. There was pleasure in his voice "You think of everything, Ma. I love you." Voices in the background meant his men were coming in from the fields. "Tell my Tinkerbell I can hardly wait."

Marigold showed Vivien and Haley the samples. "I'm thinking no drapes. They're too heavy at the windows, although it is a nine foot to twelve pitch ceiling and the chandeliers have to be replaced. The men want brown, the women want shiny brass, so I've given them a white shabby chic wrought iron. No shades. I recommend a little decorative touch on the window facings, and that will make the stained glass windows pop. They are beautiful anyway and carry their own message. Just beautiful."

She moved to the next board. "These are the samples for the pew cushions and the carpet. The carpet promises to withstand wear and I know it will, it is neither too light nor too dark, as the strands move underfoot the light plays on the color and it is just too perfect for that little country church."

"Now this," she explained touching individual sprays of pink, blue, lilac flowers, and white to ecru baby's breath. "These are to show them, weddings in any of these colors, special meetings, whatever comes their way, these colors go well with the whole color scheme and keep everything serene and open to worship. Don't you just love it?" She wavered for a moment…and if this is not satisfactory…I…"

"I want to get married there." Haley's eyes shone like stars. "It's beautiful."

"Where are the blue and brown boards as requested," Harriet asked, looking around.

New Haven

Joe paced nervously in the church yard waiting to help the designer in with her supplies. His heart was eternally grateful when she drove up just shy of ten minutes to the meeting; Ten til' five on his watch.

She had barely sit up the boards when Herm Brown asked, "Young lady where is the brown scheme? I see you have only one set up."

"Yes, sir. You called me to come down and give you an idea of what my thoughts are on making your sanctuary its most attractive appearance while not losing the worshipful spirit of our Lord."

"I don't suppose you have the blue scheme, either," Talujah Cohen spoke up.

"No, ma'am but I do have something in blue I'd like to show you."

Marigold produced the square of sheetrock painted the color for walls, applied white moldings and a sample of cut glass similar to stained glass windows, which alone cost her twenty-five dollars. "Your pastor was kind enough to set up the projector, which means I can show you rooms with the schemes you requested and we can compare them to the one I have here on the table and that will allow you to give a fair and unbiased opinion of what Shining Light Church needs."

"First, we want a serene setting when the congregation comes together to worship. The people have suffered indignities at times in the work place but mostly it is a crowded atmosphere that makes them long for a moment of serenity, no flashy or dull colors just a quiet worshipful restful background when they come to worship at Shining Light Sanctuary." She smiled. "And before the fire you had these wonderfully wide baseboards befitting a country church that I find, obviously from attention to the woodwork, the extra little touch supplied by minds that knew what they wanted, so comforting to glance toward as Brother Joe is speaking and we need a place to rest the eye…why not on the beautiful white wood that frames the stained-glass windows that carry their very own message of the Savior's love? Don't you find it all just so refreshing?" Taking up several sprays of flowers, she continued, "I want you to see how wonderful any of these colors work with what we have and yes, the beige theme would have the same effect but don't we see beige everywhere we go because people can't decide otherwise?"

She smiled on them as though they were most precious and she wanted only to find their faces wreathed in smile, their hearts beating as one and all in full acceptance of the serenity she offered. I'll step into the vestibule," She offered, "That you have a moment of discussion before you tell me your decision or to pack my bags and hurry home. Let me assure you, I have enjoyed meeting you and I will rest well tonight whatever your decision."

She stepped into the vestibule, closing the door firmly behind her when two hands claimed her and turned her around. "Refreshing, is it, Tinkerbell?" Matt's smile was all she needed, but his lips touched hers and she was in heaven. "Umm. Yes, definitely refreshing," Matt grinned. "Hello, Mrs. Langley."

She grinned as her arms went around his neck. "Hello, Mr. Langley, fancy meeting you here."

"Ma has some pretty good ideas." His eyes were bright with pleasure seeing her. "Little bold, out there, aren't you, bringing one color scheme when they requested three?" He couldn't keep from grinning, so glad he was to see her. "Just for the record, if they don't accept it, are you ready for that?"

She closed her eyes, remembering the second board in the van. "Yes, if it comes to that."

They called her back, within the hour. Their faces wore expressions of unrest and frustration. "Mrs. Langley," Herm Brown asked. "Don't you have another color we could consider? We're tied on this one."

"Actually, I do," she replied. "It's in my van. I have given you warm embracing colors, next, are more reserved; they will also go with any color one would choose."

Matt brought in the second board she had not shown to anyone.

"Ahh," Talujah Cohen was coming closer to view the carpet sample. "This one, I truly like. It's a gray but not a dark gray. Would that satisfy your thirst for blue?" She turned to the men. "I'll forget the stripes and such. I see the folly of my thinking. We want our Sanctuary to be satisfactory to all."

Herm Brown peered closely at the sample. "Gray, huh?" He stroked his chin. "I must say I believe that color would soothe a lion. I'm in on this one."

"Well, that was quick," Matt said, helping store the sample board back in the painted van. "I liked your presentation, Tinkerbelle. I have never thought about the light play on silky carpet strands inducing me to the point I can hardly keep my eyes open and when I add an extra-large pink bow, I"ve conquered the heart and imagination of every man and woman and child that participates in Shining Light's Wonder. Where in the world did you learn a speel, like that?"

Marigold laughed. "Weren't so bad yourself; bringing that board in right on time. Thank you." She giggled, "But not one word was said about an extra large pink bow, though I just might use that in the future, anything to add a touch of color in times of celebration... good job, Farm Boy."

They did a high-five before Matt gave an exaggerated bow, pulled her down onto his knee and kissed her soundly. "Wow. Tinkerbelle, you are dynamite. Can we go now?" He glanced at all the empty parking spaces. "Why don't you ride with me? Leave your van here and we'll retrieve it tomorrow."

The committee members left by way of the back door, while Levi stood in his office watching the Langleys storing the sample boards in the painted van. Their excitement in seeing each other must stem from being apart the last three weeks as Matt prepared for harvest at his parents farm and his wife ran a shop in the Cape business district. Sliding the wood shutters together, shadowing the room, he slumped down into his chair. He was weary, heart mind and soul. Leah, his mind called out but there was no answer. All he could summon was the fact prayers must be uttered, the safety and welfare of his congregation and the miracle of these new people he had met were part of the work he was called to. He leaned forward, what were they thinking? His wife's absence was as a sounding bell. Awkward.

"Stop." Marigold pointed to a hardware store. "I need brackets. I'm out of those little silver ones I use." She turned to Matt, "Do you want to run in with me. I'll finish quicker." He nodded as he pulled into an empty parking spot, climbed out and offered her his hand.

"Number eleven, I'm thinking," he said as they hurried inside, bypassing all aisles until they reached eleven. "Uh huh," Matt stood aside that she could select what she needed. "Wait, a minute, I believe those small ones are around the corner."

Marigold went the direction he pointed, making several selections, her hands full and ready to find check out when she heard a woman's voice.

"Matt?" Breatheless voice, Marigold thought. "Matthew Langley, what are you doing here in New Haven?"

Standing quiet and still, her hands filled with boxes of brackets, she listened. Matt's voice, withdrawn, careful and detached. She wondered that he didn't bring the woman around to meet her. Well, she could fix that. Marigold stepped around the end piece. From behind she saw a beautiful young woman, near her own age. Hearing Marigold, Matt and the woman turned toward her.

"Marigold, this is Britany James, my parent's neighbor." He wore a painful expression, as if to say I haven't done anything wrong. "Britany, this is my wife, Marigold."

She was an attractive woman, beautiful, in fact. Marigold found herself staring, so this was the woman who wanted her husband, whose name was linked with a married man's in an affair, standing there with her hand outstretched as if past history didn't matter. Marigold clutched the boxes of fasteners to her chest, feigning inability to make contact. "My arms are full," She said, her face void of expression and her voice leaden. The woman's eyes tightened, her mouth a straight line as she sized up the situation.

"I don't think your wife wants to shake my hand, Matt."

"I will speak for myself." Marigold turned angry eyes on her husband. "No, I don't." Now she headed toward the checkout counter. "Are you coming with me, darling?"

If he'd been a bull, Matt would have been pawing the ground. He was caught between two strong willed women and yet, his bet was on Marigold. He heard her high heels click on the tile as she marched away, shoulders squared, mind made up wearing her full body armor that so easily read, don't push my button, buster. He followed her, his eyes rolling to the top of his head.

Britany's laughter echoed down the aisles. "See you around, Matt."

Marigold paid. Matt wasn't about to question her actions. It wasn't his fault Britany was in New Haven. They walked to the truck in silence. Harriet had set up a perfect rendezvous for them; but the question whether they'd use it, now hung in the air. He opened the door for her, placed the sack of supplies in the back seat and got in. "What now?" He asked, fearing she would bolt and run home to the Cape.

"I think, Farm Boy, we have a dinner date and then a night paid for at New Haven's best bread for breakfast."

He sat there for a moment, letting the words sink in. "Bread huh? No bed?"

Marigold's eyes smoldered. "I'm working on it, Farm Boy. Your mother's choice, standing in aisle twelve at the Hardware Store, wasn't what I planned for the end of a perfect day."

Palms up, Matt shrugged, "I had no part in her appearance. I'm with you, Babe."

She scooted toward the center of the truck, "You had better be, Farm Boy, because I have no plans to release you to your mother's chosen harlot."

"That's strong," he replied but a smile played around his lips and his eyes were beginning to twinkle.

She pummeled his shoulder when suddenly he reached to pull her roughly against the console, kissed her not letting go as she first resisted, then settled down, a giggle beginning to form in the hollow of her throat, pressing its way between their lips until he let go.

"That," he said as he keyed the engine, "Was an awkward moment."

"Yes, it was." A smile played about her lips. "But I think we're going to make it through this one, what do you think?"

"I think…I know I am, as long as you are with me. I love you Tinkerbell."

Chapter Six

Three weeks passed. Leah had not seen Levi. She read about the fire at Shining Light Church. Her sister's eyes were on her as she glanced up from today's paper. "When are you going home, Leah?"

"I can find a room, somewhere," she replied. "I don't mean to be in the way."

"You're not in the way, but you are a minister's wife and I suspect he needs you to calm the restless sheep."

"The people of the church?" Leah pondered, the people filing past her mind in full color "They'll be all right. By now, I'm guessing the gossip will be on someone else."

"What have you done that they would be talking about you?" Candy slid into the chair opposite Leah.

"I left."

"That's all?"

"Yes."

Candace considered her sister's reply. Wisely she would not press but a word of caution might help. "Leah, don't let anyone sidetrack you or why you are here. I won't pry but the struggle to have a child has been a hardship between you and Levi. Just watch your step; this is where the devil will send in someone or something to replace or destroy what you and Levi have built these last seven years."

"Without a child to cement us together, I don't think you have to worry, no one would want me."

Laughing softly, Candace rose, went to Leah stooping to kiss her brow. "I've got to go to work. But remember my words, be careful. And for the record, I would love to have what you and Levi have together."

Candace had left to arrive on time at her job by eight and now at mid-morning as Leah stared out the window into the grayness, the day appeared ready for the clouds to burst. She hated being cooped up inside. Her cell was ringing and she answered before glancing at the name of the person calling.

"Leah?" There was a pause and then Jake Hutchens asked, "How about meeting me for a cup of coffee?" He was waiting for her reply. "I'm here, in a hotel. I had consultation with another doctor."

"Where?" She gave a small embarrassed laugh. "I mean, where do you want to meet?"

"Thank you for coming." His smile was welcoming as he helped her out of the rain sopped jacket. "It's a downpour out there, isn't it?" He waited for her to be seated and then asked. "How are you?"

"I'm making it." She replied. "I'm pursuing a few free-lance jobs. I don't want to be a burden on my sister."

"I'll be in the city for three days," he said. "I'm learning a new technique." He seemed to come to grips with an inner thought. "Actually, I'm learning a procedure that will either put me on the books in New Haven or cause me to have to leave." He gave an embarrassed chuckle.

"You mean, it will either enlarge your patient list or you will have to go to a larger facility to use it?"

"Yeah." He studied her with satisfaction. "You look good, Leah, not like the sorrowing wife I imagined."

"I made the decision to leave, Jake. No one threw me out."

"Do you miss Levi?"

"I do." She sighed. "I'm not sure people have to give up the love they've had for one from their past just because they feel the need to move on. Isn't there room in the heart to love many?"

"I don't know. If I left Laurie I'd worry over her welfare. But if I were choosing to love another, that love might take first place in my heart."

"What about those who lose the one they love to death? Same thing, isn't it?"

He grinned. "Not in my book. Therein lies no competition, no talking back just an open field, whereas, say I was interested in you, there's Levi waiting for your return. My pastor, a different situation, isn't it?" He reached across the table, took her hand in his. "Are you going back, Leah, or divorcing Levi?"

She tried to remove her hand but he held tight. She saw he wanted an answer. "What about Laurie? Why would you even ask? We're church family, Jake. I don't want to hurt Laurie and what you are implying is…"

"Someone to talk to, to be with that has similar needs to mine." He looked at her sadly. "Whether it's you or someone else, I'm dying inside, Leah." He stared up at the ceiling, then back to her. "I'm very interested in you."

"I never knew…well, until the last month or so, you and Laurie appear to be the happy couple."

"As you and Levi, but now the congregation, our church family is all up in arms about your leaving."

"And on Sunday's you continue to lead the music at Shining Light Church while your wife plays the piano," she said softly. "Is the whole world in such a shape that no one lives the life the public thinks they are seeing?" For a moment she appeared grief stricken, "Where does this leave us with the Lord? We both have the training and knowledge of scripture to know sitting here together is dangerous."

"I didn't ask to take you to bed. I ask for friendship and conversation."

His hand felt warm and comforting the hold he had on her at this moment. She could come to cherish the gentleness of his behavior, but he had a wife needing those same creature comforts. "Laurie needs you," she said. Maybe there was hope for her after all. This man was offering her entrance to his world but she, in her mind's eye, saw his wife who may not want a child but instead stood by his side many times singing music that lifted the weary souls at Shining Light Church to a land that beckoned full of promise and reward. What could be the reason Laurie would not want a child with this man?

"Give me the three days I'm in the city, Leah, to be with you. I think you could do with someone by your side, too." He glanced quickly at his wristwatch, "I have to be going now, but if six is not too early may I take you to dinner? Then, right around the corner there's a movie that I'm hearing is pretty good."

"I'll meet you," she said. "I'd rather not have you call for me at my sister's home."

Candace called to say she would be past nine arriving home. Leah was thankful, not having to explain where she was going. Strange, she thought, I didn't ask the name of the movie.

Autumn was in the air. Leah dressed in the set of clothing she had bought for the interviews with the newspaper. Otherwise, the three sets from her suitcase, a few casual ever day wear and a select piece of jewelry were her adornments. When she left, she had not calculated need nor day of return to Levi. She studied the simple gold band on her left hand. Not once had she thought of removing it and now, she wondered if Jake was wearing his?

She was relieved to see the band on his finger. His smile lingered as he pulled the chair out to seat her. "You look great," he said. "That scarf brings out the color of your eyes." He bent to kiss her on the cheek. "I'm so glad you have come."

Three days passed quickly. The dinners were filled with light hearted banter and the first night's movie had only one awkward moment when she leaned her head back against the seat to find his arm ready to cup around her shoulders. How could that feel so natural? For a moment she wanted to lay her head on his shoulder and feel the warmth and comfort he had mentioned. Perhaps that would have been just as well as what did happened during one particularly endearing moment when the two of them ended up holding hands.

And then it was time for him to return to New Haven. "I'll miss you," he said. "I've enjoyed our time together." He placed one finger under her chin to lift her face to his own and then he kissed her softly on the lips, their eyes so close, searching as if looking into each other's soul, that both felt mesmerized and drawn into some sort of denied intimacy.

"Are you coming home?" They were outside in the first cool weather of the season. He watched her wrap the light jacket tighter around her body, and saw the troubled expression as she dropped her head to stare at the sidewalk, her hair curtaining around her face, "To Newhaven?"

She tried to clear her throat. "We could never be together."

"Then it does mean something to you. We can make it work, Leah."

Another weekend was upon them. The weather had remained soggy and kept them inside. Candace relief in a few hours of rest was as evident as Leah's restlessness. Candace watched her pace the floor.

"Come sit by me," she patted the cushion beside her and waited for Leah to settle down. "Want to talk about what's bothering you?" Leah shook her head, no. "Then I'll talk to you." Candace grinned. "See," she teased, "You had a chance." Closing her eyes a second, she continued, "Knowing you, you've been here past your expected time-limit. You are wondering how Levi is making it with his sheep and you find it hard to return to New Haven. You think everyone's going to voice their opinion concerning your absence. Right?" Leaning forward she peered beneath the wall of hair into Leah's face. "But you're wrong on some of that. I don't think they will voice their opinion but they are going to be standing on pins and needles wondering if you are back to stay or if there's problems to be fixed." Now she laughed. "Well, how am I doing? Are you fearful of people's opinion if you go home?"

"It matters. Those sheep as you call them have been my church family seven years and yes, maybe they are entitled to an opinion… though I'd rather have understanding or maybe a prayer." Or, forgiveness, and yet she had done nothing wrong. It had been two weeks since she'd last seen Jake.

"Go home, Leah." Candace squeezed her hand. "Men like Levi are hard to find."

"Why would you say that? I imagine there are countless good men out there. You haven't looked."

"Sister, a woman alone doesn't have to go looking," she cupped her fingers around the last word. "But Levi loves his congregation and isn't that what a shepherd does? He leads and puts other people's needs above his own family's…"

"Sometimes," Leah added. "But I'm his wife and maybe he can deal with our not having a child but I can't." She sighed. "Maybe that's why I've grown tired of the weekly ritual, meetings, expectations."

"Let's pretend I don't know the answer to all you've just mentioned. You tell me why having a child would make your marriage better."

A tear trickled down Leah's cheek. "My arms are empty. I've held other women's babies and felt proud for them, but I feel empty. I don't want just to hold their baby. I want my own. Levi's child."

"Then go home, Leah. If you didn't love Levi, you wouldn't have mentioned his name. You love him."

"I don't know how to go back, now, Candy." Staring up to the ceiling Leah blew out a stream of air. "What if I've waited too long?" At that moment her cell rang. She took it out of her pocket and glanced at the caller's name. "It's Levi." She rose to go stand by the window. "Levi?"

"Leah." He said her name and then was silent. She couldn't know the relief he felt that she answered. "Leah, have you forgotten, you are to lead the association work shop for pastor's wives, next week?" She heard so many questions lining up behind the one.

"I forgot."

"Then you aren't prepared?" He questioned softly. "Who else do you suggest I call, Leah?"

"Is the concourse open? I didn't know if the fire damaged it."

"There's a decorator drives down from the Cape overseeing restoration. The concourse only suffered smoke damage and is in working order. We have seventeen ladies confirmed attendance."

"Will the people think it strange, my return for the work shop?"

"I can't answer that." The strain in his voice was evident. "Are you coming back and will you be in our home?"

A strangled laugh preceded her words. "Where else would I stay?" Irritation marked the next words. "I assume you and the church people would prefer we make this easy on all of us, wouldn't you?" She wished she had curbed the remark. "I won't be attending services tomorrow, Levi but I could be there Monday evening in time to begin the study Monday night."

"I'll take that as a yes, then." He sounded relieved. "I will be happy to see you, Leah. I'll move my stuff into the guest room." The phone clicked to silence. For a moment she stared at it.

"No goodbyes," Candace asked. "I remember when it took the two of you ten minutes to hang up."

"Life changes. People change." Leah turned to Candace. "I'm going home to teach seventeen ladies who are either pastor wives or planning to be, in be a book study. Can you image that after me leaving…."

"You will do fine. Can I help you in any way before you head home? Got a book with you?"

After making a stop at one of the better outlets to purchase necessities for the work shop, Leah drove the speed limit, not hurrying as she wondered what awaited her arrival. She stopped by the church, wandering through workmen engaged in various forms of the renovation. Some were wiping down walls, where the sheetrock in being smoothed by sandpaper had created a dust storm inside the room. "Good thing we stored the piano in the coat closet before we started," she overheard as she passed through the glass doors that separated the Sanctuary from the hall and concourse.

The manual was explicit. Pamper your pastor's wives. Try to have an indoor sitting arrangement as though you had gathered the group into your own home. Prepare, having your knowledge ready, aware of the answers to question they will ask. This gave Leah pause to wonder if she had bitten off more than she could chew. Seven years was not enough time to know the answers and surely some of the women would be older than she. Look at the predicament she was in presently. And what would she do if innocently they brought her problem to light? In a flash she silently thanked her sister for common sense advice. "Go home and simply say, if asked, that you had to get away for a while." Thankfully there was a book in her suitcase and she wondered that she could have forgotten the work shop. "Everyone has problems," her sister had said, "and they don't want people prying into their lives but this workshop will open the door for sharing." She had laughed. "Who knows the leader may learn a lot."

It wasn't Levi's fault she had become miserable. It was seven years of trying to conceive, and now this. She realized she could no more control the questions that would come from ordained men's wives than she could bear a child. This would be a chWadege. She had prayed and God had not spoken audibly but He had put a suggestion in her thoughts. She would pass the question to the more experienced wives.

She heard voices as Levi and an attractive brunette rounded the corner when a loud bang sounded. Startled, they all glanced back to where the men were working inside the sanctuary as a young woman with a little girl entered from the front vestibule. A bucket of paint had fWade from atop the scaffolding; all the while another man was pressing forward with all his might trying to counter the mishap. He had caught the bucket from on high but in his haste had knocked over an aluminum ladder in his path.

Leah wasn't certain if the mishap had created a different type of disturbance or exactly what was going on between the two women she could so easily observe. An electricity of sorts had come into their midst, almost as in slow motion Leah watched Levi, somehow knowing he, too, sensed the situation, because he was at a loss for words. Finally he said, "Miss Britany James, this is my wife, Leah, and the lady coming through the door is our designer, head of the committee in charge of restoring the sanctuary." Then Levi smiled,

"But I'm afraid I don't know the young lady Mrs. Marigold Langley has accompanying her." By now, Marigold and Ruthie stood within speaking distance.

"We've met." Marigold's cool demeanor dismissed the brunette. "I believe Miss James is a past friend of my husband's, but," her face wreathed in smile as her eyes were on Levi, "this is Ruthie Gates. Ruthie's parents are my family's good friends and Ruthie and I are partners in many endeavors. She rode down with me today to keep me company since I will be returning to the Cape tonight."

While Ruthie shook both Levi and Miss James hand, Leah stepped forward. "Hello, Ruthie," she said. "I'm delighted to meet you. I am Pastor Markel's wife." Ruthie released Miss James hand and took Leah's. For a second, Leah could have sworn, if that were allowed, that a current went through her hand and up her arm, a strange tingle that felt neither worrisome nor dangerous, a goodness, perhaps.

Ruthie smiled. "I could help you. I know you are here to do something and Marigold will be busy for a while."

"Come with me, then," Leah gave both Marigold and Ruthie a searching glance. How could the little girl know a task lay ahead of her? She gave herself a private kick, she couldn't; it was the atmospheric change between the brunette and the new one called Marigold. Did those two also know each other?

"What a coincidence, Ruthie," Leah said, "That you would come along just as I arrive to sit up for a book study." She noticed Ruthie staring out the window where the construction crew's trucks were parked with a steady stream of men crossing the lawn. "Is something wrong, Ruthie?"

"No, not wrong." Ruthie hesitated only a moment. "You probably have noticed all the activity out there. Your ladies are looking forward to being with you and they will need to focus on what you have to say, just as you need to hear what they will share with you."

She paused. "Shouldn't we turn the chairs the opposite direction?" Already Ruthie was noticing a chalk and cork board Leah could use for the banners looped over her arm.

"My goodness, Ruthie, how old are you?"

Ruthie giggled. "My mother asks me that. It is our joke."

Leah felt a light heartedness she hadn't felt in a long time. It was the Balm of Gilead, the Rose of Sharon and the Lily of the Valley visiting her soul all wrapped up in one. How wonderful that the Lord would feel her emptiness and send this one to soothe the way when her own trepidations had begun to mount there in the secret confines of her heart and mind, and overwhelm what she had hoped would take her through this task she had gotten herself into months back.

As surely as the ladder falling had created a noise, so had her own ineffectiveness hit her when she walked into that Holy place and realized it would take more than bluffing to lead in the work shop? They would see through her as surely as she saw through herself. She needed prayer and fasting.

They worked together. Ruthie placed the small bag of goodies around the two tables and chairs they had lined up to face the boards. Leah hung the banners and laid out the books on the table. Finished, Leah glanced to where the glassed doors between the hall and rooms revealed Ruthie's friend pointing to the crown molding. Leah knew it had to be done right, the crown molding in this ancient little country church was a delight to many in the congregation and a disgruntle to others, all due to the occasional sag where the cracks revealed themselves in the winter but closed in somewhat during the warmer months. Surely they would all be content once the renovation was complete.

"Ruthie, how about we step down the hall to where there's a cold drink machine? We have sacks left over, enough to have a little snack." Ruthie was following as Leah led her to the refreshment corner that entered the church kitchen. "Oh, my goodness." Together they eyed the frosted cake in the center of the free-standing aisle. 'Let's read the note." Leah was lifting the paper curled and centered on top. "To the first one who has a need for something sweet. Dig in." Leah laughed. "Mabel Hisaw. I love that woman."

"Are you glad you are home?"

Leah felt tears well up in her eyes. "I didn't know that I would be, Ruthie." She confessed. So caring and wise were the eyes that studied her from across the table. "I don't know, but I think maybe you have had something to do with it, Ruthie. Do you know what a harbinger is?"

"Yes, Momma and Daddy Daniel read a book about that and their class discussed it at church. A harbinger is someone or something that comes before something else. It can be good or bad. They said Spring is a good one because it means people get ready for the months to follow."

"Would I be asking you to break confidence," Marigold asked, "Pastor, why is that woman in this congregation, when I know for a fact, she owns land in the neighboring community and her parents attended church there?" Marigold's eyes snapped with animosity. "Forgive me, sir, but that woman wants my husband and I feel I have to be completely honest with you concerning the matter"

Blood rushed to Levi's face. He hadn't expected this "Hm…I… certainly…" he stuttered, momentarily seeking his wits. "I was, I am unaware of the situation, Mrs. Langley. I'm sorry if it seems I'm part of a machination of sorts which has made us both uncomfortable. I can only tell you Miss James is looking for a new church home due to personal circumstance and I told her we would welcome her into our midst."

"Then lock the barn door." Marigold muttered. "Let's just hope all your male congregational members have full reign on their sensibilities and their wives are vigilant." Shaking her head, she glanced around for her portfolio, "Well, Pastor Markel, I believe the men on the renovation crew are doing a great job and you should be worshiping in your auditorium, or as your members remind me, Sanctuary, within a few weeks. It is beautiful and I am very grateful you have allowed me to take part in the renovation."

She was half way toward the kitchen, when she turned suddenly, her eyes still darting sparks. "Do you happen to have any unmarried men in your membership, perhaps a bachelor or two?"

Levi swallowed. "All that comes to mind is Mr. Hobbs, but he is eighty two. Then there's James Martin, never married but so set in his ways I doubt she'd consider him. He's sixty eight and a bit hard to give up his own opinion and as I understand she is twenty six. Does that sound about right?" He turned serious eyes on Mrs. Langley. "Sorry, we are fresh out of young bachelors, but we do have Herm Smith."

"You might need to have a book study on Matrimonial Bliss. Believe me; I know what I'm saying."

He listened as her heels clicked across the tile floor in the concourse. The stares those two gave each other made his blood pressure dip. Neither was hot headed there on the last, more like calm cool and calculating, their eyes squinted, mouth in a straight narrow slit, it could've been a shoot-out at the old corral, he was thinking, except it was at Shining Light Church. He wondered if the shudder he felt was a forecast of things to come. It left him in a state of complete exhaustion. The days without Leah had been traumatic, his life, his marriage and his service to his church had all lumped together and now this.

At a loss how to follow that one, Levi made his way back through the Sanctuary aisle, the glass doors to the hall and last to where Leah was placing a picture of a family on the cork board.

"I don't know what to make of that. Mrs. Langley seems to think Miss Britany James could cause us a problem here in Shining Light Church. I can't imagine a woman that would stray away from God's will to want another woman's husband." Absentmindedly, Levi helped himself to a large piece of Mabel's cake. "There's nothing prepared for dinner. Just as well eat cake and go to bed."

Leah glanced out the window. It was not yet six o'clock. Levi must be dreadfully tired. The terrible truth of his words hit her. She had not made an advance toward Jake Hutchens, still there was a problem.

The morning the Pastor Wives Conference was to begin, Leah awoke to a flashing warning going through her head. Not only did she feel while she slept she had been run over by a train but there was some kind of problem rearing its ugly head in her mind. And then she remembered Levi's words. Suddenly it all hit home. The congregation would have a field day if they knew she had seen Jake Hutchens alone. His wife was aware of the first time, but after that she wasn't certain how Jake explained his absence.

She had to be on guard. Thank the good Lord Mabel was not in the group. The woman could pull the truth out of a lying child and maybe that was what she had become. There was little she could do now; the show must go on and it wasn't as if she hadn't studied. Not that she liked the material, considering such questions as, "what to do if one of the congregation makes a pass at you."

The women arrived, a joyous hum of introductions and hugs for those they remembered opened the workshop. Leah realized as the morning progressed, she too, was enjoying herself, worries were forgotten. There was harmony in the fellowship as the time for the questions arrived.

“I found the question about someone making a pass at you very interesting,” the pastor’s wife of Shady Oak replied. “I think, we women have to watch how we live our life right down to the way we dress.” There was a buzz of agreement. “I had been mowing, when this happened to me and Yes, I was wearing shorts. But remember, I was in my own back yard.”

“The world owns us,” Carrie Southern from The Church on the Hill, joined the discussion. “My problem has been the men who ask me if I would join them to talk about a few problems at home.” A swell of agreement rose. “You and I know we never accept those invitations. That is something that needs to be discussed in a church setting with your husband present.”

“Why is that?” All eyes turned to the newest member of the Pastor’s wives group. Looking barely fifteen, Meredith Garner from Guiding Light Church appeared to be one of the older women’s daughter. Dressed in the latest, big top with tights beneath she looked like any other teenager. But she was the wife of a Pastor fresh out of Seminary. Wearing a puzzled expression on her face she waited for the answer.

Everyone liked Kara Green. She usually taught the seminars for pastor wives. Now she spoke to Meredith. “Honey, if we accept those invitations, certainly we won’t have the gentlemen with problems into our own home without the pastor and going out into public places only starts speculation as to why we are out with another woman’s husband when we have a husband of our own. People simply do not understand the lives of a pastor’s wife. We can’t invite gossip to hurt his reputation.”

Chapter Seven

"How did you and Ruthie find the remodel at the church?"

"The men are doing a good job, but..." Marigold paused, remembering. "Ask me what else I found?"

Glancing up from the placemats and table cloths she was straightening, Harriet's curiosity was peaked. "Tell me."

"Remember the woman that wants to end my marriage?"

"That Britany person?" Puzzlement shone in Harriet's expression, "What about her?"

"She was there, in full color, and later when Matt and I were at the hardware store, there also,"

"But there was no problem.... was there?" Harriet walked closer. "I thought she lived in a different community. The odds of your running into her seem pretty nil."

"Well, I did and it probably wasn't very Christian on my part. I didn't take her hand when she offered."

"It's understandable, tho, I doubt our pastor would agree." Harriet's eyes questioned. "Is there more?"

Marigold laughed, "If you mean did I scratch her eyes out, no. But I ratted on her to the Pastor. I guess." The smile on her face disappeared. "I know, that's terrible but it was such a shock to my system coming around the corner to find her. It just popped out of me. I told him to keep an eye on his men."

I'm surprised you didn't ask about available men, to try to marry her off."

"That, too." Hand in the air, she chuckled inwardly when Harriet met her in a high five.

"So, when do I write the check?"

"To help with Britany's wedding?"

"Oh, my goodness," Harriet laughed. "You do want her out of circulation. I meant for the renovation."

"You don't have to I'm sure the church people will rally to the need."

"I want to. It's my way of giving back." She sighed. "Anonymous, of course. No recognition necessary."

"Well, I did hear someone else is going to replace the piano. All they have presently is an aged upright stored in the closet away from sheetrock dust. The other one went through the Fire Department's deluge."

"Those old ones have a wonderful sound. You know everything past sixty is not obsolete. We still have something to offer the world."

"When did this switch to people?" Marigold reached for her mother's hand. "Thank you for taking care of the shop while I worked on Shining Light's restoration. You have done a wonderful job." She kissed Harriet's forehead. "Who knew we'd be so compatible after that first year of grinding our teeth?"

Harriet smiled. "I wasn't sure you'd ever claim me for your birth mother. Sometimes I was so jealous of your adoptive parents. They were the ones who helped to form who you are, I had no hand in that." She shook her head. "They did a good job. Was your birth mother creative, like you?"

"Not at all, I get that from you." With a sudden laugh, Marigold admitted, "And I'm thinking the stubbornness and tenacity for things I like, for instance my husband. When I realized it was Britany standing in front of me, I did a slow boil. My first thoughts were, we've been through this and it is not going to happen again."

"Was Matt present?" She watched Marigold nod. "What did he say?"

"He was there when we met the second time at the hardware store. It was hard on him. I could read his thoughts and mostly they were saying I had nothing to do with this." Marigold giggled. "He was worried I would come right home…but you know, Ma, I just wasn't ready to give that woman my man."

"As I tell your farm boy, I'm not your Ma, I'm one of your mothers and it's up to you what you call me, but please," Harriet wore a pained expression, "Not Ma. It sounds so…so…Beverly Hill Billy." Changing the subject, she asked, "How was the bed and breakfast?"

"Naturally," Marigold replied, "I can't give my own mother the details, but…it was just what the doctor ordered. Matt and I truly love each other and this being apart is not what we want in our marriage."

"No, if at all possible, married people need to be together."

"Funny you'd say that I overheard a conversation, accidently, the two ladies didn't know I was working in the adjacent room, anyway, it seems the pastor's wife was not there during their Revival and there's a lot of speculation as to their marriage." Marigold stared into space. "Can you imagine that? A Pastor?"

"They're just like us, dear. Why not?"

"But they have all that church business, day and night, Bible teaching and such…"

"My point. They're human and maybe they never have time to light, you know settle. Scripture is good and being with people is fine, but sometimes a person needs a little respite to just think and be……"

"Still, don't they have as much time as us? I mean, I leave work, pick up M.J., make dinner and by the time I get him into bed it's time to do it all over again. I mean, the nights are so short."

"We all choose our path, don't we?" Harriet sighed. "Possibly there's another reason for their problem."

"Ruthie was pretty quiet on the way home. I think she sensed something and her spirit was troubled over it. While I finished with the carpenters, she helped the pastor's wife prepare for a seminar."

"You must not call me." Hastily, she closed her phone, cutting off any explanation. It was then Suze Norman entered the room.

"Gracious, Leah, do you need help." Suze was already reaching for the broom. "Where did this come from?"

"The Pastor's Wives Conference. The manual said pamper them and there were gift bags with confetti inside the wrappings."

"Well, let me help you. You must have a thousand things to do." Suze became busy sweeping.

Leah was relieved when the room was clean and Suze went on her way. Now all she wanted was to go home but where was home, a room in a house with the man she used to love and sleep with? Now he was in the guest room and they moved about as strangers. Nervousness swept through her body. It had to be hard on him, too. She was at a cross roads, what to do? One thing for certain, she could not have Jake Hutchens calling her. Speculation would run wild if anyone overheard the two of them talking.

She would take a drive, clear her head of the frustration and try to find peace in her heart. Elusive. That's what it was, elusive. She had known peace until the day she woke up one morning in her sister's bedroom to stare out the window and wonder what terrible thing had brought her there. For all purposes she had left her husband, pastor of Shining Light Church. Perhaps she should never have returned, but then she had given her word to teach the Pastor's Wives Book Study.

She drove the back roads through town, followed a small winding road Levi had shown her to a small bubbling stream. Someone had built a wooden bridge over the span of water which led to the other side where Levi had taken her to a simple wooden bench, he thought possibly the same person had built.

Immersed in her own thoughts, trying vainly to speak to God about what was troubling her soul, Leah did not hear the steps of one approaching until she heard the crunch of a twig breaking and looked up to see Jake.

"You shouldn't have come."

"I saw you leave. I needed to see you and know you are all right." He waited, studying her sitting there, shoulders slumped, a sadness in her demeanor. "What's wrong?"

"Nothing." Her head came up. "You being here. Jake, we can't do this. Too much is at stake. Laurie and Levi."

He stepped to where she sit and dropped down, knees bent, weight resting on his feet. "Look at me, Leah. Something's wrong. Tell me." He placed a finger under her chin, lifting her face, her eyes meeting his. He glanced back down the trail. "If you're worried someone will see my car, I parked it away from the highway, behind a patch of vines and downed trees. No one will see us."

"It's wrong, Jake. Don't do this again. I can't handle it. I'm so messed up, inside, I can't even pray. My words are a jumble and I can't seem to reach God. It's as though I've committed some terrible crime."

"You have done nothing, nor have I." He reached out, as if to hold her. She put her hands up. Resigned, he stood, and then motioned to the space beside her. "May I sit?" She scooted to give him more space. "I had to see you, talk to you. You are ever in my thoughts."

"Please." Her voice was stressed. "What about Laurie. Why aren't you home with her? She needs you."

"Laurie needs no one." He gave a strange laugh. "You can't get through to your God. I can't reach my wife." He scrubbed with the toe of his shoe at a half-concealed rock in the dirt at their feet. "It's been this way so long; I suppose it's a normal for her, but not me."

"How do you two perform at church as you do, the people think you have a marriage made in Heaven."

"How do you? Other than the baby thing, you both seem happy and content. I've always admired you."

"We were. It's me." She sighed. "I wish we weren't having this conversation, but since we are, I'm sure it's me."

"We can't help these times, Leah. Believe me, I've experienced them for years."

"You've had affairs, before?"

He pushed back, appearing astonished. "Why would you think that? No, I've never had an affair."

"Then why me? I'm your Pastor's wife. Isn't that what you are offering me?" She stared at him with troubled eyes. "I can never let you touch me. I might be tempted to give in. Do you understand? It is my own unhappiness and need to be comforted and I should receive that comfort from my husband."

"But you aren't."

His words sunk in. "Suddenly, the day I left to go spend time at my sister's, it was as if I had to get away. The problem was bigger than anything I'd ever encountered. I'm not sure God hears me, anymore."

"I ask myself how to resolve my and Laurie's problem, I practically plead with God. I've never been an immoral man and then you and I spoke, we seemed to connect and I began to think about you." He sighed heavily. "Too much. It wasn't about sex, Leah, though you are attractive. It was about someone to listen to me, to have the same hopes for the future. I need a friend and you fit that bill completely."

"Then why did you try to kiss me?"

He squirmed. "There was that." Throwing his arms out in desperation, he had to come clean. "I was ready to throw my marriage to the wind. I admit it, at that moment, I wanted you." He turned to her, intent, "I thought you felt it, too."

"Jake, you're a doctor. You've taken care of most of the women in this town."

"I've never felt this way, before." He shuddered. "The women in this town are past sixty, with a few exceptions. And those come in with children hanging on their hips and I am more interested in the children than any of the mothers" A thought seemed to make its way past his denial, "I'm not an ogre. I think it was a down moment, and I got tired of covering up something that bothers me deeply." He was sweating as he removed his jacket, and then loosened his tie. "I have never played around on Laurie."

"Jake, I can't deal with this on top of everything else." She laid a hand on his shirt sleeve. "Please, don't seek me out. If we should pass, please just go on by. Let us speak and forget any of this ever happened."

"What if you hear I've been finding comfort with one of those sixty year old's? Would that bother you at all?"

Leah laughed. "I'd…well, I don't know what I'd think."

He grinned. "So, you can laugh. That's what I was trying for. It's a nice sound. I wondered if you could." For the first time he relaxed, pushed his feet out in front of them and tilt his head as he took in their surroundings. "Where'd you find this place? It's pretty nice. Maybe I could lure some old girl in here."

"Remember, child bearing should happen before the age of sixty, so those ladies may be beyond."

His smile was infectious. "I like having fun with you. Are you really serious that we can't even talk?"

"Very."

"Well, on that I'll rest my case." He rose to stand looking down on her. "I guess I'll mosey on down the road. Will you be all right, here?" He extended a hand. "Can I help you up?" He sighed. "No?"

"For the first time in awhile, Jake, I feel I might make contact with our Creator. Just try not to alert the neighborhood you've been in the woods. You know, no sirens or horns honking. Please."

Taking keys out of his pocket, Jake jingled them in front of her. "You are truly a godly woman, Leah Markel." His countenance became serious. "Thanks for setting me straight. I'm sure many a man has given up good years and a good woman because some other one was flattered and took him in."

Leah waved him on. "We're friends, Jake Hutchens, speaking friends. That's all."

"Just saw your car and thought I should check to see if you are all right," he called back, whistling as he left. But climbing into his car the smile left his face and the whistling stopped. He was back to square one. What was he going to do about his and Laurie's stand off? He needed his wife. She didn't need him.

Jake never saw the figure lined up behind the big oak tree. When he was well down the road, the figure stepped out and began his walk back home. Marking trees for removal for the Landess Company could wait until another day. He'd heard their voices. Curiosity had led him to the stream where they sat on the old bench. If the town folks knew, the gossip would spread like wild fire.

Mabel was washing windows when the truck pulled to the curb outside her house. New, shining in the evening sun, white as Prince

Charming's ride, she thought, wondering if she should go to the door. No one could see her through the lace curtains and she was working on the side windows. She would wash inside, first and then out. But she wanted to finish before the evening sun started to lower.

A knock on the door confirmed the truck's driver was coming to her house. Wiping her hands on a towel she'd laid on the back of a chair, she hurried to the door. "Well, lands sakes," she reached out to pull an old friend inside. "How in the world are you, Nate? Come in. Come in."

Nates face was wreathed in smile. "I wasn't sure you'd answer the door, Mabel. It's been a long time."

"Nothing's too long for friends," she replied. "What brings you to New Haven?"

"Have you wondered how it come to be, a small town like this has the best hardware store in the county?" He grinned. "My screen door finally bit the dust and I've got a new one to replace it."

"Sit here," She pulled a matching chair close to his as she leaned forward. "Now, tell me what you have been doing since I last saw you."

"Well, you know Bill Langly had a setback in his illness and Vivien couldn't run the farm, though she tried." He gave her a piercing stare. "Matt came back to help them out and kind of got himself into a bit of trouble, not by his doing, mind you, but Vivien interfered."

"She always did." Mabel pulled back into her chair as though the memory were not many years.

"Yes, she did and I regret that, Mabel. Had it not been for Vivien, there's a chance you and I would have married and Earl would have traveled on down the road. I always wished I'd done differently and I hoped you'd forgive me." He sighed, pinning her with that familiar kindness that marked his bearing. "I don't deserve it, and it's taken me all these years to ask, but I'm asking now. Will you forgive me?"

"I made my own mistakes, Nate, and Earl was one of them. I never loved him and his alcoholic ways nearly killed us both. Maybe I was responsible for him dying as young as he did. The Lord knows I tried but as soon as he comes home from work every day he hit the bottle. Him and the bottle, I turned to the church. I had no other outlet after our Jimmy died. I had two miscarriages and then we lost our boy."

"We both suffered, Mabel. You know the story. I was just the donor. I thought she loved me, but she didn't and he was my best friend and I got caught up in something that should never have happened. It took many a year for me to reach closure with the Lord over my foolish mistake and the punishment was ever before me."

"Bill never knew, did he?"

"Still doesn't. I'd die if he did. Rather cut off my right arm than hurt him at this age."

"Do you see Vivien?"

"Yes, we suffer at the same table many a holiday. Seems someone's always feeling sorry for me and inviting me. They can't stand to see an old man alone at those times and that Britany doesn't know the story. Thank God."

"She came to our Revival."

"Did she?" Nate scratched his head, thinking. "Britany's a victim of parents too old to have a child." He chuckled. "I don't really mean that, but they were so thankful to finally have one they spoiled that girl unmercifully. Now, she thinks whatever she wants she can go after it."

"Her escapade with a married man took one of our member families from Shining Light Church. After the affair, the man's wife couldn't stand to face people and they moved back to where they came from."

"Yes sir, that sounds like her. I heard a little bit about it. Then there was Matt staying with me and she set her cap for him but you know Vivien was egging it on. Seems she don't like his wife because she didn't get to choose her but I've met the girl and she's a fine person. A beauty, inside and out."

"But Matt and Britany grew up together." Mabel relaxed again. "You know all about Matt's childhood."

"That they did and she thought because he was always kind to her he belonged to her."

"Matt's wife is in charge of renovating Shining Light after the fire's damage."

Nate sat straighter in his chair. "Now how did I miss that piece of information?"

"She comes every Friday and checks on the progress. She's different, I'll say that. Knows what she's doing though. It's looking really good."

They talked for over an hour, the evening sun dipping low and Mabel knowing the windows would not be washed outside. She didn't care. Talk with an old friend was better than washing windows and Nate, well, Nate once meant the world to her, until Vivien Langly stepped in.

It was all water under the bridge after this many years. Nothing could erase what happened. Perhaps years had reduced the hurt Mable had suffered. But then she'd married Earl and his world was a whole new way. He'd not known to be kind as Nate had, before Vivien when he'd allowed her to take him away from the only woman that had ever loved him.

Chapter Eight

A week filed past, another taking its place. The renovation of Shining Light Church was coming to a close. The workmen had done a wonderful restoration. The moldings had all been placed, the carpet installation went smoothly and the gray paint was found in the swirl that lightened when footsteps brought the nap a certain direction. All in all, Shining Light was beautifully done.

Levi stood admiring the serenity of the room, secretly glad the designer chose not to install curtains to the windows of the sanctuary. She had somehow appeased the people on the decorating committee by bringing a new paint into the glassed-in foyer and applying the material they wanted at that window. A small table was centered, where the Bible remained open at all times, the two tall candlesticks on each side stood guard, an attestment to the rather large piece of wall art to one side that claimed God's word a lamp unto one's feet. But something was just a bit off balance, he thought, one hand rubbing the bristle of his chin where he was attempting to grow a beard in preparation for the annual Christmas program.

He heard the front doors open and the rustle of papers in movement before he saw the person, rather persons, behind the commotion. The designer and her accomplice were coming toward him, their arms filled with items. He rushed to help. "Here, let me take that, before you drop it." He shook his head in disbelief how women would carry as much as they could to save a trip. There was a bulging purse and an object rather haphazardly tucked between her body and one arm. "This was rather large to be tucked under your arm, wasn't it? My goodness, it's an oil painting." He admired the work. "Beautiful."

Marigold's laughter filled the sanctuary, as she nodded. "Well, Ruthie, we made it, but I have to admit that was a load." She turned to Luke, "Thanks, Pastor. You remember Ruthie, don't you?"

"I do remember Ruthie. My wife has told me she was very helpful. How are you, Ruthie?"

"Good." Ruthie smiled, waiting for Marigold's instructions for what she was carrying.

Unloading the remainder of parcels on the front pew, Marigold turned toward the foyer where Levi had been studying the wall with only one side adorned. "Have you noticed something's missing in the foyer between the Sanctuary and the Concourse, Pastor?" She nodded toward the door. "Come with me." A smile on her face must mean whatever she had in mind was good.

"Ruthie, you have the sack with the hardware, we'll need it too." She was carrying the oil again and the purse handles looped over her arm. "Now, let's hope I have everything," she said. Levi watched as she brought a stud finder and a small drill, from the purse. "Ah, yes, perfect. You have the screw, Ruthie?"

Evidently they had done the procedure before. A screw was drilled into the wall exactly where she had found by the stud finder. The wire attached to the back of the frame was finished and then the painting hung on the opposite side of the Lamp Unto My Feet hanging. Levi was mesmerized by the colors in the painting, umber, cobalt and the white robe of Jesus. "It's breathtaking," he said. "Where in the world did you find it? It's perfect." The three were now standing back to study the full range of color in the painting.

"It's the story of Jesus when he was tired," Ruthie explained. "Matt told me. When Jesus grew tired, the people still wanted to be near him and listen to his teachings, so he sit in the boat, a short distance from the bank where they could all see him." She paused. "See his hands? Matt said in Jesus day they did not have the Bible, they had scrolls, but Jesus hands are empty so he can stretch them out to the people. Jesus is the word. He offers salvation to those who accept him. His hands are not empty when we believe in him. They are stretched out to us, welcoming us. He holds us in his hands."

"I could not have said it better, Ruthie." Levi's voice held reverence. This child. This child, he thought, explains the scripture with love and wisdom. "You have captured the meaning as surely as the artist has captured the picture." He turned to Marigold. "I ask again. Wherever did you find this painting?"

Marigolds laughter filled the sanctuary with joy. "I have an inside track on a very good artist."

"It's Matt," Ruthie chimed. She pointed to Marigold. "Matt is her husband."

In the following moments while Marigold was explaining finishing the renovation to the Pastor, Ruthie studied him. Her heart told her he was not as sad as before but still the matters of his heart were not complete. It was not a problem with God. She sat there, and in the quiet of the Sanctuary Jesus spoke.

"Pastor Levi," she called across the room to him. "May I visit with your wife?"

Levi glanced Ruthie's way, a sudden sadness overcoming him. "She is in the back yard, Ruthie. You might find her with her hands dirty."

"I know she is planting tulip bulbs."

As if something shadowed his words, Levi wondered how could Ruthie know that, but his thoughts returned to Leah. "I'm sure she would love to see you." If Leah were leaving, why would she plant the bulbs Suze Norman had shared? But then, Leah was not one to shirk a job nor waste anything.

Sometimes Levi wondered if the people in his congregation knew more about his marriage than he did. They seemed to wait on Sunday mornings until Leah took her seat near the front before they were mentally prepared for worship hour. It was probably all in his mind, but with Leah in one room and him the next his mind conjured strange thoughts. If a congregation could take one deep breath, all breathing at once, Shining Light Church did. Such foolish thinking; he shrugged his way out of the depths of despair and looked to see if Ruthie had found Leah. Yes, there they were. Leah with her tulip bucket sitting nearby was now leaning on the tulip punch Suze had loaned her, talking to Ruthie.

"There's a nice swing on the other side of the house," Leah said. "Why don't we sit there?"

"I'd like that," Ruthie replied. "Do you need to take your bucket since it's empty?"

Leah laid the tulip punch on the ground by the bucket. "I'll get them later," she said.

They began the motion, feet to ground, touch, push, only the squeak of the chain made sound. "I like your husband," Ruthie said.

"I like him, too," Leah replied. She gave Ruthie a hug and when she did she felt something more than the warmth of a small body. "Ruthie, do you always pick up on how people feel?"

"A lot of times, I do," Ruthie said, meeting Leah's direct stare, for a moment Leah's hug made her think of Bitty and how much she missed her, but she would think about that later. "Why are you sad?"

"I have a decision to make, Ruthie, whether to stay…" She caught herself. "I am so sorry, I should never have said that to you, Ruthie."

"Jesus told me if you stay until the tulips bloom, you will be happy. I don't know why, but he says you must trust him and lean not to your own understanding."

"What does that mean?" For a moment rebellion surged through Leah. "That is all I've ever done, wait and trust… but there's very little I understand." She stopped the swing's movement. "Why would God… or Jesus tell you something about me when I'm older and have always put my trust in him?"

Tears swarmed in Ruthie's eyes. "I don't know. Momma says I have a gift. We don't tell people."

Leah saw her sadness. "Oh, I'm so sorry." Immediately she put an arm around Ruthie and drew her close. "I didn't mean to hurt you, little one. I'm in such a mess and there's no one I can confide in."

"Jesus knows your heart," Ruthie said. "Tell him. He wants us to talk to him."

"Oh, Ruthie, you must come to see me more." Leah wondered that at this moment she felt a peace in her heart she hadn't known in a while. "You have a calming effect on me, Ruthie."

Ruthie smiled. "No, that's Jesus. He knows your heart and he wants to help you."

"We have time to run out to the farm to see Matt," Marigold said as she slid into the seat and turned the key in the ignition, "How do you feel about that, Miss Ruthie?"

"I imagine Matt would love to see you, Tinkerbell," Ruthie teased.

"Oh, a girl after my own heart," Marigold quipped. "So how was your visit with the pastor's wife."

"She's sad."

"Really." Marigold's voice was hushed. "Can you let me in on it, or is it a secret?"

"No, there's no secret. What time of the year do tulips bloom, Marigold?"

"All the months of Spring, I'm guessing." She gave Ruthie a glance. "Is that Important?"

They went about the daily routines of life, breakfast together, Sunday worship, Wednesday night Bible study and at end of day each retired to their own room. Levi was losing weight. Leach noticed his clothes were practically hanging off his bones. Like a dutiful wife she was preparing meals. Aware of his problem she had begun to cook his favorites. Was he ill or losing weight because of their state of matrimony?

Before she left food had been her last temptation but now, having returned, though she did not know what the future held, she was able to function almost normally. She had encountered Jake once with Laurie on his arm. They had spoken and moved on. For that, she was grateful.

There was no remorse only thanksgiving and relief that nothing had happened between them. In the first weeks she had known paranoia that someone might have seen them and reported to Levi. If anything had calmed her nerves, she supposed it was the sweet encounter with Ruthie. Whether because Ruthie was a child and she longed to have a baby, or Ruthie's words to wait until Tulip time, Leah resolved to stay. She did ponder on Ruthie's words. Stay until the tulips bloom.

"I can't get this tie to cooperate," Levi came into the kitchen, his face wrinkled with dissatisfaction, the top button of his white shirt open, a tie dangling around his neck and tucked beneath the shirt's collar. "Can you help me?"

"You have it twisted in the back and the collar is holding it." She reached around his neck to straighten the tie, her body touching his, so close they could kiss. Quickly, she stepped back, but not before she saw the longing in his eyes and then the slump in his posture as if to say, it's hopeless, don't go there.

"Thank you," he said, walking away. "I'll get my jacket."

"You understand," he was waiting for her to join him. "We will be thrown together, today. This seminar is to refresh how we handle our congregation and to enrich our own lives as a married couple who present an example to them as leaders?'

"Does it seem the focus is heavily on pastor and wife relationships this year, or has it always been that way?" She slid an arm into the olive colored jacket that matched the skirt she was wearing.

"I think it's an annual presentation the association plans for all the churches, but that's why I wanted to warn you, everyone will be expecting us to be the happy couple. They still see us…"

"As honey-mooners, perhaps?" Her expression was as cool as the sound of her voice. "Because we have no children we represent the picture of what all newly married into the ministry expect to see?" Not waiting for his reply, Leah snatched up her purse to head out the door toward the car.

It was as Levi said, most greeted them, "How's my favorite couple, so good to see you both." They were there a few minutes when Leah saw Laurie Hutchens across the room. "Why is she here?"

"Who?" Levi scanned the room, finding Laurie. "Oh, the Hutchens? They are considered as Shining Light's Music Ministry. Of course they were invited." Studying her, he asked, "Do you have a problem…"

It was only natural she would encounter Laurie by end of day. Laurie hugged her in greeting. "Are you headed to the last session? Come on, I'll open the door for you. Your arms are full. Jake took my stuff to the car." She followed to the seat Leah chose, sliding into the next. "How has it been for you?" Laurie's eyes shone with pleasure. "You know how I love music, Leah and the music directors from all the churches combined to try out the new praise material offered. Oh, Leah, it was beautiful. I think we all felt God was truly in this place today."

Before she could reply a lady, Leah didn't know entered the room. "My goodness, where is everyone?" She glanced toward the door. "While we wait, I'll hand you two a sheet to fill out, like if you haven't done this all day." She smiled. "By the way, my name is Connie Price, I'm in charge of the music department at Liberty on Forrest Park road, and your association ask me to come down and share this last session with you. My credentials are mainly that I was a pastor's wife for fifty four years and when my husband died last year, to keep me from losing myself in grief, our church's association put me to use leading in sessions such as you are attending today."

Mrs. Price began to share her life with the two, glancing at the door occasionally, finally to say, "I believe our ladies attending have left early, and a few may have come into the previous sessions." She sighed. "It has been a long day, I've already led three classes and now that there are only two of you, how about I give you a quick rundown, because I know you are tired, also."

She gave them a small booklet titled, Sharing. "This is a lovely little piece of God's blessing. It has brought meaning to my life these last months. I hope you enjoy reading it in the days to come. As we begin our review, it asks the question, have you ever felt the need to voice a concern you have carried within yourself for fear no one would understand and if so, what effect has it had on you?"

When neither of the two spoke, she pulled a chair closer. "As they say, where two or more are gathered the Lord is with us, so I'm going to get off my feet and enjoy just the two of you as we become better acquainted. I can share this with you because the incident is many years past and the young lady in what I'm going to share with you has grown into a fine Christian woman. She has put the problem behind her and now helps others who have similar circumstances."

"In one of the churches my husband pastured, in a rural area away from the grind of city, a young girl came to us, in our home. She was crying and said she needed help but she didn't know where to turn because if people found out the problem they would think it was her fault. Cassie's father had died a few years earlier and her mother had remarried but still worked and often returned home late. Cassie's stepfather's job ended earlier and he was home near the same time Cassie arrived each day from school."

"Now the family attended the church my husband pastored, but he was not a member. Still, most of the congregation thought of him as a fine man. He was always willing to help with maintenance to the church. As you know, looks are often deceiving and good works can be an avenue to throw us off guard and such was the case. The stepfather was sexually using Cassie and threatened if she told he would make her the laughing stock of the community and he would say, "you do not want to hurt your mother." But the very seriousness of the act was turning Cassie into a nervous wreck and she needed someone to talk to, someone she could trust."

"What did you do?" Laurie's eyes were moist with tears. "That is a horrible thing to happen to a young girl."

"There was little we could do, if she was unwilling to press charges against her mother's husband. My husband told her we must tell her mother. Cassie was scared for her life but she was also relieved. She needed someone to stand up for her. My husband called her mother at work and asked her to come in before she went home. At first, things did not go well, the mother refused to believe her husband would do such a vile thing, but then with Cassie's sobbing she took her child into her arms and asked her if she would be willing to go with her to a doctor and let him tell her his findings."

"How old was the girl?" Laurie asked.

"She was eleven."

"This means when the doctor examined her, he knew she was a child and had not been with a man." Laurie's tears gained force, running down her cheeks. "And the report proved she had been abused, didn't it?" She swiped at her cheeks, almost in an angry gesture. "What did the mother do?"

"She confronted her husband. Of course he denied any wrong doing. But she wasn't finished, she had the local Sheriff's office run a check on him and she was able to do it discreetly since she cleaned house for the Sheriff's wife. The report that came back was not good. The man had a record for the same…"

Laurie interrupted, "These tears are not only for that little girl, Mrs. Price, but for me. I have never told this to anyone, not my husband, not my pastor, no one." Her eyes rest on Leah, "I'm sorry, Leah. I had no idea I would be telling this." Her voice broke for a moment. "Maybe it's because the music sessions were so moving today, all of our hearts were touched. We felt the presence of the Holy Spirit and my heart has been full." A sob caught in her throat. "I've had to come to grips with so much today and this last session was not what I wanted at all…I've never wanted anyone to know."

Leach was experiencing remorse of her own. "I won't tell, Laurie. Please, believe me I won't tell."

The words were rolling out of Laurie. "I was ten. My mother had been divorced since I was six and we had wonderful times together, then she met this man. He promised her the world…and he did take her out of a simpler life than the one he lived, but I was part of the bargain, you see, and since my mother was a nurse and had always stood on her own, she wanted to give back to society a part of what she was neighborhood wouldn't play with me, folks would say I was lying. He told me all those things and more. When you are ten years old and afraid you believe strange things."

"What happened?" Mrs. Price was holding Laurie's hand. "How did your mother find out?"

"I was ten when it started and in a few months my birthday and the doctor said later some girls do start having periods at eleven and I did. Then there were no periods at all and my mother became worried and took me to the doctor. I was eleven years old and pregnant and I was too immature to even know."

Fresh tears ran down Laurie's cheeks and Leah felt her own emotions building. Mrs. Price was handing tissue to both of them. Leah felt a sadness that was nearly unbearable along with the guilt that was hammering in her mind. Why wouldn't Laurie have told Jake? Everything would have been different.

"You had the baby?"

"No," Laurie shook her head, "whether it was the trauma of my mother losing her marriage or the abuse I had suffered, I was not yet three months along and no one knew unless the doctor told, but my mother asked him to not put it on the record in his office, so I would be protected. It was her plan that we move away. But by the time the doctor and my mother finished with her husband he left town and the doctor told him he would be checking on his whereabouts and notify the authorities."

"There should have been punishment," Mrs. Price said. "But the doctor and your mother were protecting you."

"I know," Laurie wailed. "My mother did not remarry until ten years ago. She was fifty nine when she met George and they had a lovely life but she died three months ago and I miss her every day. Maybe that's what's wrong with me, my missing her because I've kept the secret all these years."

"What happened to the baby?" Mrs. Price asked, gently.

"I lost the baby that week. I've often wondered if it was all the crying I did, being so young and all."

"This must have affected your life, Laurie." Mrs. Price's voice was soothing as she stroked Laurie's hand. There were tears in her eyes and her expression relayed her desire to comfort Laurie.

"I haven't told Jake. He has always wanted a baby but I just couldn't. It seemed wrong when I'd lost that one." She stared up at Mrs. Price. "Wouldn't it be wrong, trying to replace one I couldn't have?"

"We never replace people we have lost, dear." She let the words sink in. "Your baby was one little individual and should you ever decide to have another, that one will be a different little person that is born out of the love between you and your husband and the past has nothing to do with it at all."

"But the past robbed me. I've put it in the farthest corner of my mind trying to forget. It robbed me."

"Don't let it." Mrs. Price took Laurie into her arms. "You are young, my dear. Years lie ahead of you. With God in control there's no telling what the future holds." She leaned back to gaze into Laurie's face. "If you desire, I believe you will make a wonderful mother. Why don't you talk to God about that and dear one, please tell your husband what you have told us. It wasn't by chance you came into this session today, nor the fact that there were only the three of us."

She turned to Leah. "I'm so sorry we haven't discussed whatever is on your mind. I'll willingly stay, if you two have the time." She glanced at her watch. "The others are just now ending session. What would you like to do?"

"I have to meet Levi," Leah said, "What about you, Laurie?"

Laurie nodded, blowing her nose. "I need to go. Do I look terrible, Leah?"

"No, you are always beautiful." Leah took a tissue to wipe mascara from beneath Laurie's cheek. "But you don't want to start a new trend, now do you, really dark mascara under the eyes?"

"It's wonderful to see your friendship." Mrs. Price smiled at the two, "If there's nothing more you wish to discuss, let us hold hands and pray and don't forget to read the little booklet."

Levi met them in the hall. "Jake wanted me to tell you he's waiting in the car, Laurie."

Giving Leah a quick hug, Laurie headed toward the door, calling back, "Thanks, Leah."

"What's that about?" Levi was concerned. "Had she been crying…and you? What's wrong?"

"The session on sharing was pretty intense," Laurie replied. "Our hearts were softened." She could tell he didn't understand. "Didn't you have any earth shaking moments today?"

Scratching his head, Levi felt something was missing in the conversation. "Evidently, not as profound."

The ride home was quiet, each lost in reflecting on the day, but Leah's was more. Guilt was having a say. She glanced at Levi. Was the time she spent with Jake something she should tell him, or was it better left unsaid? Surely there was no way he or Laurie would find out. His knowing could bring repercussion best left alone. And she promised Laurie she would not tell her story to anyone. The whole matter left her ill at ease. Then, too, there was the day Jake followed her to the woods but he honored her request, there would be no contact between them. That was probably why he waited in the car for his wife.

He had become a watcher. This was his church. That man was his pastor and all he wanted was to see the peace a church represented magnified in his congregation. They pulled into the drive, the Pastor and his missus. If he thought for a moment he was misguided, he would give it up. He hadn't seen the pastor's wife in the presence of Jake Hutchens since. Maybe they were doing no wrong, but then why would she be sitting on a bench in the middle of the forest when Jake Hutchens parked his car down the lane to hide it behind trees and sought her out? Something smelled foul and he would wait until he knew which way the wind was blowing before he gave it up. He turned to hike back through the woods when the thought struck him, maybe he should check on the Hutchens. It was a short distance away. When he arrived, protected from their view by a tangle of vines and downed trees, they were getting out of their car, arms laden with sacks that clearly read Marlins Grocery. So, they had undoubtedly attended the same Associational meet as Pastor Markel. Yes sir, his instinct was right, they bore watching. Satisfied the day was closing he turned and went quietly through the forest to his home.

The arrival of the new piano caused much speculation as to who was the anonymous person that donated it. Then, there was the question where to sit the instrument as the designer, one Mrs. Marigold Langley, had not signed off on complete restoration of the Sanctuary.

"She assured me there are only a few necessary tweaks and then she will be gone and we can resume services in the sanctuary," Pastor Levi told the various groups questioning why they weren't already allowed to use it. "Be patient," he said. "Instead of proving yourselves impatient, prove yourselves grateful that someone donated this beautiful piano for the worship of our Lord."

"Yes, yes." Herm Smith nodded, "But the question remains who donated the piano? Maybe it's someone trying to pay off their sins." He was aware Levi was staring at him, an incredulous gleam in his eye. But Herm was not backing down. "We can't go messing with the Lord's blessing, Pastor."

"Let me understand this, Herm. You think the piano would be tainted if the one who provides that lovely instrument had sin in his or her life."

"Something like that."

"But Herm, we all have sin in our lives. That's why we pray and ask forgiveness every day. Would you rob someone the blessing of giving Shining Light Church a new piano, that is already here, ready to sit in its place of service?"

"Maybe we should take a vote. There's a business meeting coming up this Wednesday night."

Levi shook his head. "I disagree with you Herm, but if that's what you think necessary, speak with the other deacons and if they so deem, we shall vote on the piano, whether to keep it or not. In all my years I've not come upon this." Levi felt heartsick. It had been his observance, if one problem cropped up there were probably two more to follow. At the moment he couldn't imagine what that might be.

"No sir, and I imagine you've looked the other way a time or two when something came up that brought disagreement to your congregation, but there's always the matter…" Herm paused. "The matter of establishing the church belongs to the people and it's the people's voice that sets the standard."

When Levi turned to walk away in order to avoid further discourse he did not see the anger that flashed across Herm's face. Few people stood up to Herm Smith. All the land around the church belonged to him. "You might say Herm's generosity is not to be questioned," was the saying. "Everyone will be taken care of in due time as long as it's done Herm's way." But Herm didn't volunteer to purchase a much needed instrument for the Sanctuary when it nearly burned to the ground.

When Sunday arrived, Levi's sermon was based on first Corinthians thirteen. "The key verse would be thirteen," he explained as he searched the congregation for Herm. "And now abideth faith, hope, charity, these three, but the greatest of these is charity. It will enrich your faith and you will grow in spiritual maturity when you grasp the true meaning of these verses. God has laid this scripture concerning love, on my heart for today's message. Let us pray the Lord will bless the reading."

"Heavenly Father, we ask you presence as we study your word. Help us to find the true meaning and apply it to our lives. Lord we thank you for each person in our midst and ask you open our hearts at this time. And all the people said. Amen" He was aware, Herm had entered during the time of prayer.

"What is the most extensive form of God's love that comes to your mind as you read this verse?" He paused as the rippling of pages in his member's bibles lessened in sound and he believed they had found the passage. "Is it gifts we give to those we love, a mindset toward others, or is it a visible obedience to our Lord that reveals a benevolent disposition toward our fellow man? Toward our Christian brother?"

The congregation was quiet, waiting. "Though I speak with the tongues of men and angels, and have not charity. And if I have not love, I am become as sounding brass, or a tinkling cymbal." His eyes roamed the pews, gentle and kind, taking in each person. "If a person spoke with the most studied eloquence, and uttered the words of an angel but had no love in his being, would not his words fall on your ears as useless? Without reason, would those be… just words to ignore and put down?"

"Do we set value on unnecessary things, unnecessary attitudes that disrupt harmony among believers? As the apostle speaks to the people of Corinth, what is he seeing? Do the Corinthians love their brethren or value themselves and disdain others? Are we sometimes guilty of throwing out those with pure hearts in order to achieve the esteem of those who can do good for our lives, even if that good does not come from God but through the intensity of those who would help us in order to receive our loyalty in other matters?"

"We studied faith, faith as a grain of mustard seed, faith that is the essence of things not seen but hoped for, faith that can move mountains, and yet here is the apostle telling us, love is the greatest of all and if we do not have love we are as sounding brass…not a pleasant sound but an abrasive vibrating sound that puts our body in a state of unrest when we could have the sweetest melodic ring of love, a sound that has soothed the minds of kings, settled the lamb in the fold and captured the heart of man."

"Why would God give this message to me?" Levi stepped down from the podium, to stand on the same level as Shining Light's people. "Soon, we will move into our Sanctuary. But this space represents God's heart for us. Everything we needed has been provided, but God always wants the best for his children. Our sanctuary will be like new. We want our hearts to be as refreshed as the paint on the walls that cover charred places plastered over and washed clean. We want to live at home what we speak in church. It is our desire to love one another, as Jesus loved us. That is why we study first Corinthian thirteen, today. To remember the greatest gift we can give to God and to each other is to love one another, because he first loved us."

A prayer of dismissal found Levi by the front door, people shaking his hand as they left. Smiling people thanked him for the reminder of God's love and then there was Herm, offering his hand, looking Levi in the eye as he said, "Nice, Pastor. I feel you were influencing the people in a subtle way, toward Wednesday night's business meeting. They will never know they have been coerced into a vote."

His words stung. Levi fought within his own spirit not to withdraw his hand from Herm's. "Herm, is there anything we could possibly bring before Shining Light's people to hurt them? Wasn't the fire enough? The devil stumped his toe; let's not let him take us down."

Herm's laughter was no comfort; Levi felt the ripple of fear course its way up his spine. Get thee behind me, Satan, his spirit whispered silently. What was happening when Shining Light should be rejoicing? Instead of joy, Levi felt the batter of discontent forming. Was God preparing him for something else?

Sunday night services were as usual, half the attendance of morning worship. Bible study finished without mishap, but Herm was absent. Levi forgot the offering and the offering was important. There was the matter of the renovation expense. Leah could count on one hand those who sensed Levi's troubled spirit. She had seen the wheels of despair multiply when the new lady walked in and took her seat third pew from the front but Levi continued with the order of service presented in the bulletin. His sermon was not moving but an honest application for life. And when the visitor went to the altar, Levi's manner was difficult to read. Leah was unsure of the problem but acutely aware of Levi's desolation.

They were still in separate rooms; careful, lest occasional visitors would detect their arrangement. Accepting that fact in the beginning had become an embarrassment. Now, they felt unable to work through the problem and each felt there was no reason they should. "We've not eaten," Leah reminded Levi once they were home. "Is there anything in particular you prefer?"

"Nothing." He replied, "I'm going to my room."

"Are you ill?"

"Perhaps," he said, "but not physically." He was loathe to explain, at the moment, but she should know. "I believe there's trouble brewing in our church." He put a hand up. "For now, that's all I can say."

Leah's mind went into over-drive. Levi was clearly upset. What could be the cause? A nagging thought stayed with her as she sliced cheese to go on crackers. Could it be someone knew about her and Jake? The Hutchens were not in either service and Alice Morrow had led singing morning and night. Now their absence wore on her nerves. She had hoped Laurie would explain her early childhood to Jake. If there were any doubts that she wished only happiness for the Hutchens, at this moment she realized she had in Heaven nothing had happened to ruin their lives forever. Their foolishness would possibly have severed ties not only with their spouse but the church would have had to act on their behavior.

Shivering, Leah passed by Levi's room and through the open door saw him on his knees by the bedside.

Did a man cry? How often had she wondered if Levi cried? He seemed strong. Strong in his walk with God and strong as he stood before the congregation. But small things add in number and beat at a person's will. Was she part of the sadness she saw in Levi's countenance? It had begun with her own unhappiness over not being able to bear a child. Was she Sarah in the Bible, bitter, ready to hand her husband over to another woman? Or was she Leah, the one Jacob loved less? Had their love been as Jacob and Rachael in the beginning?

The hours of the night filed past and she did not sleep. The crackers had made her thirst. She crept from the bed, not turning on the light, down the hall she came to Levi's room, where moonlight streamed through the open shutters enough to see Levi was still on his knees and she heard his prayer. Standing there, unnoticed, listening, her heart ached to hear his words. Distraught, within, she wanted to go to him but how could she?

Hadn't she longed for human comfort? Hadn't she prayed God would ease the pain and fill the void of her soul? Perhaps her own unrest had caused Levi's suffering, and now to hear his prayer that he still loved her when she had spent hours thinking his only concern was the church, and wondering about Laurie's heartache so deeply rooted she had not told Jake her deepest secret.

The day had pressed such misery upon her that she could hurt another, though Laurie was unaware and called her friend, and now Levi's pain so evident, his words caring for her when she had done nothing to deserve them. She, who judged Laurie, now found herself floundering in the aftermath of her own creation and she knew not how to correct it.

It was as if God spoke to her standing there. You have read the story of Ruth? Leah was momentarily dumbstruck. Think about it. You will know what to do. Leah went on down the hall to the kitchen. What did the story of Ruth have to do with her and Levi? Her mind was playing tricks on her; she had considered Jacob and Rachael, not to mention Sarah allowing Abraham to have Hagar. She had begun a flow of Bible that would not turn loose.

The clock on the wall showed three. Outside the world glowed softly. Down the street, there were street lamps that shone dimly where they stood. If she walked to the front window, the security lights would be on the church yard. She had seen Levi on his knees praying. God intended for her to see him. Then the meaning came to mind. Laughter, silent but joyful lit up her soul. God provided the answer. Surely he had a sense of humor. She padded down the hall, her step a little lighter. She wondered if there was a smile on her face. Levi had climbed into bed. She heard the soft purr of his breathing as she lay at the foot of the bed, and in his sleep Levi reached down and pulled her into the hollow of his side, his arm around her as he had done so many times, and she snuggled close knowing this was where she was meant to be. I didn't last long at his feet, she thought, and God said, I know.

He couldn't sleep. He was to meet the logging crew at day break. On his way he passed by the pastor's home. It was early morning and there were no lights on. He had seen them before in the guest room. It was his opinion they were no longer sharing a bed. Did this mean soon there would be a divorce?

Chapter Nine

Ruthie was excited. “Momma, will you be all right with the twins?”

Ellen laughed. “Yes, Ruthie, I will be fine. Go with Marigold and don’t worry.”

“Will Daddy Daniel be home soon?”

“He will be home in time to help me get the twins ready for dinner.” Ellen came from the boy’s room where they were playing and she had been putting clean clothes away. “Now, go, don’t worry. I heard Marigold pull into the drive.”

“She will say hello, she told me.” Ruthie smiled as the door opened and Marigold peeped inside.

“How are the Gates ladies?” She twirled into the room, her black and white dotted dress whirling around her body. “Oh, look, Ruthie and I are twins.” She winked at Ruthie “We planned this, didn’t we? That should make the committee sit up and take notice, huh?”

“The committee has a voice?” Ellen was grinning as Marigold had taken Ruthie’s hand and the two were doing a step they’d used together in the last dance routine. Clapping her hands, Ellen laughed when Marigold tilted Ruthie backward until her hair was touching the floor. “Bravo.”

“How are you?” Marigold gave Ellen a hug. “Wanna go with us? We could use your support.”

“I’m afraid we don’t go anywhere without two days notice. Can you imagine packing for two sets of twins with various needs?” She shook her head as she settled onto the sofa. “But Ruthie’s excited.”

“It’s fun, Momma. There’s Pastor Levi and Leah, his wife, and then the committee has these strange old people. They make Marigold do everything twice and she doesn’t even get mad at them.”

“I bribe them,” Marigold admitted. “They love the goodies I bring and you know the shop has a lot of goodies.” She kissed Ellen’s cheek. “All right, Momma, we gotta hit the road…and not come back no more, no more.” She and Ruthie started out singing, until Ruthie remembered and ran back to kiss Ellen.

“We will be there in no time, flat,” Marigold promised. And they were. “Here you go, Ruthie, one bag of doughnuts from their favorite shop. Two liter of sparkling water, we will add the spice too, once we get inside. There’s a scarf for each of the women and ties for the gentlemen. Now, for pastor Merkal…” She smiled. “What do you think about this? A book I know he will enjoy. And for Leah, I want you to give this to her, the softest yarn, fit for a lady of means, a shawl for those times at home when she is cold. Whatta ya think, girlie?”

Ruthie stroked the shawl’s softness. “I like it. I know she will. A little baby would be sweet wrapped in it.”

Stooping, Marigold peered intently into Ruthie’s face. “Are the Merkal’s going to have a baby, Ruthie?”

“I don’t know, Marigold. Someone is.”

“That’s like muddy water, child. Of course, it could be that I’m the sole owner of that. This bump under my belly button is not going away. We will have a new bambino pretty soon.”

“You’re not very big, Marigold. Momma was huge.” Ruthie paused, thinking, “Maybe that’s why Momma always says, “Yes, you go help Marigold and don't let her carry big or heavy items, but you do."

"Carrying more than you should at one time, as usual," Levi greeted the two, opening the door for them. "Hello, and how are you two this fine evening?" He was helping Marigold unload the packages. "The Committee will arrive shortly; it seems they decided to drive down to the Junction and look at the New Methodist Church."

A frown creased Marigold's brow. "Is there something, in particular they are interested in?"

Levi chuckled, "No, they wanted to compare workmanship on the two projects, ours and theirs."

"Should I be alarmed?" Momentarily, she had visions of having to tear out something; the thought was disconcerting. "I've sought agreement each step of the way in your renovation."

"No, no," Pastor Levi comforted. "You have given us everything we've asked for. There's not a lot of entertainment around here. I'd say the Committee went as much for that as anything."

"Well, Pastor, I'm relieved, but there's one last thing. It's rather large, so I may need your help carrying it in. Follow me."

Ruthie went as far as the door. "I'll open for you," she said as they passed through to the entries foyer.

Returning to the van, Marigold opened the side door. A sheet wrapped item came into view. "If you will take one end, I'll manage the other," she said. Together they lift the object from the van and began a sideways walk back to the Church.

"Isn't this too much for you?"

Marigold managed a smile. "Actually, it isn't heavy, just awkward and large to carry by one's self."

Ruthie opened the door and once inside they sit the frame on the floor and Marigold removed the wrap. Ruthie and Pastor's sighs were enough to know the painting was perfect on the foyer's center wall that divided the foyer from the Sanctuary.

"Perfect," Pastor Markel was saying. "Oh, my goodness. The woman at the well has never been more beautiful and how perfect that people entering our building will see Jesus talking to her and offering her eternal life." His face wreathed in smile, Pastor reached out for Marigold's hand first and then Ruthie's. "This is a moment of praise." Levi Markel looked up to the one he served. "Father, blessed be thy name. Let us praise him," Pastor said. "Bless his holy name."

"And all who dwell within," Leah's voice added to the praise. "Hello. Good to see you." Her eyes rest on Marigold as her arms opened to Ruthie. "Come, here, my dear little friend," hugs were in order as the two come together and then Leah noticed the painting. "Oh, my goodness. Oh……"

"Her husband is the artist," Levi explained. "Isn't it wonderful?"

Leah's enthusiasm matched Levi's. "And then there's this little girl. She is wonderful."

"I'm so happy to see you, Ruthie." Leah was leading Ruthie away, through the doors to the concourse and down the hall. "What have you been doing since you were here last?" And as always, she had noticed and Leah wanted to ask Ruthie if Shining Light's designer was expecting a baby. As usual there was a twinge of longing sprang into her thoughts but she would save that conversation for later when they sit down to have their tea.

"So much for that," Levi murmured as the two disappeared down the hall. "I hope I'm an apt replacement for your helper because those two seem quite enamored of each other."

"Everything is in order, Pastor Markel, but I have noticed the piano is not in its place. Any reason for that?"

Levi felt a rush of embarrassment. "Well, we were to have a meeting on that, after Wednesday night services but just as we were closing down Bible study, one of our elderly got strangled and had to have medical attention, so that item of discussion was tabled."

"You mean there's dissension over the new piano?"

"I'm afraid so." Levi gave her a rueful glance, and then busied himself picking up the papers that had covered the painting.

"I thought members only quibbled over the color of the carpet and we covered that, didn't we?"

"Yes, we did, but in this instance it's more who bought the piano, as that person wished to remain anonymous."

"Anonymous is a problem, then?" Marigold sat down, "Join me for a minute, Pastor." Marigold reached into her purse and brought out the billing for supplies she had spent replacing items for Shining Light Church's burn out. "My mother has graciously paid for all expenses and we have donated our time." She held his attention, as she ripped the billing into. "It is our hope your members will allow us to contribute to your great fellowship and here is a check to cover the cost of the workers because we realize that has been a major expense and could possibly set Shining Light's operating cost back considerably."

Marigold laid a hand on his arm. "Pastor, you have to let people help where there's a need and from my observation, with the count of, what, say three or four young couples, your church as far as I can tell is mainly elderly people on fixed income and while I know they give from their heart, please accept this check." Marigold considered what was on her mind at the moment, and then taking a deep breath, continued. "Pastor, stick to your guns, allow the payment by anonymous people and set the piano in place and continue praising the Lord. Doesn't scripture say, every good gift is from the Lord?"

Footsteps interrupted Levi's reply as they turned to see Britany making her way down the aisle. "I came to see how the piano I purchased looks in its place and if you don't mind, I'd like to play it."

Levi suddenly had a need to thread his fingers through his hair. It must be standing straight up.

"I think I will go find Ruthie and visit with your wife a moment before we leave, Pastor."

"What?" Britany spread her arms wide, a smile on her face that chWadeged. "You don't want to hear me play? It's a very fine instrument; only the best for Shining Light Church." Laughing, she glanced to the piano's customary place, seeing the old upright? "Where is it? Pastor Markel, you and I will shove that one aside and set the new one..." She saw him shaking his head. "No, Pastor. I demand. The piano goes right here," her hand was on the old upright. "Don't tell me there's a problem. Now, let's move it."

So that's how it's done, Marigold's mind was in a whirl. God was no respecter of persons. Still, she lingered on Britany's Cheshire cat smile and the intimidating laugh that followed. Both were aimed at her and she ...being shocked at Britany's sudden appearance had let the moment pass by.

Now, following the sound of laughter she found Leah and Ruthie across the way, following a stone path that lead to the Parsonage, a modest white siding home that matched the demure of the church. Though adequately remiss of frill the present occupants had made the landscape interesting and attractive. Leah motioned she was to come join them and Marigold stepped onto the gray painted floor of the front porch and took the seat offered. The small round table bore a pitcher of lemonade, several thin crystal glasses and a plate of crust-like pastries.

"Do you always pull out the southern flair for your visitors?"

Leah laughed. "I knew Ruthie would be here and we are girls after each other's heart, so I found these little glasses that are hardly ever used and this beautiful plate that was given to us …and voila, here we are in party mode."

"Do you have a lot of visitors, from the congregation?"

Leah sighed, "not nearly enough, lately, but everyone's busy from the regular church schedule."

"Do you have children?" Immediately, Marigold saw the sad expression on Leah's face. Thinking there must have been loss, she added, "I've miscarried one child."

Leah glanced from Marigold to Ruthie.

"It's all right. My Momma says I'm older than my years. But I can go somewhere if you want."

Marigold reached over to hug Ruthie. "This one has a gift, Mrs. Markel. If ever there was one to read between the lines, it's this one."

They met Matt. Instead of Marigold driving out to the farm, he came to them. "I needed a few supplies," he explained. "See, it all works out." He tweaked Ruthie's nose, "How are you, Kiddo?"

"What about me?" Marigold pretended to pout.

Matt grinned and planted a big smooch on her lips, then stood back to study her. "Didn't the doctor tell you to leave off the high heels?" He pulled her close, and laid his hand on her stomach. "You are no bigger than a baby…." He stalled for a word.

"Pumpkin?" Ruthie giggled, pointing at Marigold. "That's what she used to call M.J."

"A little pumpkin, then," Matt said leaning in to whisper in Marigold's ear. "You all right?"

Nodding, Marigold's eyes were squinted. "I just had a little encounter with your old girlfriend."

Hands up, Matt shook his head. "I'm innocent until proven guilty. Where?"

"At the church." Marigold's head dipped as she stared at her hands.

"Why?" He rubbed a day's growth of whiskers. "Why would she be at Shining Light Church?"

"Good question, but the answer is she bought the new piano that everyone seems unable to accept."

"Why's that?"

"One of the founding fathers, obviously objects, seems Britany may be thought of as a harlot."

"That's harsh. She may be many things but I doubt that."

"Not my saying." Marigold turned toward the painted van. "Coming, Ruthie?"

"Did I say something wrong?" He came strolling behind her, looking gloom. "I can't help if you run into her, Tinkerbelle. It's not my doing."

"I know, Farm Boy." She gave him a searching stare. "It's just a reminder of a terrible time in our lives and for some reason I feel sad that it ever happened."

Matt leaned close as she was getting into the van. "Come here, Tinkerbelle, if I can't take you home with me, at least you can give me something to think about." He had his arms around her. "Now, lay your head on my shoulder and just relax. This is us. We love each other. We have a healthy little boy and a new one on the way."

"I thought you were having a girl," Ruthie said. "After two sets of twins, I was really excited to think…"

Matt interrupted. "What do doctors know, huh, Ruthie?" Then he grinned. "He says it is a girl."

They were miles down the road when Ruthie asked, "Marigold, are you sad over the baby or Matt?"

"I miss him, Ruthie. Matt's trying to help his parents and that's good but it keeps us apart."

"Will he come home when the baby is born?"

"I hope so. I don't think I could do this without him since I had such a hard time having M.J."

"It's a year for babies, Marigold."

Glancing her way, Marigold asked, "Is the pastor's wife going to have a baby, Ruthie?"

At that moment a deer ran across the road and Marigold had to use the brakes. Ruthie never answered but in her mind it wasn't the Pastor's wife she was seeing. She had no idea who the woman was.

"How did you and the little girl get along?" Levi was sitting in his favorite chair reading the paper.

Glancing up from her spot at the table, a distant stare came into Leah's eyes. "If all women could be as pure as Ruthie and all children as wise, then our world would be a better place." She gave a deep sigh. "There's such calm in that child, it's catching. When she leaves I can't explain it, but I feel I've been blessed."

"There's certainly no calm when those two women meet. I wondered if I should run this afternoon. What do you suppose has created such hostility between them? That Britany and Marigold?

"A man." Leah started toward the bedroom. "I think she warned you." Stopping she asked, "Do you find yourself enamored by the beautiful Britany?"

"No, I'm enamored by the beautiful Leah," he replied, "but that hasn't worked out so well for me. I'm allowed to hold her…and that's all."

Leah blushed. "I thought…it doesn't matter what I thought. Thank you for holding me, Levi and allowing me back in your bed… that night I saw you praying and knew what a good and just man you are, I could not find one more faithful…" She sighed. "It's me, Levi. It's always been me. Do you want me to leave?"

"Never." Levi shuddered at the thought. "I need you and I'm a patient man, only because God answers prayer. I'd rather just hold you the rest of our lives, than to be without you ever again."

"You deserve much more." Her eyes were moist. "I don't know what's wrong with me."

His heart was breaking for her sadness. "We will weather this storm, Leah, and grow old together."

Sometimes, his own nerves felt frayed. He prayed continually to the God who had called him to this life. Lord, don't let me disappoint my people, help me to bring in those who are lost and don't know you, and help me to love Leah, Lord, so much that she will one day love me. He looked toward heaven with a tiredness that was seeping into his bones, knowing tonight there'd be little Bible study, the people were waiting to hear everyone's opinion, whether to keep the new piano or press on with the old upright. It seemed foolish to him, weren't there more important things than their labeling the woman who bought it a sinner? We're all sinners, saved by grace and not by works lest any man should boast. The words popped into his mind. Where was she? The beautiful Britany and how had he listened to Mabel Hisaw calling her that until the words were fixed in his mind, too? She wanted to be present for the meeting. When his mother was well, he often asked her opinion on such as the matters Shining Light was facing, but his mother wasn't well and while Leah was away he had moved her to the local nursing home. He had not felt at ease performing the necessary rituals to care for his mother's present needs.

The conversation with the piano lady had hung in his thoughts to rethink over and over.

"Ma'm," he'd said, wringing his hands, "You are not a member of the church. They'll ask you to leave."

"Pastor," she had pinned those smoldering blue eyes on him. "Is that any way for a church to behave?"

"No, ma'm, I preach against it, I have scripture in prayer meetings to curb the problem, but it stays."

"Then let's see if we can entice them to keep the piano and perhaps they will allow me to remain, also."

He was beyond frustration. What was causing the work of the devil in his congregation? If he wasn't any more effective than this, perhaps he was the one should leave. But where would he go? Sinking down on the front pew, head in his hands he was praying again and when he looked up, Lar Smith was standing in the aisle.

"Am I going to have to take you fishing again?" Lar sank onto the cushioned seat beside him, smiling satisfaction. "Sure beats that old tractor seat," he said. "But what's going on, you were in pretty deep there."

"Did I speak out loud?" Levi felt embarrassed. "I didn't realize it."

"No, no, you just groaned a time or two; I could tell something's bothering you."

People were filing in. Herm Smith took his place in the second row on the left side of the building.

"We'll talk, later, friend." Lar reached out his hand. "I know what this meeting's about, but not your problem. I thought maybe you needed to open up about your own…"

"One and the same," Levi replied, opening his bible. "I can't believe the things that disrupt harmony."

"As I recall men have created dissension over a bowl of soup," Lar whispered, "and women just cut men's hair." Satisfied, when Levi chuckled, Lar walked to his spot mid-way of the church and sit down.

It was when Leah came in from the back, the usual babble and banter became a hush. Slipping into her seat, she wondered that they could all hear a pin drop in the silence. The number present meant someone had been on the phone, attendance never exceeded one third of the membership on Wednesday nights. As the opening prayer for Bible Study was offered, Leah peaked a glance to see exactly who all was there and to her surprise found Laurie and Jake Hutchens seated across the aisle. Laurie smiled and wiggled her fingers in recognition.

With the prayer completed, Levi stood before the people, clearing his throat, Bible open to the chosen passage, when Herm Smith rose up. "Pastor, if it's all the same to you, let's get on with the business portion of this meeting, then we'll read the scripture."

There was a murmur of approval. Levi turned the floor over to the church clerk who also served as secretary. Almost every aspect of Shining Light's meaning to the community lay in her hands. She might be getting too old for the amount of responsibility she served, but her mind was sharp and Shining Light was protected as a mother protected her child. Now, as she read the minutes of the last meeting, a slow churn of resentment boiled in her veins, that someone dared question a gift given to glorify the Lord or for that matter her pastor, Levi Markel…and his wife, well, it meant they questioned the validity of herself, too. She practically lived at the church and ran her part of the business with an iron fist.

"That's the minutes," she said, her words staccato crisp, "Here's the financial report, and now," her eyes roamed the group sitting before her. "Why don't we get to the real meaning of this meeting? Half of you never darken the door on Wednesday nights and don't start protesting or I'll call you by name. Someone has created a stir over the piano, an instrument donated to the church, a much-needed instrument and some of you," She paused, her eyes had become mere slits and her countenance, if possible, more stern. "Some of you, those who quibble at every turn of the way, think there's a problem with the donation." Drawing her shoulders higher, she sniffed disdainfully, "and some of you have more troublesome meddling things on your minds. Some of you never enter the door until you hear there's a little problem needs settling. Well, just remember when you meddle, what goes down comes round." Those stern eyes settled on each one, again, daggers darting straight to their souls. "All right, Larry, you are the Deacon in charge this year, come up here and do your job. I said what I did because I knew you wouldn't. I want you all to remember, it's for the betterment of Shining Light, God's church."

"Will someone make a motion we accept Talulah's report, as read?" It was done, followed by a second and Larry opened the floor for discussion of the piano. "You all know Miss Britany donated the piano, a very fine instrument."

"What's the reason a stranger comes into our midst and buys an expensive instrument, right off?"

Mabel Hisaw glanced around to face James Green. When no one spoke she said, "Now, James, you know Miss Britany grew up around here and has been attending Shining Light."

"I know other things, Mabel," James Green murmured, a yelp ending his words as his wife poked him.

"Shall we take a vote?"

"Now hold on here." Herm Smith rose to his full height. "We haven't fully discussed this."

"Have you heard, Herm, silence is golden. These people don't seem to want to discuss the problem. Silence usually gives consent. We need only to take a vote."

The silence was deafening. Herm stood his ground, scowling at the moderator. "What about you, Pastor?"

Before Levi could answer, although he scrambled from the seat, the sound of piano came from the hallway where it had been closeted. Everyone looked toward Jake Hutchens who always led their singing and to see if his wife, Laurie, was by his side. She was. And she was listening enraptured. "Absolutely beautiful," she said. "Listen to the sound. Oh, yes, we need the new piano and I'll step down for whoever's playing it to take my place."

Jake stood up, extending a hand to Laurie. Together the two walked toward the sound and only moments later the three pushed the piano into the presence of the congregation.

"Open your songbooks, people," Jake invited, "to page three-seventy-six. How Great Thou Art."

Laurie seated herself to the right of Miss Britany, the two giving the hymn an arousing opening. So infectious were the three, Mabel rose, Suze Norman joined her and James Green's wife came to stand with them as they sang. Soon everyone had joined in, except Herm Smith and James Green.

The spirit of the Lord moved upon the people, following, as the two at the piano moved into a liturgy of hymn of thanksgiving and when the songs ended, Larry Smith asserted his authority being in charge of the business session. "Would anyone care to make a motion as to whether we keep the piano donated by Miss Britany, or send it back?"

"The singing has been wonderful," Mabel Hisaw exclaimed. "I haven't felt this wonderful in ages. I make a motion we dismiss any doubt and keep the donated piano for Shining Lights glory."

Suze Norman and James Green's wife spoke in unison, "I second."

Herm Smith stalked past the three women. They heard the door slam behind him.

"That was absolutely exhausting," Leah practically fell into the chair opposite Levi's recliner. "You must feel elated. Those women took the bull by the horns and pushed the vote through."

"I feel like I've been punched in the gut."

"Why?" Leah felt a quick intake of air. She leaned forward to stare at Levi. "What do you mean?"

"Yes, I'm thankful for the piano matter to be settled but after the service ended, Larry was listening to the men talking outside and he said there's talk there's another matter of a more serious nature facing Shining Light."

"What were they referring to?" Leah registered his grave concern. "Surely you would have a hint…"

"No, I haven't the slightest idea. They say it could mean asking someone to leave the fellowship."

"Oh, Levi." His hands were clenched and his lips pressed so tightly together they had turned white.

"I won't do it, Leah. I will not ask anyone to leave the church. I will leave myself and no one will care."

Chapter Ten

At the Cape, Christ Church windows were dark when Ellen pulled into the parking lot. "Ruthie, are you certain the program committee told you to come tonight?"

"Yes, ma'm," Ruthie was searching the lot, looking for another car. "Mrs. Lola said she wanted all children to be ready to try out for parts and that anyone that didn't get a part must not be disappointed because she has an even more important job for them to do." Digging in her back pack, Ruthie brought out a paper, "here's the number she said to call if anytime we can't attend practice."

Taking the paper, Ellen found the number and dialed. Mrs. Lola Duggins answered. "Oh, Ellen, I saw your Daniel's name on caller I.D. I must apologize for not reaching you but a pipe burst and the church basement is flooded. That's where we were to meet and we will next week, I promise." She gave a nervous chuckle. "We didn't want to risk the children going near the water and getting hurt."

"Well, Sweetums," Ellen stared across the console, "Here we are, Daddy's with the twins so it looks like you and I have a few minutes to ourselves. What do you want to do?"

"We could pick up hamburgers and fries," Ruthie's eyes twinkled, "and milk shakes and go by Marigold's. I haven't seen her this week, have you?"

"No, and she has those new candles in that I like." Ellen's nose wrinkled, remembering, "the twins put play dough in mine…somehow it just isn't the same, especially after daddy wasn't paying attention and lit it." She reached down for her purse, "Can you find a twenty? That might do it."

Marigold heard the doorbell jingle as she came from her office. "Hey, hey." Her face wreathed in smile.

"We come bearing food; it may be a bit early for you, but how about a hamburger?"

"Praise the Lord, I've had to do book work and it gives me a headache. Food sounds good." She turned to go to the back room. "Yep, it's clear. Come on back, we can spread out on the wrapping table."

"So what's going on with you?" Ellen was folding her sweater over a chair, proceeding to hunt napkins from beneath the burgers. "We brought shakes, hope that's all right."

"All right? That's wonderful." They were all seated. "Who's saying grace? Ruthie?"

"Thank you Lord for this day and keeping us safe and letting us be with Marigold. Thank you for the food. Please bless everyone in your Holy name. Amen.

"Amen," Ellen and Marigold said in unison. "So what brings you out?"

They ate and talked. And as they were leaving, Marigold said, "Ruthie, the committee from Shining Light called and ask if I would come one more time to tell them what they should do to spruce up the pastor's office." She laughed. "It no longer matches the rest of the building. They said I should give them pointers and they will do the work. Want to go with me?" The grin spread as she finished, "We can go by and see Matt and while we're there you can see Miss Leah." To Ellen she said, "They hit it off immediately." Catching Ruthie's expression, she asked, "What is it, Ruthie? Is something wrong?"

"I don't know. When you mentioned Miss Leah a feeling of sadness came over me." Quiet for a moment, Ruthie seemed to be listening to an inner voice. "I hoped Miss Leah would have a baby but that's not it, something is wrong with the church."

"Oh, no," Marigold slapped a hand to her forehead. "I pray it isn't because of something I've done."

"I don't think it's material things, Marigold," Ruthie replied. "I think it has to do with people's feelings."

"You know, don't you," Marigold turned to Ellen, "That Britany person is trying to attend Shining Light Church." Closing her eyes, she shuddered slightly. "Let's just pray Matt Langley isn't there."

"Speaking of babies," Ellen was pushing an arm into the sweater, "What is going on with you? You just aren't gaining weight with this one and your time is almost up, and too, should you be wearing those wedges?" She helped Ruthie into her jacket. "Do I need to buy you some flats to wear?"

Patting her stomach, Marigold grinned. "Doctor says I'm doing fine and as for the shoes, I gave up the heels. I know. I know. They were a danger, could cause me to stumble, all that stuff, but these are what, an inch high? For Heaven's sake, El, I'm not a granny. Which by the way, the granny has M.J."

"And you have to pick him up. Let's go, Ruthie, it's shop closing time and Daddy will need relief."

They were into the drive home when Ellen asked, "do you want to tell me about Miss Leah?"

"She wants a baby really, really, bad, Momma. I ask Jesus to give her one and I always feel him smiling but it's not a picture of Miss Leah I'm seeing."

"In time, God will reveal what he wants you to know." Ellen reached over to squeeze her daughter's hand. "Sometimes the gift is confusing, isn't it?" She sighed. "That's why we have to learn patience and follow the Lord's leading."

Suddenly Ruthie was laughing.

"What's so funny?"

"We forgot the candles."

They arrived home to find the twins all sitting in high chairs at the table and Daniel on the phone, pacing as he listened to the caller and nervously threading his fingers through his hair, which was already standing on end.

"Yes. I got that and I'll be waiting to hear from you. I'm sorry this is happening. We love you guys."

"It's in the papers," Daniel turned to where Ellen had taken his place stirring the huge pot on the stove. "It hasn't stuck in the bottom, has it? I was so stunned by Andrew's news I completely forgot the soup."

Ellen gave him full attention. "That was Andrew on the phone and his news must be upsetting but please, tell me, what are you talking about? I haven't seen Anne in two weeks."

"I know, we've all been busy and then we couldn't have dinner with them because the twins had colds." Stopping to take stock of himself, Dan stared up at the ceiling. "You remember when Waldin died it cleared Andrew because there was no one to press charges," he sighed. "And we were all extremely happy after all that man put Andrew through, leaving damaged toys hanging on their front door knob, calling Andrew and threatening to find him at a time Andrew least expected Waldin."

"Yes, it went on forever. How could there be a problem now that he's dead?" Ellen was removing two bowls from the table. "Ruthie and I ate with Marigold. We needed to touch base, you know, with Matt gone."

"That's what worries me." Daniel slumped into his chair, glancing at the twins involved with the new sticker books and as expected they were plastering each other. "What a waste, well let me rephrase that, if it keeps them occupied and quiet when we talk those stickers are worth every dime."

"Buster," Ellen stood over him, a wooden spoon in her hand. "You are killing me. Get on with the story. What's in the paper about Andrew? He was about to take a new job, wasn't he?"

"Until today's news, then the firm called and told him due to recent media coverage that would be damaging to their practice, it was best they withdraw their offer."

"Someone is making charges against Andrew?" Ellen wore a troubled expression. "What are they?"

"Whether Andrew set up the plot to kill Waldin. Now they're saying it was no accident."

"Who would do that?"

"Andrew is pretty sure it's someone on the local level, or the auspice of the Attorney General."

"My goodness." She slid into her usual place at the table her eyes on Samuel and Daniel. "Oh, Dan, they resemble the soiled pages of a catalog, where you know the object was there but you're not sure what you're looking at."

"Well, it kept them quiet while we had this conversation. There's something in that." Dan began to pull the stickers off, the boys yelping and wanting to keep them. "No, son. We have to eat and you don't need paper in your soup." The twins clatter rose to a new pitch. "No, boys. Now let's say grace." He was a little flustered. "Ellen, I'm troubled over what Andrew has told me, will you pray?"

"Close your eyes, boys." Ellen waited. "Now." Reluctant the twins bowed their heads. "Father, we come to you thanking you for another day and for the blessings you have given us. Our hearts feel the burden our friends must be bearing, but we cannot know to their extent. We lift them up to you now, that whatever lies ahead, you will be with them and we give praise knowing you are always with us. We ask now, a blessing upon this food, our family to your care, and strength to always be found serving you. Amen.

Chapter Eleven

They were all in attendance. New Haven's Women's Society of Shining Light Church had grown and it was all due to the gossip going round. Mabel Hisaw counted fifty two. "I can't believe this," She murmured.

"What's that?" Suze Norman was digging in the material crate. "We've about come to the end of our donated material that is of any size to make lap pads. Who knew Shining Light could pull fifty two women into its holy portal to do anything, other than eat at socials." Straightening up, she gave Mabel a wink. "Of course we know why they are here. They hadn't darkened the door to help before, now they're here."

"And all for the wrong reason," Mabel huffed. "When word got out someone might be asked to leave the church, the gossip went like wild fire. That's wrong. Some are even speculating it's our pastor."

"You think Herm Smith is behind this?" Suze shut the lid to the chest, piled the material she had salvaged across one arm and asked Mabel, "Are you going to help me cut these out?"

Mabel, tossed her head, as a prim expression settled on her face, "Just look out there who's talking the most. I'd say if you put her in charge of that pile of material and a pair of scissors in her hand, well, now, she just might slow up. It takes a bit of doing when you're aiming for two things at one time."

"You haven't changed a bit. Always a salty reply when we were teenagers." Suze paused for a moment. "I heard Nate stopped by your house last week." She saw Mabel's roll of the eyes but pressed on. "Rumor had it last year that Vivien's boy, our designer's husband, was staying with Nate and not Vivien and Bill. You got any comment on that?"

"Like if it's any of their business, but since it's you asking, "Yes, Matt is staying with Nate."

"Don't suppose you two got into that business concerning Vivien's boy being Nate's son." Suze saw Mabel's reaction, "I'm not prying, Mabel. I may be younger than you but my sister was right there by your side when it all happened. News travels fast and she called, said she'd heard he came by your house and was there any chance the two of you would make amends. I already knew it was Vivien broke you two up." Suze sighed heavily. "I miss Wade so much, if there's any way you and Nate could make a future together, then I'll say go for it." She gave a hurried glance Mabel's direction. Seeing the tears, her heart was properly contrite. "I'm sorry, Mabel. I'm just now realizing I've hurt your feelings. Again."

Mabel forgave Suze. Widowhood was a hard task to accept. She'd been there but she and Earl hadn't loved each other as Suze and her Wade. Making sure no one was listening, she replied, "Yes, Suze we spoke of it and Nate apologized but it's all near fifty years too late, don't you agree?"

"Moving on to a new subject, then," Suze leaned in to whisper. "What do you think about the new woman? She's talked around, if our designer don't want her husband, her words are, "She sure does."

It was bad timing, all the way, as if the Women's Society Group had lost their mind, talking about the possibility of someone being churched, when the Pastor or his wife could pop in any moment. "I hope that designer woman doesn't show up, too." Mabel said.

"But it's Wednesday and she usually comes on Saturday."

Mabel felt the hair on the back of her head crawl. "I saw Miss Britany pull in and another van that has Angel Tuning written on its side door. I suppose she's having the new piano tuned." She turned to the lap pads laying on the center island, ready for delivery to the Nursing home. "I'm telling you this is some of our best work. That means our new gals have been holding out on us."

"Oh, mercy, me." Suze exclaimed. "I just happened to glance out to see the van you mentioned." She grabbed Mabel by the shirt sleeve. "Look." She pointed to the second entrance of Shining Light's drive. "Isn't that our designer lady?" Suze checked her phone. "But it is Wednesday."

"How could two women dislike each other so much?" Kathleen Tanner stood behind them. "Don't mind me, I've been listening to you two, when I could understand, that is, and its life isn't it?"

Suze appeared disgruntled. "Sometimes, Kathleen, conversations are private and I can say that since we are cousins."

Kathleen smarted, "Only through your dead husband, maybe since Wade died, we're not cousins."

"Oh, Kathleen, I apologize. I didn't mean to hurt your feelings. I just got caught up in this church thing." She reached for Kathleen's hands. "It bothers me, our church people are at odds."

"It bothers us all, Suze." Kathleen's eyes welled with tears. "Our sisters in Christ are a bit dramatic."

"When you lose your husband...well, you spend more time at church," Suze admitted, "and for some reason it becomes so dear to you it is a great concern when there's a problem."

"Isn't that the way it's supposed to be, girls, putting ourselves aside for the greater cause, which is in our case the Lord's house... but sometimes we get a little side tracked and feud among ourselves."

Mabel smiled on them. "Let's finish up for a walk. Before long, we won't have the pleasure. One day this warm weather will turn cold and we'll long for these times, with the leaves turning all orange and gold."

"What about the people," Kathleen pointed to the hall, "that's coming together and may have …"

Mabel interrupted, "That's not our concern, is it?" But their attention was drawn to the two there.

Britany stood defiant; staring at Marigold, Shining Light Church's designer and rectifier of the burn out who was loathe to pass by. Words came to their ears. The one who purchased the piano sounded demanding, "Don't you ever finish your projects, eems to me you've had plenty of time." The designer merely stared back. They heard her say to the little girl, "Come, Ruthie, let us find the Pastor's wife."

The ladies from Shining Light's Women's Society, turned down the sidewalk, sneaking a peek toward the designer and her little companion who were already on the path toward Pastor Merkel's back yard.

Running ahead, Ruthie found Leah was not alone and she recognized the woman with her, instantly. Still, she listened as Leah introduced her. "You said you had good news to share, do you still want to?"

Laurie's laughter rang with happiness, "I came to tell you, Leah, you were instrumental in my reconciling with Jake. Poor man, he never knew what was coming his way…but after seminar, that day, you remember my heart was so emotional." She turned to Marigold. "My husband and I weren't separated, or anything like that, but let's just say…our marriage was pretty dull. And it was my fault."

"Aww, I doubt that," Leah offered. "It takes two to tango, isn't that what they say?"

"And we did," Laurie blushed. "I mean, we got on solid ground after I made confession." She saw the puzzlement in Marigold's expression. "I'm doing a terrible job at this…and we just met. What I'm trying to say is I had kept things from my husband…that would have helped him to understand me…"

At that moment her cell rang and she answered. "What? Oh, my goodness. I'll be right there. Yes, now." Her eyes were large with surprise. "Either I left in a hurry, or someone else has used the front door, left it open and the neighborhood dogs got in, but that's not all, I had made a cake…you can guess the rest… I've got to go. I'll talk to you later, Leah." She was twinkling her fingers as she hurried down the walk to her car.

Leah was trying not to laugh. "Would you believe, we just recently became really good friends." As though the car speeding away gave clue, Leah said, "I wonder what her good news was…?"

"She's going to have a baby." Before her words registered on Marigold and Leah's face, Ruthie realized she had spoken out loud. "Oh, I shouldn't have said that. Please…"

Marigold was cupping her arm around Ruthie's shoulder. "You knew that the last time we were here."

"But I didn't know who was having a baby." Ruthie stared down at the ground. "That's the first time I have done that. I'm not ever supposed to speak out loud, but I kept seeing this lady in my mind. It's her."

"It's all right, Ruthie." To Leah, Marigold explained. "Our Ruthie has a gift. She knows things. It seems when someone needs a blessing really, really, bad, God gives Ruthie a word of wisdom."

Remorse filled Ruthie's heart as she remembered Momma saying be patient and careful in what God reveals to you because all people did not believe in her gift and then there were others Momma said would want to use her gift.

Ruthie stared up into Leah's face. "Be happy for your friend. God knows our hearts. Yours is sad."

"If you only knew," Leah wanted to say but she didn't. There was a happiness for Laurie and Jake and possibly a relief she hoped would wipe away any guilt she felt over those early days of the year when she met Jake. But she did hang on to the fact nothing happened. Then why had their relationship been strained?

Suze waited until Kathleen turned on the street to her home. When she was certain there was no one to hear, she said, "Mabel, what if it is our pastor's wife someone wants to remove from fellowship? Now, don't pull that you don't know what I'm talking about on me. I'm pretty sure we both saw that exchange of words between Leah and Jake Hutchens and he was asking her to meet him."

"All right, so I heard it. I never mentioned it to you because it could be harmless and it is months past, Now, do we have to discuss it?"

"I think we better, unless you want to discuss you and Bill Langley. I sure didn't know about that."

Mabel rolled her eyes. "For heaven's sakes, Suze, you should know as well as me, she has it mixed up. Bill and I were just good friends. When Vivien thought she was miserable and left those few days, Bill called me to see if I knew anything. Of course I didn't but then he came to my home to inquire and all I could do was tell him the same thing all over again." She shook her head. "How can things from the past rise up to haunt us? I pray, and you must too, that nothing comes from any of this."

"I want to know if it's Herm Smith. He's been around my place more than he should, lately. There's something spooky about him."

"Maybe he's interested in you."

Suze twist her hands together, nervously. "Mabel, he's younger than me."

"What's that got to do with anything?"

Tears welled up in Suze's eyes. "I still love Wade, Mabel and I don't want another husband."

"Maybe Herm just wants to befriend you, Suze. There's no one his age in New Haven and he did live most of his life with his mother. I'd say he just wanted to talk. Maybe he cares if you are all right."

Suze went into a tether. "I can't believe you would dishonor Wade's memory with such nonsense."

"I've not dishonored Wade at all. You are sad, you can't get your mind off of your grief and possibly there's a man who has noticed." Mabel snorted. "Just forget I said anything."

"What about if Pastor finds out his wife and Jake met?"

"Suze," Mabel's hands were on her hips. "Do we know what they talked about? Do we even know if they met?"

Suze burst into tears, a sob escaping as she turned away. "I've wanted to cry all day, Mabel. I can't seem to control it. What if Herm came to visit and I cried the whole time. I don't want him to visit." Her sobbing escalated. "I don't want anyone churched, no one sad and most of all me always crying."

Mabel guided her up the sidewalk to her own front porch, sat her down in one of the old rockers and took the other herself. "Dear, our group letting go and out of control upset us all, and then we see those two young women at a standstill, and it brought us full circle to ourselves. Herm is not part of this equation, unless you want to listen to him some time, instead of me. And Suze, you are going to quit crying one day. Time has not evolved enough. Now, I'm going in to get us both a nice glass of peppermint tea."

"You are awfully quiet. What are thinking?" Marigold reached across to pat Ruthie's knee. "I've been around you enough to know when you get quiet, something's going on."

"I know, but I don't know why I'm keeping Anne and little Andy in my mind. Momma says when times like this come I must listen. God will work it out. But I worry because I don't know what I'm listening for." Ruthie sighed, her sober eyes meeting Marigold's. "Are we far from where Matt works?"

They were on the way to meet Matt. "Our time has run out, Ruthie." She gave a deep sigh, "I was hoping we could spend a little extra time with him, but leaving after you finished school, and the brazen interference of that heifer," Marigold shook her head. "Well, all things working together were not perfect this afternoon. But you and Mrs. Merkal seemed to have a few pleasant moments."

"I like Leah. She said it made her feel old if I called her Mrs. Merkal." Glancing her way, Ruthie asked, "Did you know they put Pastor Levi's mother in Sleeping Shades Respite? She needed better care than they could give her." Marigold nodded and Ruthie continued. "It made them sad. I would be, too."

Finding the field road that led back to where Matt said they were working; Marigold made the turn. A cloud of dust rose up behind the van. She realized it would be covered and in need of washing when they returned. Her thoughts wandered to Matt's parents. His father was in ill health and the longevity of his illness had to be causing his mother to tire out. She wondered who would care for them when the time arrived; the illustrious Britany or a Nursing facility since his mother had no use for her, Matt's wife.

"Did you say something?" Ruthie was peering up at her.

"If I did, I didn't mean to." She grinned. "There's my man. I cannot tell you how glad I am to see him."

"He must be happy, too." Ruthie clapped her hands. "He's climbing down, look…he's running."

The minutes passed. "I know you have to get on the road, take Ruthie back to her parents, but I needed to see you." His arms cupped around her. Pulling her close and the baby kicked. Laughing, "Matt said, "that was a hard one." He kissed the top of her hair, something she remembered he did in the beginning of their knowing each other. "I love this woman," he said to Ruthie and they both laughed. "So what do you know about Andrew's problem? It's on the radio. I heard it on four o'clock news. A warrant was issued for his arrest. He's at County…"

"What?" Marigold turned. "I didn't know. What about poor Anne and little Andy?"

"It was two hours ago, Babe, I can't tell you. Maybe you should go, then, you can call me."

"It's not good is it, Ellen?" She reached for her friend's hand. "Ruthie was quiet on the way home. She senses more than we can imagine. The whole afternoon has had too much drama. I have one more trip back to Newhaven for the church and then I can put those people with unrest in their congregation behind me."

"Problems?"

"If they decide to make problems, yes, but nothing like what Andrew and Anne are facing." She hugged Ellen. "Thanks for letting Ruthie ride with me. She is such a little keeper. But I must retrieve my child."

"I have a feeling Anne will be at Harriet's. I called and she was crying. None of us could go to her but I told her to pick someone and let them be with her tonight to give comfort where it's needed."

"I agree. She and Harriet became close after the accident when Anne and Andy stayed with her." Shaking her head, Marigold gave a deep sigh. "It is almost unbelievable that the rich lady on the block became mentor to Anne and me. When I came here after my adoptive parents died, I was looking for my birth mother…but meeting Harriet Becker…I thought she was the meanest woman I ever met and then to find out…she was and is my mother."

"That situation is good, isn't it?" Ellen examined Marigold closely. "My friend?" Marigold was nodding. "So you and Harriet are mother-daughter examples, now, but you are looking tired. Go home and go to bed." With one hand on the door knob, she motioned with the other. "Out. Drive careful."

Anne's little blue car was parked in Harriet's drive. While climbing down from the seat, Marigold realized she truly was tired. The baby must sense her mother's unrest because she was in constant movement.

"Hi," Anne met her, welcoming the open arms Marigold offered. "Whoa," she leaned back. "What was that?" They both glanced down at Marigold's stomach. "You sure there's a girl in there?"

"No," Marigold gave her a tired grin. "If I'm not mistaken, there's a whole football team."

Harriet came from the kitchen, wiping her hands on a striped towel and dripping flour on the floor. "You girls have to come in here with us, cookies are in the oven. All three dozen." She registered their puzzled stares. "I know, but Andy and M.J. want to take some home. So we needed that many."

Marigold collapsed on the nearest stool, leaning her elbows on the island's counter top. "Tell me."

Anne sat opposite, blowing out a spew of air, her hands on her cheeks, the gray circles prominent beneath her eyes. "They arrested Andrew. He's at county jail with no right to bail and I can't even see him."

"What else?" She studied the evening newspaper opened on the counter top with pictures of the two accomplices to Waldin that had been blamed for his death previously. "There's more."

Anne nodded. "They took him. He won't be coming home. As a lawyer he told them there are procedures and they said not with his previous record and there was enough evidence to hang him."

"That terminology?" Marigold was watching emotions play out on Anne. "What…?"

"They are charging him with first degree murder." Tears trickled down Anne's cheeks. "Now they are going to reopen the investigation and since he is suspect he has to be in jail."

"But what can they prove? The body was burned beyond recognition. Walden was missing from his jail cell and they said he had escaped. These men in the newspaper are the ones' Walden hired?"

"They are changing their story. They told the police Andrew hired them to help Waldin escape prison so he could kill him."

"And the police believe those two?" Disbelief shown on Marigold's face. "Have we come to this?"

Nodding Anne lifted sad eyes to Marigold. "He has that stuff on his record, from before, and it counts."

"But he's a lawyer. Doesn't that count?" Marigold was stacking the papers, "Come stay with me if you want so that you won't be worried and alone all the time. I don't think anyone will bother you, but we never know."

Harriet came to where they were sitting. "I've asked Anne to stay here, trying to keep Andy's schedule as near normal as we can." She shrugged. "It doesn't matter to me, I was thinking of the child."

Marigold reached out to hug her. "You are so right, Ma. You are such a good mother." Yawning, she turned back to Anne. "It will work out. God knows Andrew is not guilty of murdering Waldin." She reached for keys to the van. "Little fellow there, and I, have to go home. It is nearly time for bed."

Chapter Twelve

Bethany pulled into the Langley drive. The home resembled an old southern plantation style with its tall pillars, the curved bricked steps to the front entrance and not at all like Matt's sister, Janis, modern ranch style that sprawled widely over the landscape. Successful in their own right, Janis and her husband were constantly on the road, traveling to speaking conference. That led to an opportunity to stop in to check on Janis parents and, Britany thought drop a word here and there to emphasize the need to have their son nearby. She was waiting the first opportunity to pull the rug of confidence from under Matt's wife and she knew just how to do it. Matt was now her choice and she meant to make it happen.

Vivien answered the ringing of the doorbell and pulled her eagerly into the room. "Where have you been? I've missed you." She led Britany to the sofa that faced two high backed Queen Elizabeths. "Sit here by me so we can catch up. Bill is napping."

"You know I've changed churches. The Shining Light had a fire that destroyed the outer sanctuary, which means the pews, the piano and smaller items were damaged. They needed a new piano and it was the least I could do." She sighed, an innocent expression on her face. "I drove by today to see if they had set the piano in its necessary place...well, who do you think I accidently ran into?"

"I have no idea who would make an impression on you, dear. The members there would know your parents."

"Marigold was there. Matt's wife." She noted the change of expression on Vivien's face. "She was called in to oversee the remodeling."

"Hmph." Vivien's dislike was completely evident. "I knew that was her calling but down here, who needs her?"

Britany giggled. "We had a little run in," she grinned, "I guess you could call it that. Nothing mind bending." Leaning forward, Britany lay a hand on Vivien's. "You know she's pregnant again, don't you?"

Sitting straighter, Vivien absorbed the news. "Why am I not surprised. How far along?"

"It's hard to tell. She is small, though tall enough I suppose, but she wears those flowing dresses that are in right now." She mused, "but I did notice…so maybe six months?"

"You know the crops are almost out of the field. I understand Matt will be leaving soon. For good."

"How do you feel about that?"

Vivien's eyes flashed. "This is where he should be, taking his father's place to run the farm. I don't know if Bill will ever gain enough strength to take charge." Her voice dropped off as she stared at the single gold band on her left hand. "I thought by now we would be finished with this mess of Matt leaving."

"Don't be discouraged." Britany's hand tightened on Vivien's. "You never know what's around the corner."

"Why are you attending Shining Light Church, Britany? Without you and Bill having to stay home on Sundays, I feel so alone here in our own community church. I really do miss you."

"It was those awful rumors, Vivien. People snickering behind my back but still in my presence where I could hear, claiming I broke up another woman's home, why you know they moved away. Lock, stock and barrel." She shivered. "It was awful. I wish it had never happened."

"I know dear. It would all have been different if Matt hadn't married that…that…."

"Marigold."

"What are you going to do about it, Britany"

"But you have grandchildren to consider, Vivien."

"I think of them as hers."

Britany left a short while later, a smile on her face and a devious plan in her mind.

Levi closed the door to the office, retrieved his suitcase from the floor and turned toward the back door he took when he wanted to slip away quietly to his home. He hoped for peace and quiet tonight. The women always unnerved him. He could feel their dislike of each other. If Matt Langley was living with his wife, then why was the other woman intent on disrupting his marriage? He paused for a moment trying to let it all sink in. The designer lady, Marigold, was very bold in exclaiming she wants my husband and that just is not going to happen, unless over my dead body. Was she really threatening such chaos or was that a mere matter of speech? Whatever it was, he was left helplessly inept each time he encountered them and still, he felt if he hadn't been present, mayhem might happen.

He was so into his own thoughts he didn't hear his name being called, until someone touched him on the arm and he jumped. "Oh, mercy, Herm, I didn't know you were there."

"I could see that. Deep in thought, there, pastor. I guess I called you three times before I reached out."

"Are you fellows up to something?" Levi saw his deacon board standing a few feet behind Herm. "Or, were you looking for me?" He scratched his head, perplexed at his own tiredness and desire to go home.

“How about we step into your office, Pastor, we have a few things to discuss.”

“If it’s about those two women,” now Levi scratched the side of his forehead, he was beginning to itch, “Anyway, I sent them home. I don’t understand their derision. They just plain don’t like each other.”

“Fraid it’s not about them. Let’s take a seat.” Herm was ushering everyone into Levi’s office where he took the chair behind Levi’s desk and Levi found himself like a schoolboy looking for a seat for himself. “This meeting will come to order.” Herm said. “As chairman of the deacons, I’m asking James Green to take minutes, Larry you might want to scoot to your left a bit, I’m sure Jake Hutchens will be coming in soon. I personally contacted him.”

Levi leaned toward Larry. Surely his best friend would know what the meeting was about. “Lar?” But Larry shook his head as though he knew the question. “I got no clue why we’re here, Levi. Herm seems all heated up to do business, as he says in the Lord’s house.”

A ripple of indignation coursed Levi’s veins, growing stronger as Jake burst through the door, wearing his usual golf clothes, a sweat already on his brow. “This better be good, Herm. I was…”

“Sit down, Jake.” Herm’s usual high tone ways were not missed by any one present and a restlessness was fast gaining momentum. “We can begin, now we have a quorum.” He sighed heavily as though the words he was about to speak were wearing him down. “I know you heard the rumor Shining Light Church needs to,” he sighed again, drawing it out, heavily, “Church someone, I believe were the words.”

Larry rose up. “Herm, that would be the pastor’s place to bring this business before us.” Larry’s face was red, “I mean, this is no time for you to stir up trouble, Herm. Lord, man, don’t you have anything better to do?

Herm gave his usual squint-eyed smile, dismissed the last comment Larry made and addressed the first. "In this instance, it is better I take the floor, and pastor remains seated."

"Am I on trial, Herm?" Levi's voice came so quiet, not a wiggle, cough or clearing the nose was heard. The men sit stone still.

Herm gave a gurgled cough. "I don't know, Pastor. Let's get on with it. It has been brought to our attention a certain man and woman of our congregation may be having visits with each other outside their marriages and we've never encountered that sort of thing, nor do we intend to.:

"Then, Herm, before we stone the guilty parties, why don't you let me do my job and speak to the parties. Let us leave the members of Shining Light out of this debacle and keep harmony and brotherly love in our midst. This the very thing that could divide our congregation and we don't need it."

"Well, Pastor, maybe we do."

Levi stood up. "Men," he said, stepping to the center of the floor, peering intently at his deacon board. They now numbered four, two of the older ones had died, those with wisdom, he thought now. "Men, if there's any truth to this matter, I beg you to treat it with the utmost care. If ever your being chosen to lead in this congregation had meaning, it is now. Your very title of deacon has come into play in a most significant way. What is said and done here can be the keeping or the breaking of fellowship in this church. It is not ours to judge, nor malign, nor break the spirit of any man or woman, but to love them, encourage them to do right and nurture them in the love of the Christ who died for each of us on the cross of Calvary. By his blood and his stripes are we healed and through his love we love others."

"You won't speak so eloquently, Pastor, when you have their names. I assure you. I assure you."

Levi sank onto his chair, noticing as he did that Jake Hutchen's expression belied Herm's assurance.

"Well, get it over with, Herm." James Smith, crossed his legs and tilt his head just so. "I've things to do."

Mabel heard Suze step on the porch, leaving her post at the window to grab Suze arm and yank her through the door. "Lord, help us all, Suze. Did you see the cars lined up over at the church?" Recover-ing from her rude admittance to Mabel's home, Suze could only nod. "I'm telling you," Mabel went on, Herm is dredging up trouble." Mabel's agitation was catching. "It's not right, just not right what he's doing."

Suze began to tremble. "You think it's what we know?" Suze was grasping for straws, trying to understand. "You think the deacons are meeting?" Mabel cast a disfavored eye her way. "Well," Suze demanded, "do you think Herm knows. You know, what we know?" Catching Mabel's dubious stare, she defended herself, "Well, you did tell me not to say names. You know what I'm talking about."

"I want you to run to the church and tell those men, my living room is on fire. Can you do that?"

Suze glanced around. "But it's not."

"Suze," Mabel's patience was thin. "Just run to the church and tell those men my living room in on fire. It seems to me, the Hutchen's are happier than I've seen them in years. I don't know why and I don't care what ever it is, but Herm Smith needs to keep his greedy little nose out of their business. So, hurry up, go tell them my house is on fire."

Her face beet red, Suze drew herself to full height, "Mabel Hisaw, your living room is not on fire."

Consternation was drawing Mabel's face to resembled a puckered pin cushion. Taking the lighted candle from the center of the table, she dumped the contents on Ralph's chair and then she opened the door to fan the flames. "It is now," she muttered. "Run, Suze, tell them before those men make the biggest mistake of their lives and unchurch someone."

It was dark when Levi stepped into the shower. "Merciful God, wash me white as snow," he whispered. The water ran rivers of smoke and soot from his body. He didn't know whether to pray at the moment or just give thanks. "What in the world," he said aloud, "did that woman have in her dead husband's chair that smelled like the dregs of hell?"

"Are you talking to me, Levi?" Leah stood in the doorway. "Is Mabel's home going to be all right?"

Sinking onto the built-in seat of the shower, he nodded and then realized she couldn't hear a nod. "We were in midst of a meeting, Leah." His voice was husky, whether from the smoke or weariness, he didn't know. Barely audible, he said, "Herm Smith was hell bent on removing someone from church membership. Can you believe it, off the membership role of the church."

An incredible thought entered Levi's mind. "I don't know if it was me or John Hutchens. He didn't seem to have much use for either of us, the way he talked. Why he lumped us together, I don't know. By the time we beat the fire out of Mabel Hisaw's dead husband's chair, he was on his own, the rest of the men had had enough and wanted to go home. They didn't care who he wanted to hang. They're sticking with me and brotherly love."

Levi gave a long sigh. "I'm too tired to even wash my own body. I'll just sleep in here, tonight."

Leah slipped out of her robe and opened the door to the shower. "Let me help you, Levi. It seems Herm's intention to harm the church has worn you out." She took the wash cloth and began to wipe the grim from Levi's body. "For some reason you smell like chicken feathers."

"So that's it." Levi muttered softly, "The seat of that chair was padded with chicken feather." He thought to chuckle but it came out more of a windless snug of a sound.

Levi's tiredness reminded Leah of the stay at her sisters. Comparing his exhaustion with what she experienced gave her an insight that possibly even men of the cloth often felt the wrath of the world. Tonight, she would be thankful her own sins were hidden and she prayed no one ever found out.

Using the hand spray she rinsed Levi's body cleaned. Towel drying his body she wondered what was Herm Smith up too? Surely… not, no not that? She helped Levi into pajama bottoms and watched as he slid between the sheets. Stooping to kiss his forehead she heard him saying thank you before he settled. "That must have been one big chair and cushion to need the church pastor and his deacons to put out the fire.""

Between snuffles, Levi managed to say, "Somehow the linoleum floor caught fire, too. It was ready to eat up the furniture."

"Poor Mabel. Now she needs a new chair."

"And a yard." Levi managed to say between snuffles.

Leah remembered when Levi took pastorship of the church, he was warned sometimes Herm Smith was known to go off the deep end. The deacons seemed used to it, but Levi wasn't. Still, she felt a relief, no one was cut off from fellowship. It was practically unknow people being unchurched these days.

What had broken this strong man tonight? She slid into bed. All she could do was hold him and wonder who was Herm Smith really trying to remove from church membership and would he stop now?

Across the street from the church parsonage, Mabel and Suze settled on two of the blackened kitchen chairs, their own faces smudged with soot, their hair straggly and the kitchen a complete mess.

"Spend the night if you want," Mabel said. "We could talk about this one all night."

"You had a good plan," Suze replied. "Light up the chair and then push it outside onto the porch. Let the men put out the flames, but you didn't count on the fire catching on as fast, did you. Them feathers were dry and ready to burn. Lord help us, that it didn't burn down the house. You didn't know the men would push it out on the yard, instead, did you." Suze began to giggle. "Lord, help us all, I'll never forget those men running around flapping this and that trying to put out the flames." She doubled over. "Lord help us all." Tears ran from her eyes, making little riverlets down her cheeks.

Mabel studied Suze's expression. Somehow Suze laughing was a thing of joy. Mabel felt the laughter bubbling inside her chest. She bent over to stare at the melted linoleum. "To think I did this to save two marriages." She began to laugh. "And me and you, we ain't even got a husband and here we sit looking like a bomb went off inside the house." Mabel's laughter began to build. "I must have inhaled more smoke than I thought…them chicken feathers are powerful stuff."

When the two calmed their self of laughter, reality set in. "This is a terrible mess," Mabel said.

"I'll help you clean tomorrow" Suze replied. "That's what friends are for. Right."

It wasn't easy cleaning soot from every single thing in the room. It had taken them from seven in the morning until five o'clock that evening. They were worn through. There was nothing they could do for the linoleum but rip it up and leave the bare boards beneath.

"I've got to go home and get out of these clothes," Suze said. "I need to burn them."

"We need to take a minute. What I did has finally sunk in."

"It was a good plan except it backfired on you."

At that, Mabel began to laugh. "Yeah, it backfired. It was awful."

"It was stupidity," Suze agreed. "I could not believe you would do that and then tell me to run tell the men your house is on fire?"

"You did good." Mabel stared at Suze. "The problem was that feather pillow on the chair. To think, out of one pillow every one of us smelled like burnt chickens. To think, we did this to save the Hutchen's marriage because they have a little baby coming to their household. It got those men out of Herm's meeting designed to destroy them."

"And maybe saved our Pastor and Leah." Suze sweet smile turned to consternation, "You could have lost more than this." She spread her arms wide. "We were as unstable as teenagers. It's been forty years since we did anything like this. I hope it was worth it."

"I guarantee you; it was. The chair served its purpose. What do you think, will I get any stars in my crown? Greater love hath no man than he lay down his life for a friend. All I sacrificed was a chair."

"A whole house to soot and grime and the smell it will take weeks to erase. Your home."

The phone dispelled the moment. "I'll get it." Mabel held the receiver close to her ear. In the background, she heard music. She chuckled, hearing a man saying her name. "Hello, Nate. Yes, I'd recognize your voice, anytime." She paused to listen to his question as a wave of shyness washed through her body. “Why, yes, Nate, that would be lovely.”

Quietly she returned to where Suze was studying a photo book from the pile they salvaged. “Those were my mother’s.” Suze glanced up. “That was Nate on the phone, Suze. He asked if I would have dinner with him, tomorrow night.” Suze’s face lit up for a moment to recede in a sad expression.

“I’m happy for you, but I must go home and you need your beauty sleep.” Mabel started to speak but Suze put her hand up. “I’m fine. Don’t worry.” She couldn’t explain. Maybe Mabel understood. Something had set off the sadness again.

She walked home. All she wanted to do was cry and when the crying ended, she couldn’t sleep. Remembering Hannah and Mabel encouraging her to write down her emotions, Suze went to the computer. Before she began, she checked her messages, and there it was, a message from the man she shared conversation one lonely night.

She had prayed about this. Yes, she had asked God to give her something to ward off the loneliness she felt in losing Wade, and if it was a person to talk with, she would accept that too, but she hadn’t expected this man. The crying spells had increased and she thought surely communicating with this man would bring no harm, but it did embarrass her to think if the women’s group found out, they would tease and make fun of her unmercifully. Thus, she decided to tell no one. She tapped on his message.

“Hello, my dear. Are you well? You have been silent, too long. I have missed you.”

Suze caught her breath, in wonderment. He had missed her?

Herm was searching the internet, mumbling all the while. “Where does one go to find how to rid one’s self of such foul smell?

That woman's chair must have been stuffed with chicken feathers. The smell remains in my nostrils. I feel like my throat is full of feathers." Glancing down at his clothes, he wondered if he might as well burn them, shoes too, for that matter, all caked with grime and the rubber souls appearing melted from his run across that yard on fire.

The evening was a complete loss, not at all as he planned. His intention was to rid the church of a pastor's wife that would embroil herself in a tryst with one of the deacons. It wasn't right. If he had to be the judge and jury, so be it. Just as he clicked on foul smells and how to rid them, the cell phone he'd left in the kitchen was ringing.

"Mr. Smith," the hushy voice inquired. "I've observed you while visiting your lovely church and I realize you are a man who will fight to your last breath to keep the holiness of your place of worship secure." The hushy voice gave a low amusement of laughter. "I believe, Sir, you and I are kindred spirits and we should meet. Sir, I believe you and I share knowledge not common to the others on your church deacon board. May we meet?"

Herb's demeanor perked up immediately. "I'm assuming you know a few of our church discrepancies?" Glancing around, even in his home, to be certain no one was listening, his body began to shake with excitement; he felt the other person that seemed to live in his body taking over. Where did that leave him? The voice spoke in his head day and night, seeming never to rest, and now here was this person on the phone making him believe what that other one thought wasn't right at all.

"You want to meet with me?" He asked.

"Indeed, I do," hushy voice acknowledged. "I know your plan failed tonight."

Chapter Thirteen

At the Cape

A solemn group moved into Marigold's storage room. Although the shelves on the wall were filled with various items, the floor around the wrapping table was free of clutter. Sensing the importance of being called together, they assembled themselves and waited for Harriet Becker to open the meeting.

"I thought with this being a busy mainstream business, meeting here, we would not be easily conspiçable to people passing by." She gave a deep sigh. "We are Andrew's friends, and that is why we are here. First we need to glean whatever piece of information is out there, and try to come to conclusion why, after all this time the Feds are looking into his business. No one seems to know why they picked him up and took him directly to jail." She sighed again. "Most of all, Andrew doesn't have any idea."

"My first thought has been this," Brother Joe, said, "Are we one hundred percent certain Walden is dead?"

"We know there was a funeral, with a body present," one of the group offered, "though I understand the body was unrecognizable."

"That's interesting," Marigold replied, knowing not one of them had attended the funeral. "Did they have a closed casket?"

"I don't know, Marigold." Dan's glance met Marigold's. "I'm surprised his wife buried him. After all, he disgraced her family."

"What we needed was Andrew here to fill us in on what happened previously and any information he has." Harriet was genuinely concerned over Andrew's incarceration. "We are just treading water here, unless someone remembers something that hasn't already been investigated. Of course, you remember it was spread all over, in the newspapers."

All eyes turned as Annie whimpered.

Joe was studying Andrew's wife. "How are you holding up, Anne?"

Anne tried to regain composure. "We are all right." She scrubbed away fresh tears. "I don't want to cry in front of everyone. Andy keeps asking when is daddy coming home. If," she swallowed down tears, "if they allow visitors...I'm trying to decide whether to take Andy to see Andrew. I don't know...what I should do, but I think seeing his Daddy would help...I don't know."

Brother Joe brought the group into a circle around Anne. "In times like these, we have to turn to the Lord to give us faith, strength, and a mind of fairness, only God can provide. Let us pray." Andrew was their fWade soldier and where their hands were tied, Brother Joe's prayer reminded them, "We serve an all-seeing God, omnipotent God, who knows every detail." United, the group ask for their heavenly father to protect Andrew and his family and to bring answers to a problem they were unable to solve. Harriet was hiring a detective and Anne was to speak with Andrew's lawyer. There was little else they could do but pray unceasing.

Marigold stood by the door as each one left, pressing into their hand a small metal button that read, "the effectual fervent prayer of a righteous man availeth much." Dan read the writing aloud and pinned the button to his shirt pocket. Leaning, he kissed Marigold's cheek. "Thanks, Sis." Marigold grinned. "If you have a moment, my sister in Christ, I have a question for you."

"Well, my brother in Christ," Marigold quipped, "Let's have your question. Seeing as everyone has left, except you, Ellen and Harriet, let's join them and we can all hear your question. She led toward Harriet and Ellen in deep discussion. "Who's watching the kids?" She asked.

"We haven't talked with you in the last week, have we? We found a reliable person." Ellen lay a hand on Marigold's arm. "There's something we need to ask you." She looked to Dan to continue.

"You know we led singing for Joe's revival with the church you have been helping?"

"Yes. Shining Light. We are ninety percent finished with their renovation," Marigold replied.

"But you probably don't know we have received invitation to come to your mother-in-law's church to help with another revival." Dan paused. "What was the name of that church, Ellen? Misty Vale or Mission Vale?" Ellen was nodding, as both she and Dan peered intently at Marigold. "We haven't accepted the invitation, yet, because we want to know how you feel about it and your opinion."

Gripping Dan's arm, Marigold feigned a fearful expression. "I don't have to attend, do I, Brother?" Removing her hand, she pulled Ellen into a fierce embrace. "If you are one hundred percent certain I won't be needed in any capacity, I will even come to your house and sit with you children while you are away leading." She gave a relieved chuckle at their grins. "It's the least I can do. Serve on the safe side and if I recall, correctly, the name of Matt's childhood church was Misty Vale." She nodded, "Yeah, I'll sit with the kids. At your house."

Ellen and Dad were laughing. "We may have to take you upon that. This is a three-night weekend Revival and we haven't checked with the new lady as to whether she can stay."

"Just let me do this for you. Ruthie and I need some time together and I can bring M.J. to play." Hearing the phone ringing, Marigold said, "Just give me one minute and I'll be right back."

"I have to go to work, Babe." Daniel leaned in kiss Ellen, as Marigold returned.

"What?" Marigold's voice rose. "I can't believe it. Why or who would do such a thing?" She finished the conversation and lay down the phone, turning to Ellen. Dan, was at the door but he waited, having heard the distress in Marigold's voice. "Matt painted the most beautiful scene of the woman at the well for one significant place in Shining Light Church and a second painting of the open Bible for the church concourse." She shook her head in disbelief. "Someone has stolen one and slashed the other painting. All the work he put in to it, and Pastor Levi is beside himself."

"That was Levi, that called?" Dan's eyes were piercing as his mind had gone into a dozen spins. "Just knowing Levi and the situation he just worked through with his wife, I can only imagine his pain."

"I'm caught in the despair of seeing one beautiful painting slashed, the other, stolen," Ellen said.

"I can only wonder if Britany has anything to do with this." Marigold's eyes were smoldering. "It's just the next thing she might do, but she would need an accomplice to have entrance to the church and to carry out the one painting. In the frame it is quite heavy. The church has an alarm system, due to the fact some kids vandalized the property, once. A lady told me, Pastor Levi was against the alarm system but they had no choice. He felt a sanctuary should always be open to the people."

"I can see Levi would believe the church should be open. But these days life doesn't allow that."

"But why would anyone steal a painting they cannot display and where would they hide it?"

Dan and Marigold considered Ellen's question. "I guess you'll go back to check out whether the work you have done has been left along, won't you?"

"I'm beside myself, knowing what I should do, it's the work of a self-centered person, and I know one." She motioned, "Come let me show you another picture Matt has finished." She sighed. "But I will have to say, in the woman at the well and the Bible, he accomplished perfection, they were beautiful."

Later, when the shop was quiet, Harriet stood in the center of the room, with her arms up, toward Heaven, and asked out loud, "What in the world is going on? Andrew jailed over the death of a man he couldn't possibly have killed and now someone is stealing paintings from a church?" Her heart was heavy for Marigold and Matt. "Lord, I don't understand...what is going on, who can benefit from it?"

Newhaven Church

In spite of it being the monthly meeting of those who made lap pads for the residents down the road, in New Haven's only nursing home, gossip flourished. Hannah Noyes was sitting up shop; Sewing machine, twelve pads, and a small container of spools of thread in various colors. The cutting crew waved as they headed down the hall to the room with the saw horses bearing a large sheet of plywood on top. Once, Mabel said, "we just as well be shearing sheep's wool, the way we are set up." It was true, they were equipped. The Sewing Group had ample places to hide out and gossip about what was going on in Shining Light Church. It read like a hot novel. Mabel enjoyed hearing the different opinions, but hoped the hot topics didn't come back to cast blame on the group, because women will be women.

Hannah had no one to blame. When she made a mistake, she owned it. "So, Mabel?" Seeing Mabel across the far end of the room, she paused and cried out her name. "Maabelll. What's this I hear about your yard on fire and the elect deacons and our pastor of Shining Light Church, trying to put out the flame?" Boisterous laughter followed Hannah's question. "Oh, excuse me ladies, maybe we aren't supposed to know about that little situation." She continued laughing, as Mabel came closer.

Standing in front of Hannah, hands on her hips, Mabel studied the group. There was an unfriendly expression on her face. Mabel asked, "What in the world are you hollering about over here? They can hear you all the way to the corner of the street, not this building, but the corner, outside."

"I wanted to hear the real story about your yard," Hannah replied, "And why Pastor and his crew felt led to put out that fire?" Hannah leaned forward. "Noone caught you in a compromising situation, did they?"

Mabel had started to walk away but stopped suddenly. "Mercy, Hannah, you must be desperate to start false gossip, In case you haven't realized it, this is a church environment and we could do without. out such rash statements…or ridiculous questions."

"Well," Hannah replied. "I always say, where there's smoke there's fire and in your case, I heard there's a lot of fire." She seemed unable or ready to shut up, as she continued, "I also heard Nate's truck was parked in front of your house."

Blushing, Mabel replied, "Hannah, do you love making public announcements? Why don't you let people find their own information, since you really don't know what you are talking about. Really, Hannah, this group was formed to bring us closer together, not push us so far apart we will never get back together. If you wanted to know about the fire to my yard, why didn't you come to me and I would have told you what everyone here already knows. It happened, Pastor and the deacons were in a meeting and came running to help. I had a real mess as it started in my house and I had one friend came to help me clean up that mess. I'm very grateful to her for the kindness."

Hannah sniffed, dawning a new expression, trying to look contrite. "I see I've made you uncomfortable, Mabel. I'm sorry about that. Why don't you just light awhile and tell me all about Nate." Hannah pat the bench beside her, as though they were best of friends.

"Actually, Hannah, I'm supposed to meet the other crew in chapel to pray, right now. It is on the agenda that there's been back biting among our group and before it becomes damaging, it has been suggested we take time to pray that problem through. I'd love for you to join us, if you have time."

"Seems to me, some things are best left unsaid. I don't think we have to pray about that, the Lord will take care of anything that has been said that's untrue."

"I can't agree with you more," Mable agreed. Lifting her head she walked away, but her heart hurt that she had been confronted over a simple time Nate parked in front of her house, while they enjoyed a brief visit.

Later as she and Suze walked the short distance to their homes, Suze asked, "How was your dinner with Nate? Will he be returning?" Suze thought of her own secret, knowing for now, she could not share.

Mabel turned to face Suze. "After all these years, I wouldn't have thought Nate and I would enjoy a dinner and conversation together. But it happened and that's about it. What did you do that evening when you left? How do you fill your hours?"

"You and Hannah encouraged me to write down my thoughts, hoping I might discover why I'm so sad and want to cry." Suze sighed, deeply. "It doesn't come easily. Mabel, every word I typed came stilted and hard to come by, but I did try." She wanted to discuss things with Mabel, but fearing criticism she let the questions recede. She often found herself praying for someone she could talk to that would understand, even asking God to send her someone that would understand she was trying to work through grief over Wade, trying to understand if she had a place in the world with him gone. Who was she? She used to be Wade's wife and it didn't matter what anyone thought. Now, she was the woman that walked in the woods and cried.

She and Mabel parted ways. Mabel had seemed quieter than usual. She had worked in the office and missed a part of the sewing hour. Maybe it was her imagination Mabel was quiet. Mabel was strong. Now, she quickly stepped inside the house, Slipped the hook in the eye on the screen door and left the wood door open. Almost running, she went to her room, turned on the computer and found a message from him.

"How are you today, my dear lady? It seems you are busy and I have missed you. I will try again, tonight, at eight o'clock."

Almost paranoid with fear, Suze considered that she, who loved Wade with all her heart had admitted into her world, this stranger that she could not discuss with anyone. She felt it was that wrong. They would tell her to block him. But she enjoyed texting with him and he called her, dear lady. No one else cared how her day went, but he seemed to care. He always ask and if she elaborated at all, he seemed to understand and say, "I see," or maybe, "really?" and often he said he chuckled and she especially liked his seeming to laugh, though she could not hear him. Her mind gave his voice sound. Yes, she best keep him secret to save herself of ridicule and embarrassment and this man, she thought of as a gentleman did seem to settle her down after a day of second guessing everyone and everything.

Through the eyes of a stranger, Suze was learning to enjoy different music, discuss poetry and even movies they had seen. Time passed and Suze felt the constraints of loneliness begin to slip away. Where she had felt bound up in hopelessness, she now had hope; Hope, that one day her laughter would be genuine.

Often, she mused, we all have secrets and she prayed. Father in heaven, I ask your watch care over me that I do nothing to bring harm or embarrassment upon myself. Please remove doubt and fear, and Lord, let me enjoy this escape from the terrible bondage of loneliness and depression. I need you Lord and I thank you that you are always with me. Amen

Mabel had prepared a salad for her evening meal and having a few moments, decided to spend time communicating with the Lord. Life was becoming busy again. She needed the Lord's blessing. Just as she settled down to pray, the phone rang. It was Pastor Levi.

"Mabel, I understand there are times the ladies sewing circle suffers a bit of unrest. I was wondering your thought on bringing a lovely and godly woman I know of, to one of your meeting to present the idea of being worshipful while in the midst of making those much-needed lap pads, you ladies so graciously put together for the Nursing homes in our area. What do you think?"

"Someone told you about my and Hannah's confrontation, didn't they? Really, Pastor, that is Hannah's way and perhaps I'm as much to blame as she is, though I do try to keep my personal life to myself."

"As is your right," Pastor Levi replied, "But others feel the sting, Mabel. Why not let this lady come for one session? You have already met her. That's why I value your opinion."

"I have?" Mabel's curiosity was peaked. "You would have to run this by the others, Pastor. Not just me." An idea came to mind, as she wondered still who Pastor was speaking of. "Pastor, we have adequate supply of lap robes presently. Should the lady you speak of, perhaps know in her facility another place that might benefit from our work sessions, that might be a perfect reason for this lady to come speak with us, and the possibility of serving others will keep from setting Hannah on edge."

"Wonderful, Mabel. I think its worth doing. I'll fill you in on the time as soon as I know, myself. And Mabell, I never doubted you."

HE arrived home to find Leah busy in the kitchen. "Leah, would you join the ladies if Mrs. Gates comes to speak to them? I'm told she is a very good speaker?"

From the kitchen, Leah heaved a great sigh. Pastor's wives were not always taken in on what happened in every little group gathering, no matter their effort was considered important to the Lord's work. In truth, it would wear a pastor's wife, out, if they had to attend every meeting and they were never asked to head the event. There were those that offered a higher level of caring and friendship; Friendship, was a gift, earned as both parties established trust. "I don't know," she replied.

"I was hoping you would head the event."

There were several meetings that day. He shift, from on foot to the other as he waited for her to drive down the road, turn around and park her car deeper in the woods and walk to this magnificent spot he had found the day he followed Jake Hutcheson and saw him speaking with the Pastor's wife. He could not abide anyone's tardiness. If he could be on time, so could she. Then he heard the sound of twigs snapping under foot. Ah, there she was. Beautiful. If only he was her type, but already he knew, he was not. Still, they were equals. "What have you done? He asked. "I have heard the rumblings of evil." He withdrew his hand from her pro.

"Wicked, perhaps." She replied as she sized him up. Here, he appeared different than when he stood in the pew. She took his hand, turning it palm up, studying the pattern of lines. "I'm never evil," she said in that hush-hush voice. She gave a throaty laugh. "Shall we sit?" From the concrete bench, she turned to him and ask, "What happens next?"

"Open accusation, I think. Closed doors with the deacons did not work. She is still there. What do you want?"

"I want Matthew Langley. It doesn't' matter that he is married. He has been mine from the beginning. I don't care that his wife is pregnant." She cast a cold stare on him. "Stealing the oil painting was only the beginning. Slashing the other was a statement. It will take his wife a day or two to realize this is directed at her, but when she realizes, everything will begin to fall into place."

"What's in it for me?" Her prolonged study caused him to remove his hand where it was touching hers on the concrete bench. "You have no idea who I am or what I am capable of doing."

"Do you think I'm a fool? I observe you every Sunday. You are in love with that mousey little woman whose husband died, that man they called Wade, but you are too weak to make a move. You want the pastor's wife out of the picture because you see in her, your fear, that all women commit adultery, though it's possible they met by chance and it appeared otherwise. You are the weak link in the human chain. You want but you are afraid to go after what you want, in one regard, using what you have to intimidate others, in another."

While she spoke, he had taken back her hand, putting pressure on it as her words grew lengthy, until finally she winced. Her eyes squinted as she jerked, "Let go."

"Be careful how you speak to me," he said, his eyes boring into her own. "I believe you are evil. You barely winced. I don't know that I want anything to do with you. You are evil. The woman you spoke of, is ten times worth more than you will ever be."

"Then, why would she want you?" Her laughter peeled out of her painted red mouth, as her eyes seemed to mirror the fires of hell and damnation." Her laughter rose to a damning pitch he would have sworn they heard in town, beyond the trees to the church's highest steeples.

"Lord, God, what have I gotten myself into," he cried out. "You are demon possessed."

"I am," she agreed, rising, her hand on his cheek, caressing now. "And you will do exactly what I want." Leaning in, she kissed his cheek, her eyes smoldering and the laugh gurgling its way past her throat and curling between them. "Remember, I know you, and your desires."

He wasn't aware of how much time passed in her leaving and him sitting mute on the bench. Shaken, he arose to walk silent through the woods he had known since a boy, until today his safe place.

What if she were right? He was a weakling, using his parent's wealth his parents earned to intimidate others, trying to make them see worth where there was nothing but an empty shell that seemed to exist best when making others feel worthless. And that woman? Had she always been evil, for he truly believed what he had seen that day was evil. It made him rethink himself. Was it that Judas kiss?

Her words concerning Suze struck to the bone. Why would she want him? He saw nothing mousey about Suze. She was a lady. Few made him feel capable of great abilities, but Suze did, always saying to him, "Herm, you are so smart. You should be in Politics and make a difference for all of us." She always spoke with kindness and did not turn away at the sight of him, giving that sweet hint of a smile. Damn this woman, with the red lips, taunting him and making him feel less than nothing, trying to reduce him to nothing. Damn her. Yet, through her eyes he saw a side of himself he had never seen before.

Afraid? Intimidated? Words not in his vocabulary. Was there a chance, the pastor's wife and Hutchen's meeting in woods was nothing more than that? Anger course through his body, ripped open his mind. He wasn't having it. He would take them all down. And this woman? He threw back his head and laughed. It would be his pleasure to reduce her to nothing. She deserved it. Until that hour, he would play along with her plan to take from that designer, her husband. He was neither blind, nor stupid. Now he must find her weakness. Then the pain hit his head and he wasn't certain which one he was. It was never his plan to be two people, only himself but when the pain hit, he was never the deacon, he was majestic, a man among men and it was his job to bring justice where there was nothing but evil in motion. That woman had no idea who he really was.

Chapter Fourteen

Levi placed the phone in its cradle. He had not been able to reach Mrs. Gates. Joe had given him her husband's number. Daniel Gates seemed a good man. It was his opinion; his wife would be pleased to address the Women's group but he would pass the information on to her and she would contact Levi.

His mind turned to Leah. She had not left, since returning to give the book study, and there had been ample opportunity, had she wanted to leave. Then there was that one night. He turned his Bible to read the story of Ruth. Why Leah had lay on his bed remained a mystery and he in his weariness had felt her presence. Without thinking, he had pulled her into his arms and the sweetness of earlier days had taken hold……

Why, then, had they reverted to keeping each other at bay, when every night he longed to hold her, tell her he loved her and feel her hand caress his chest in the old way as she smiled into his eyes. Stretching his legs, full length, he laid his head against the back of the chair, trying to find on good reason he had lost her. She was not well that morning. A flu bug, no doubt; Tully said the Hutchens were down with it, too.

Ready to prepare dinner, Leah came to ask what he would prefer, to find him sleeping with his body at a strange angle in one of the high-backed chairs. Her heart quickened at the sight of him; Just a good-looking man stretched ridiculously askew, when he had the most comfortable chair to recline in…and yet, there he was, a neglected man, sound asleep, appealing to her senses. How had they come to this? She turned toward the bedroom, strangely tired herself. She would rest a few minutes before dinner. Evidently the virus of the morning had left her exhausted, otherwise the vomiting had stopped.

It was nine o'clock when Levi awakened. The house was dark and he had an uncomfortable crick in his neck. Thinking not to disturb Leah, if she were asleep, he stepped out of his clothes by the bed and slid onto the sheet to find her on his side. Sleep induced, he folded her to his chest, closed his eyes and slept. Light filtered through the blinds to awaken him the next morning. Leah was in his arms. He lay there to contemplate how this had happened when he realized, slowly she was awake and staring into his eyes.

"Good morning, Beautiful," he said, as he leaned down to kiss her lips, a butterfly kiss that deepened when he felt her response. "Where have you been all these months?" Her arms crept around his neck as her head settled into that familiar hollow. "I missed you," he said. Her smile made his heart skip a beat.

"I missed you, too," she whispered, melding into his body. His finger was tracing here cheek. His eyes were luminous with love, and she was feeling all she had been missing, when suddenly the urge to purge hit her full force and she was scrambling to free the covers and race to the bathroom.

"Oh…." She heard him grown. "You still have the bug. I'll probably get it, too, and here we have this big weekend planned, not to mention; the Gorman Trio, worship hour, the dinner after and the Old Time Races on Saturday." He was still groaning as she emptied yesterday's dregs of dinner into the commode.

"Can you take me to the doctor?" She could barely speak; she was that weak. "If the schedule is that heavy, I need something to calm my stomach. Can you…."

Levi slumped against the pillows. "Yes, but promise, I won't get what you have."

Stumbling across the room and falling on the bed, her hair fanned out on the pillow, Leah reached for his hand. Somehow, I don't think you are disappointed due to the church schedule...."

He raised up, on one elbow, to stare down at her. "No, I have to admit, I'm not." He buried his face in her hair, for a moment and then raised to study her. "Did I sound convincing?" a whimsical smile was playing on his face as he planted a kiss on the tip of her nose and then scrubbed his lips, vigorously. "The story of my life, is wait, hurry up and wait again."

Another trip to the bathroom left Leah hanging to the side of the bed, too weak to raise one leg off the floor. There she lay, seeking solace for the weariness that had come unexpectedly upon her.

"I'll call Jake," Levi was reaching for the phone. "Maybe he can get you in first thing."

The call finished, he turned to Leah. "You have a nine thirty appointment," but she had drift off to sleep. The urge to snuggle up to Leah was strong, but the church pulpit meeting was at eight. From there he would be pushed to meet Leah's time for appointment. If, he hurried he would not be late.

An hour later, through the glass door panel he saw Leah coming up the walk. "I have to finish this meeting, People." With those words, he left the room, without noticing most of the committee members were startled that he did not linger, as usual, nor did he tell them goodbye. "poof." And he was gone, leaving Tully to whatever explanation she cared to give.

"Hello, again." He swooped down, to pick up an envelope lying on the floor, rose up and placed his hand beneath her elbow. "Let me lead, you, to your chariot. Right this way, Ma'm."

"Feeling chipper, are we?" She asked, closing her eyes as he opened the door and she slid onto the seat with his help. She let him maneuver the seatbelt, tuck her purse beside her and close the door. It was a short ride to the Medical Arts Complex, leaving her nauseous and grateful when he practically lift her from the seat and guided her up the walk. They passed through the glass doors and started down the hall, pausing once while he read the various locations. When she thought she could no longer stay upright on her feet, he said, "Here it is," and there was the boom of a familiar voice.

"This is wrong," the words formed in her brain but struggled to come from her mouth. "Not here." She whispered, "Jake is a baby doctor, Levi." Tears came, unbidden, rolling down her cheeks.

At eight o'clock the next morning, the burdensome task of trying to wake up began. For some reason she was longer nauseous. Instead, her body felt heavy, moving her legs was a chore. She believed she had died some horrible death and returned this…this…person who could barely hold her eyelids open, and yet she knew something was either terribly wrong or terribly right, possibly even wonderful.

"I've never been on a bender," she moaned, pulling the covers over her head. "Never drank."

"Really?" He began to laugh. "That girl I met in t hose short shorts and low-cut tank top, that hung out with that tough looking group, never drank?" He pulled the sheet away, to see her face. "Hmmm, I dunno, they were known to be rough stuff…and you….?"

"Trust me. They were my friends. They drank. I did not." She sounded grumpy. "By now, you should know. You were a ministerial student, not supposed to observe skinny girls in short shorts."

He kissed her forehead. His hand on hers, their fingers twined, his voice turned gentle. "You'll feel better by noon. Jake promised." She heard the smile in his voice. "Who said anything about skinny women, anyway?" He grinned. "Curvy, may be a better description."

She pulled her knees up, letting her body form a fetal position. "Why did you take me to Jake? I was sick and vomiting. No woman wants to go a doctor that is her friend." Her voice was indignant. "I could barely hide my embarrassment." Her words became stilted. "All those questions about private things."

"Not to worry, my love. Jake will call you around noon to tell you what type virus you have, or don't have and why you are feeling so hostile." She tried to kick him off the bed. "Or, maybe have you come back for them to draw more blood, I saw you liked that part of the procedure." She kicked again and nearly rolled off the side of the bed. "Nah, nah, my darling." He caught her, lifting her up, midair stopping to hold her still a moment and look into her eyes. That loopy grin spread across his face. "I'm so glad we found each other again. I do wish you weren't sick and I don't know why you are, but we can get you to feeling better, together, and we have the rest of our life ahead of us."

"Get you to feel better, is a phrase?" she asked, tiredly. His eyes had turned serious with deep emotion. "What?" She stared at him, sulking. "What?"

"I'd love to kiss you, but I don't want your puking virus." Turning her head into the shelter of his shoulder, she was finished talking. Let him rage on. She was too tired to think. He pressed her close to his body, kissed the top of her head and lay her back on the pillows, as he tried to unscramble the sheets. "I'm late. Tully will have the Janitor searching for me. I don't know why, there are no places to hide. Believe me. I know."

She missed the twelve o'clock call. "This is Jake. Come to my office, you and Levi. Five, this evening."

Ellen dialed Marigold's shop number. "Marigold, speaking, It's a great day to be praising the Lord."

"Well, yes, it is, Miss Sunshine." Ellen laughed. "Hello, to you too. Marigold, this is Ellen. Are you still planning to go to New Haven about Matt's paintings?"

"Yes, I was going to call later to see if Ruthie wants to ride with me. She and Leah, the pastor's wife have developed a nice friendship. Why are you asking?"

"If our new sitter can stay with the twins, I would love to ride along with you two. Do you mind? I have been asked to do a one day study with Shining Light's ladies."

"Great. That's wonderful, Ellen. I'd love for you to join us. "We'll pick Ruthie up from school and head out."

On the ride down, they reminisced, discussing times past when Ruthie was abducted, when Haley was kidnapped and found the love of her life. Those days had been terrifying and they all faced fear but through it all they had felt God's presence. Ruthie had decided to sit in the back, thinking she would go to sleep on the way, but now she sit listening to them talk.

"Remember," Ellen said, "One of our worst times was after Ruthie was taken; you were hospitalized during the time you were carrying M.J. and we worried whether you would lose your baby, but again, we were locked in prayer.

Marigold was nodding, watching the road but remembering vividly those days of unrest. "I know. It was troublesome. At the time, I was fighting to live, things became a blur." She sighed, heavily. "Can you imagine, Anne is in that same limbo, presently, not knowing what's going to happen with Andrew." She glanced quickly to Ellen. "Think about their history. They lost their marriage, had to rebuild trust in each other." Again, she sighed, shaking her head at her own painful memories. "It goes on and on, doesn't it? Life holds many mysteries we don't understand until we walk completely through them."

"People change," Ellen replied. "That's the good thing. We have choice. We can change."

"You're referring to Andrew. He went from being known as a bad boy," Marigold clicked her fingers in italics on top of the steering wheel, "to community watch dog," trying to live down his past and now look where he is." For a second, she paused, thinking. "What do you think, El, on this deal with the oil paintings. If there's a chance in a million, it was Britany did this. In some weird way, she is trying to push her agenda to have Matt.... but I can't see slashing beautiful art work, he did, can you? Is there a hope in heaven, that someone could speak to her and change her way of thinking, like Andrew did?"

"Anyone can change if they want to, but with Britany, I wonder if it would take more than one opportunity of witnessing to her. I'm not judging her, Marigold, but from what I have been told, Britany has been used to having her own way, all her life, and she has let things get out of control. Now, she feels entitled to walk over other people's rights, in your case, you to have your husband, because she usually gets what she wants, She is forgetting one thing, Matt loves you."

"In the beginning, I thought it was the fact they grew up together. Maybe she hero worshipped Matt, but the things she and Matt's mother concoct... let's just say, sometimes I feel a sniggle of danger in Britany's actions. That she is not beyond hurting someone. That's also, why I think she slashed one painting and took the other one."

Ruthie raised up and asked from the back seat. "How would she get in and out of the church?"

"I don't know, Darlin', that's one of the reasons why we are driving down to Shining Light Church. We haven't a clue and we know the paintings in those large frames were heavy, if she took the frame."

Thirty minutes later, the three were sitting in Pastor Levi's office. Ellen's introduction was completed and they discussed Ellen's leading the Ladies of Shining Light Church in a day of worship and contemplation. It was then the subject of the paintings came about. Ruthie kept staring at the door, until finally Levi realized she was waiting for Leah to join them in a visit, as usual.

"Ruthie, Leah has had a stomach bug. Some kind of virus, we suspect, so I'm not sure you should be around her." He glanced to Ellen. "That's up to you and your mother. Whatever you decide and if it is a visit, I know Leah would be happy to see you."

Ruthie slid from the chair and stood before her mother. "May I whisper?" Ellen nodded and Ruthie leaned in close. A smile broke across Ellen's face. "I think it will be a blessing for you two to visit." Ruthie made a bee-line for the door. Through the window the three watched her cross the lawn to the parsonage. In a matter of minutes, they saw her knock on the door and Leah was hugging her and welcoming her inside.

Marigold was not insensitive to the fact; Ruthie had delivered good news to Ellen. The gift one shared, the other understood. Sometimes, Marigold marveled at God's goodness in giving the gifts of the spirit. Ruthie's calm had worked wonders in their young friend, Haley. She remembered Ruthie saying Vivien Langley was in the hospital the day she was admitted in difficulty for M.J.'s birth. Ruthie said she sit in the waiting room sharing God's love with a tattooed biker and his wife. Vivien had felt intruded on by the couple's presence. Ruthie had loved every moment. She later confided to Marigold that the Biker and his wife, come to know the Lord, but she said, "I'm not sure Matt's mother did."

Now, Ruthie was with Pastor's wife. No doubt there would be a healing. Keeping her thoughts private, Marigold said a silent prayer… 'oh, dear Lord, if only Britany would wake up to your love, before someone gets hurt. Her obsession to have her way is hurting my little family.' But her own next thought was a surprise to even herself. How would Ruthie handle Britany? One thing all of Dan and Ellen's friends had agreed upon, they would protect Ruthie and her gift, no matter the cost. Suddenly she was aware, Pastor Levi had called her name, several times.

"Sorry, Pastor, I was doing a bit of wool gathering. It came to my mind, an hour with Ruthie would change the outlook of whomever the person was that destroyed Matt's painting. May I see it?"

Leading the way, Levi took opportunity to point across the way, the concourse where Ellen might speak with the ladies, "or," he said, "If you choose to hold your meeting in their work room, they will be happy." Coming at last to the spot where Matt's paintings previously hung, one spot was completely bare and beneath the second sit Matt's painting of the open Bible, slashed into ribbons of canvas, the picture was now only strands of color. "The person who did this, meant to completely destroy the obvious meaning of the painting. Do you see the one strip that is hanging only by tattered strings of canvas? Read what it says. These words are visible. "Whoever believes in him has eternal life." Wouldn't you say the most important part was left. Look further, "but whoever does not believe is condemned, all ready." Pastor shook his head, "If I were that person, I would be shaking in my shoes."

Marigold pressed her fingertips to trembling lips. She knew now, what she had wondered. If the act of mutilating or destroying something her husband created would affect her as this did, she spoke without realizing, as a tear ran down her cheek. "Pastor Levi? Matt is a good man. Is this someone who dislikes him?"

Levi was not one to judge another. He had to think this question through and as he did, Ellen spoke.

Ellen's composure revealed the depth of her thinking. "It is bordering on a deal with the devil. When one allows the act of discord to depths that would harm another, that person has lost touch with their Savior. Or, else, they never knew him." She reached down to touch the lifeless strings that still bore the words that would etch on someone's heart. "Someone has pledged to have what is unattainable. In this case, Marigold's husband. If, indeed, it is Britany. In so doing, perhaps she has forgotten, the Lord gives and the Lord takes away. Blessed be the name of the Lord."

Levi shuddered. "Mrs. Gates? You believe in our world, today, there are still people making pact with the devil?" He heaved a deep sigh and continued. "We were told this in seminary. Yes, we were." He gave another deep sigh as though the weight of the world was on his shoulders. "Yes, I believe there are those willing to sell their soul to have their own way."

"Do you, Pastor?" Ellen was nodding agreement. "In cases, where we break the law and go against our Lord's teaching, doesn't it merit consideration? We are breaking his commandment, thou shalt not steal, thou shalt not commit offense against thy brother or sister?"

"God help us," Levi muttered. "I can see why churches ask you to come lead their women in worship." He turned to Marigold. "She knows her bible scripture, doesn't she?"

Marigold patted his arm, as if to comfort him. "That she does."

Marigold had stood there, listening but studying the wall and the doors that entered to the area. Britany would enjoy such a chWadege. "It is your new lady in the congregation, Britany. She will use whatever means at hand, and whoever is a willing accomplice that will stoop to her level, to achieve her goal."

Levi felt he must give the benefit of the doubt. "Let me play devil's advocate, here." He struggled to clarify, a task he personally wasn't accepting, "There are levels, aren't there? We may resent that we are never one to purchase a new car, but I'm not going to run out and destroy my friend's car just because he can buy a new one and I can't."

Marigold gave a scornful laugh. "That does not compare to this, this was done in secret, if you destroyed your friend's car, surely some evidence would lead to your punishment for the act."

"But how could we condemn one of our own people when we have no proof? Isn't that a bit harsh?" The whole thing troubled him. "Isn't that like saying if we don't go to church, we wish Christ dead?"

Marigold stood her ground. "Not at all. If I'm right, Britany has decided it is past time to test the water. It's not the first time she has tried to destroy my marriage and her best friend is Matt's own mother. She has done this to bring attention to Matt, for some crazy reason I can't decern, but I will. She's vicious, Pastor. When it comes to things or people and it is something she wants, she goes after it. I find myself wanting to help, but I know how she is. This is God's matter."

Levi was still struggling to grasp the evil done by a person. He had to think this through. He was the shepherd, the people were to be led as sheep, not followed. "Could any person be that blatant, to do something like this in the house of the Lord? Surely no one would go that far. There is hell and damnation to those who go against God's word."

Ellen heaved a deep breath. It is God's matter, pastor, as Marigold said. "This situation requires much prayer and God's attention."

"Have you considered the story of Judas, Pastor?" Marigold asked. "She thinks this more simple."

Levi felt caught in the midst of a summer storm, the sky felt gray and troubled, the clouds in conflict as he glanced out the window. He tried to pray. He and Leah had just emerged from days of darkness. Oh, that they never again face the heartache they had been through. One word appeared in his mind and he reeled wanting to be away from it. Cloven. His lungs, his heart, his mind was trying to shut down, so terrible was the stench he was smelling, "Please, God," his mind cried out, "don't separate me from Leah." His situation was never cloven. Why had the word come to his mind, the slashed painting? They had studied that word in Seminary. It meant split or divided in two; but he reasoned, not aware time was passing. Cloven tongues appeared on the day of Pentecost and sat upon each of the disciples. He remembered, it was in Acts, when the people witnessing the event believed the disciples drunk and Peter explained the Lord was pouring out his spirit on the disciples. Through the disciples, he would show wonders in heaven above and signs in the earth below....there the word cloven was good.

"Pastor, Levi?" Marigold had called his name. Her hand was on his arm as if to awaken him from a dream. "Are you all right? Your color has turned ashen, what happened to change your countenance?"

Something pricked his memory. He glanced at his watch. Twenty til five. "Ladies, I apologize. I'm supposed to have my wife to the doctor's office in twenty minutes. Will you please accept my apology?" Obvious concern played on his brow. "She was quite ill this morning. She has already seen the doctor once this week but we missed a second appointment and now the doctor insists she must return today."

"May I take the frame, Pastor?" Marigold waited for his nod, claiming Matt's mutilated painting and the frame, she said, "We will walk over for our Ruthie and then be on our way. I am sure Matt will want to replace this shredded painting."

Within the next few minutes, all intact, the painting loaded and Ruthie secure in the back seat, Marigold's feathered van was ready to pull away from the church drive as the pastor walked Leah to the car and they watched the couple leaving. Marigold glanced to the visor mirror to see Ruthie waving, a smile of happiness on her face. "What's going on, Ruthie?" Knowing Ruthie could see her by way of the mirror, Marigold winked. Glancing to Ellen as she pulled out on to the highway, she saw the same smile of contentment on Ellen's face. They were three little women who knew God was going to give someone a miracle that day, in spite of the ugliness that had happened to Shining Light Church God was still in control.

Ruthie could no longer contain the joy she was feeling. "Momma, is it all right if I tell?" With her mother's consent, Ruthie began. "I'm so happy I have goose bumps." She giggled. "When I knocked on Miss Leah's door, she was glad to see me but she said she was sick and waiting for Pastor Levi to come take her to the doctor. "Come sit with me," she said, "I know I'll feel better with you here." We sit in her big old rocking chair and my feet didn't touch the floor, but hers did. She patted my hand as we rocked and it was a while when she said, "Ruthie, I feel such peace in my heart. I was so weak but now I feel stronger. Let me go put on a dab of lipstick so I won't look so pale." Miss Leah laughed and said, "before I didn't care." After she put on the lipstick, we sit and talked until Pastor Levi came for her."

Marigold listened to mother and child sharing the experience. Ruthie was feeling such joy. There was more to the story than these two gifted people would reveal. Ruthie already realized she had a special anointing and the two now sharing would take their secrets to the grave, but she in her own way felt a discerning that Pastor Levi and Leah were going to receive word that Leah's illness was not a curse, but a blessing. Now, Marigold knew she had to accept the task that lay ahead. Surely Britany was in the grips of the devil, as Ellen believed. Why else would she willingly give herself over to destroy items in the house of the Lord? Wasn't it more than vandalism? How did one immersed one's own self into claiming their own desires at the expense of another? Did she not acknowledge the other person at all?

It was tearing her apart. To think, she must let go of her own feelings toward Britany when she had been treated with such disregard. Matt was her husband. Britany was a woman who would stoop at nothing short of murder to have what she wanted. This made Marigold feel shaken inside to the highest realm of fear for her and Matt's family. But in the presence of Ellen and Ruthie, she knew in the last hour, God was performing a work in her heart. No longer could she harbor resentment and revenge. Yes, revenge. She had become a tool to do what was right in the sight of the Lord and though she questioned why, she realized what Ellen said was right. Britany changing could only happen with the Lord's help but if he called on her to pray and give a Chistian example, as hard as it was, she must.

"We must be tired," she said, after musing some thirty minutes or so. Ellen smiled. In the back seat, Ruthie was sleeping. Still, they were miles from home. Marigold's thoughts turned to God's way of bringing his people together. Sometimes, it wasn't an easy task and the people he chose to fulfill his work might balk at being called. It was not by chance, but by divine intervention God had chosen her to help restore Shining Light Church's fellowship. She knew that now, because Britany was there, all the while Marigold was chosen to lead in the renovation of the building, it was not by chance Britany decided to attend Shining Light when she was a member of Misty Vale Church where Matt's mother attended. No, Britany would try to bring dissension using the ploy of Marigold as the one in charge of that renovation and in the process try to destroy her marriage to Matt. How foolish the plan.

Then, there was the fact Brother Joe and Pastor Levi knew each other and Ellen's invitation was to lead in women's worship at Shining Light. It was all an orchestrated plan, the two women would be in prayer with the pastors, and in turn the church would come together and bless others. The rumblings of dissension were that and nothing more. God could take a problem and turn it in to blessing. Marigold's own life bore witness. What were the odds of a young woman adopted as a new born baby would years later move to a small town in a different state and find her birth mother?

For a moment, her heart raced with inner joy. She and Harriet had found a sweet relationship. It had not been so in the beginning; at that time, they were like oil and vinegar. Yes, God could use a community if he chose, to turn lives around and the folly of one's own way might be revealed. Drawing a deep breath, the thought flashed through her mind, what if Matt belonged to Britany and not her? She dismissed the thought as quickly as it had come. It was as if she felt God's smile. "Oh, ye of little faith, have I not told you, my plans for you are good and not bad." She and Matt loved each other. His mother might try to lead them through the fire, but it was God who led the Israelites through the river, creating a wall of living water on each side to protect them. Now it was time to bring a second baby into her and Matt's life. She reflected on the child she miscarried. She hoped Bitty had met that baby and found heaven a happier place, because he was there. Somehow, the thought gave her peace.

Staring out onto the landscape, Ellen's thoughts were on Anne. In the beginning, Andrew had treated Anne badly. After many wrong doings, being the victim Anne felt she must divorce Andrew for the turmoil young Andy was witnessing and their child needed a better environment. Ander soon realized few women could live up to the standard of is former wife. It had taken two years to rebuild trust. Haley's parents had taken him in and made him look at himself. What Andrew saw; he did not like. Thus, began his pursuit to win back Anne. It had taken ample time for him to convince Anne to remarry.

Now, the Feds had burst into his business and taken him away. His friends were told Andrew would have his day in court; the judge would decide his fate and if the Judge was having a good day, Andrew might be allowed to return home to "get his business in order." That would be before serving sentence. Ellen shuddered. It was wrong. Everyone knew Andrew was not around those last day when a woman living with Walden reported Andrew was the man killed her lover. She was present, she said, and Andrew was to blame. What was going on, when a person that was the guilty one had more pull than one who was innocent? Andrew had changed, but past offences were recorded, who could prove his innocence?

Marigold interrupted Ellen's thoughts. "Well, it was a good evening, being together, anyway. I guess your boys will be fed when we arrive home, and in bed and everything in place? Did you and reverend set the date of blessing when you will meet with the women's group at Shining Light?"

"Concerning the part of fed and in bed for the boys," Ellen grinned. "Daniel has a way of settling them down. I'm sure he is in control, but I can't guarantee what the house looks like and yes, we did set a day for the Women's group, on a day that Ruthie can go with me."

"Gotcha," Marigold replied, pulling into the Gate' drive. "So, you think Shining Light needs Ruthie?"

Daniel came bouncing out of the house, opened Ellen's door and planted a kiss on her forehead. Raising his eyebrows, he grinned across to Marigold, acknowledging her presence. "Good day?"

"It will work, Brother," Marigold replied, raising her own eyebrows. They laughed together.

Daniel pulled a sleeping Ruthie into his arms. "What did you do to knock this kid out?"

Ellen opened the door and followed him carrying Ruthie to her room, watched as he lay her on the bed where he had turned back the covers, and now was removing her shoes. "Can she sleep in those clothes, or will she wake up for food in a while?" Ellen nodded. "So," he walked her back to the family room, sank into his chair and pulled her onto his lap. "How was the trip?" She lay back, her head on his shoulder. "Will you be speaking to the women's group?"

"We set a day when Ruthie is out of school, to attend with me. There are all kind of vibes going on down there, Daniel. I'm not certain one day meet with Pastor Levi's people would make a difference."

Three miles down the road, Marigold turned off the ignition and lay her head back for a minute, surveying the outside landscape of Harriet's home. She was mentally and physically exhausted. Pushing out a huge breath of air, she let everything go; Britany threatening her marriage and the situation at Shining Light Church. If she had felt the stirrings of discord, then Ellen and Ruthie must feel swamped.

For all his worries concerning the church, Pastor Levi seemed more positive and when he spoke of his wife, the man fairly glowed. Some inner sparkle of Levi Markle came through and she wondered how that was happening, they were another couple who had been through the fire, according to Daniel. She must go in. No doubt Harriet would be tired from keeping M.J. and tired trying to keep up with him.

Harriet met her at the door. "M.J. and Andy are napping. Anne's at a meeting. How did it go?"

"Honestly. There's a feeling of darkness hanging over this, my feeling, except where before the pastor seemed cowered, it's a mystery to me, you know in the beginning I felt someone had let him down, but today, in spite of the vandalism, he was more upbeat. Matt's painting that was slashed had not been removed. You will see it at the shop. It is shredded. I can't understand why anyone would do that and it feels to me that it is Britany's work."

Harriet's eyes snapped. "Why, Marigold? Why would that woman set out to destroy your marriage? She can have whatever she wants. Why does she want your husband? It's diabolical."

"Strange you would say that. Ellen came to the same conclusion." Slumping down into a chair, Marigold ran her fingers through her hair. "If that's the case, we can't pass judgment, can we? We have to care."

Harriet stooped to kiss the top of her daughter's hair. "It takes a woman of strength to say that. I know it all cuts you to the bone and without Jesus in your heart, you probably would want revenge." She gave a tired sigh. "It's similar to Andrew's case. We know he is innocent, but a lot of people think he is guilty. God will bless you for having this insight as to Britany needing the Lord… but it's tough."

"We can't even long for the good old days, can we, Ma?" Marigold slipped into Matt's name for Harriet. "They weren't that good with all of us trying to settle into life, but then we learned a lot along the way and now we realize we went with the flow and God was with us. But, we are back in a situation where our hands are tied, all we can do is trust in the Lord and try to be honest. It is not easy, praying for a woman who wants to destroy my marriage, but it is what it is."

Reaching down, Harriet smoothed Marigold's hair where she had ruffled it, running her fingers through. "Let's remember, God works in mysterious ways, his wonders to perform." Again, she kissed her daughter, this time on the forehead, looking into her eyes. "I'm so glad we found each other. God is good, isn't he?"

Chapter Fifteen

Shining Light Church

Laurie Hutchen's smile was brilliant. She was wearing one of those flowing tops, like all the young women wear these days but Laurie was proud to show off the little bump around mid-waist that some said would be a little boy. Mabel and Suze were speculating, maybe not, since the baby was riding high, but then, again, they said, there's time. Then, we'll consider a boy. Everyone was caught up in the couple's happiness, except maybe the new lady who bought the piano for Shining Light Church.

Miss Britany was prone to come in at last minute and slide into the second pew from the back. Which she did today, but after a few minutes of Laurie's piano playing, she stood up, glanced around with those furtive eyes and walked up to the front where Herm Smith sat, second pew from the front on the left side. "May I sit with you, Sir?" Herm, completely surprised, dropped his hymnal as he nodded, assertively. "I asked to play piano, today," she said, loud enough Mabel and Suze sitting on the other side of the aisle heard. "The nerve of that pastor. He said, Miss Britany, Miss Hutchens is the duly recognized pianist of Shining Light Church. She has been loyal and faithful. I would not hurt her feelings for anything. Do make yourself comfortable and feel welcome to Shining Light Church. It is our honor to count among our dear church family."

Herm Smith barely grunted. Not one to make an embarrassing spectacle of himself, Herm saved all his exposure to times when business meeting was called or if there was an opportunity to undermine Pastor Live. "You, are a deacon, are you not?" Miss Britany's voice carried all eight rows to the back. "I'm asking you to intercede for me. Since I purchased the piano, I do believe I should be welcome to play it."

Mabel and Suze would later say, the conversation became a bit difficult to hear at that point. They believe Herm Smith, asked, "What are you doing? You are simply out of control." This inferred to the two ladies that Herm and Miss Britany must know each other.

Jake stepped to the pulpit and asked everyone to rise as they turned to page one eight six, Victory In Jesus. Three songs and two prayers later, the report on Faith groups was read and Pastor Levi took the place behind pulpit. The past months had found him slumping in his walk with the Lord, but today he was a new man. His handshake was firm. Shoulders squared, with the hint of a smile on his face, he looked out into the congregation, found his wife, Leah, and the smile became full bloomed.

"If you will, please stand for the reading of God's word. John 6:37. "All that the Father giveth me shall come to me and him that cometh to me, I will in no wise cast out. For I came down from heaven, not to do mine own will, but the will of him that sent me. And this is the Father's will, which hath sent me, that of all which he hath given me I should lose nothing, but should raise it up again at the last day. And this is the will of him that hath sent me that everyone which seeth the Son and believeth on him, may have everlasting life; and I will raise him up at the last day." Everyone said amen. "You may be seated."

Levi stepped down to floor level. His head tilted, thinking a moment, he set his eyes on his friend, Larry. "When Jesus walked the earth, there were those who embraced him and those who hindered his work. Now, let me explain, embracing and hindering are two completely different ways. The renovation of our church is almost complete. Two weeks past, beautiful oil paintings were placed in particular places. One beautiful painting was of the Word, an open Bible. The second painting, depicted The Woman at the Well. It was equally well done. It spoke to our hearts because we know the story. Jesus offers his love and salvation to those who ask and are willing to take up his cross. That person, believes Jesus died on the cross. Yes. And that person believes not only did he die on that cross, but he arose again. After death, he arose from the grave. The stone had been sealed to the tomb where his body lay. Jesus arose, again." He paused, letting the words sink in. Jesus defeated all the ugliness of death and the ugliness of those who hindered him."

Levi addressed those sitting on the first pew. "Now. The word, such as the painting of the open Bible, finds many unwilling to be saved. Some of you embraced the paintings, saying you not only understood their message, you felt the message of each painting. And though not one of you said, I don't like the paintings, evidently there was someone who did not like one." He paused, letting the words sink in. "Because, you see, one painting is missing, completely. The Woman at the Well is gone. The other painting, The Word, was cut to shreds." The gasp arose from the congregation and swished around the walls. "Yes, shreds."

"Now, who would do that? Not one who has received the Lord, as the woman at the well did. Not one who rests upon the promise of salvation, believing Christ died on the cross for our sins, rose from the tomb and lives again, to sit by our heavenly Father…where one day they will meet the Father, face to face, knowing that which was done on earth, was right, or, that which was done on earth was wrong."

Levi stepped before the pew across the aisle. "Don't get me wrong. The act of slashing the painting was not the unpardonable sin, but I ask you, what person that loves the Lord would do this? Our Father's will is that those who come to Him will never be cast out. That one, who comes to Him, receives the grace He offers and the promise of eternal life. That means, no hindering. Right?"

"Then, who would do such a cowardly act? Does that person know the Lord? Do we need to sit down, together, and study the Word? Scripture that defines Christ love for us, and love for Him? Obstruction of church property does not deal exclusively with me, nor our deacon body, but with you who sit in these pews as Sunday arrives; it sets with who you sit beside, rub elbows, have fellowship, and take the Lord's Supper with. If we are truly saved, scripture tells us we will not be cast out. What does the Bible tell us about one who says he loves the Lord, he knows the Lord, but truly does not? Will that one be cast out?"

Levi stepped back to center of the pews and for a moment glanced down the center passage to the altar. He closed his Bible and paused as if pondering the next step. Finally, he looked his congregation in the eye. "We are dismissed."

The expression on faces changed from listening expectation, to puzzlement. This was new. No song? No nothing?

Mabel laughed and then clapped her hands. Suze joined her. Soon most of the congregation was clapping. On the second pew on the left at the front, Herm Smith wore an expression of consternation. The lady beside him, turned to face him. She kicked his shin, though no one was aware of the action as she departed the pew. She neither spoke to anyone nor shook their hand.

Herm Smith made his way to the Pastor. He neither extended his hand, nor expected Levi to. "That, was different," he said. "I don't believe that's in accordance with our ways, Pastor."

Levi laughed. Good naturedly he replied. "Today, it was." Herm limped by without another word.

Mable was standing behind Herm. “Go home, and think about it, Herm.” She then turned to Suze. “I won’t be home this afternoon, Suze. Nate’s picking me up to go with him to check on the progress of his farm.”

Suze walked home, dreading entering the house. Sundays were a reminder of how she and Wade had spent the day together. In her mind she reviewed those days, unaware when her attention turned to Levi’s sermon. What was the unpardonable sin? She always thought it was rejection of believing Jesus Christ died on the cross. But the sermon was not the unpardonable sin…and yet, in a way it was. No one wanted to be cast out of the presence of Jesus Christ, did they? Was the sin of wrong doing, as in someone slashing the beautiful painting the sin that led to disbelief and rejection of the Lord? Pastor Levi had left the thought in the minds of his people, why would a person want to hinder the work of their Lord?

What was next? Lonely and restless, Suze was drawn to the computer. He was there. “Hello, Suze.” Now they called each other by name. “I had such a fear you would not come today. It worried me, Suze.” It was nice to hear his concern. “Dear Lady, why are you silent? Won’t you reply, so I will know you are there?” She sent him a smiley face. “May I call you?” He asked.

His voice was smooth and rich at the same time. He told her of his native land. He spoke of his wife who died six years past. No, they had no children. Perhaps it would have been easier losing her if they had. Please tell me of your life, he said. I feel you do not trust me. I will not hurt you. I am just a lonely man seeking conversation and I saw your profile. Why are you afraid? Today is our anniversary. We have been talking three months. Suze sat straighter. He made notes. He knew when they began texting? Someone might think she had done wrong, if they knew. She closed the computer and hurried from the house. She would walk and clear her mind, but she didn’t, she thought of him.

The next week she grieved. Mabel was spending more time with Nate. Theirs was a relationship that spanned time, it was safe. It had history. She would not be surprised if Nate ask Mabel to marry him. On the other hand, she knew only Wade. She was aware, the computer friend had text her daily and tried to call her, but Suze had shut down. She was afraid. Afraid of what to do about his constant attention, but she had no one to talk the situation, no one she trust, like Mabel. She had asked God to send someone and the man had appeared soon after, to text and talk as she requested but was he of God or the devil? She heard such terrible stories about on-line relationships. Still, she missed the kindness of their conversation. Finally, she sit down and opened the computer.

"It hurts me," she read, "you do not trust me, Suze, and I have come to care for you."

Suze bolted and run. It was hours later, she text, "I do not want you to care about me. I simply enjoyed our conversation." She did not say, I long to hear someone's voice at the end of the day. That was too personal. Suddenly, she was writing daily in the journal as Mabel and Hannah suggested. The writing was filled with sadness, loneliness and the heartache of losing Wade. Only months later, looking back, would she see where she had made a smiley face here and there and mentioned, 'but God does have surprises for us, sometimes our prayers are answered in the most unusual ways, not always unpleasant, but nice and help us to see He has more for us. It is His way of opening us up to life again.'

Misty Vale's revival weekend arrived. Mabel said, "Suze let's go. You and I. That's Nate's church and he has invited us. It might be interesting to hear the young man sing again. As I understand he and his wife are leading the music. The Gates? Yes, that's it, the Gates.

Who knows, we may even see Vivien Langley and if I know Miss Britany, she will be hovering over Vivien." It was another beautifully kept country church. Tall steeple, bell tower all enclosed in white vinyl siding. Suze had viewed all the good points, and decided it probably harbored the same sins and secrets as Shining Light under Levi's care.

Nate told them goodbye. "Good to see you, Suze. I'll see you this coming weekend, Mabel."

Driving out, Mabel ask, "I don't think Vivien Langley has any idea we know her son through our decorator, do you?"

"How could she, Mabel?" Suze replied. "Sometimes, I think we are so reserved we dare not advertise ourselves. We come from a little country town and we don't want people figuring that out, like if, we are, you know?" Mabel waited for Suze to explain. "You know," Suze struggled, "We're the examples. We are supposed to be good wholesome people, no room for sin, nothing but good people."

"Suze, you don't have to answer to anyone," Mabel said gently. "There may be something you want to do. Don't fret. Do it. Life is short. We know that, losing our mates. But God gives us strength to go on, and we have enough sense we try to act wisely, but Suze, sometimes we step out and take a chance, if we mess up who cares what the next-door neighbor thinks? It's between us and God. Enjoy opportunity that comes your way, that's what He expects of us. You won't make a wrong decision."

But was that true? Suze went over the conversation, wondering if Mabel had any idea. She agonized over the question whether she should continue speaking online with a man she had never met. She was drawn to his voice. It mesmerized her with that foreign accent. She was finding more and more she was waiting for his call and he was sending her a yellow rose each morning and calling her every night. "I honor your wishes, my lady, to treat you with care and not overload you with sentiment but I anticipate calling you each night. I am learning the progress of your day by the sound of your voice."

Suze lay in bed laboring over the secrets she kept and she prayed continuously that God would forgive her is she uttered one wrong word. She considered how many lonely people lived in the world and how many secrets, like hers, were kept because of that loneliness. Herm Smith continued to stop by and she treated him with respect. Still, nothing drew her to him. She had seen him meeting with the beautiful Britany who was attending Sunday services and wanting to play the piano because she bought it. She could only wonder about their connection. It was a strange match, but like her, maybe they were also lonely. She would never have known if they had not chosen the spot she and Wade used to call their own. Wade made the wooden bench the two sat on that day. Sitting on a little concrete pad he poured with words he scratched into the dampness. I will love you forever. No one had ever known it was their place. There was a concern remained with her, about Herm. There were times he was not himself. She and Mabel knew this for sure.

On this Sunday evening, Mabel had ridden the field roads, sitting next to the center console, in order to hear Nate's explanation of various crops they were viewing. "You know, Mabel, this should have been our life, except for my bull-headed ways." He sighed. "But we were young."

"Did you have a good marriage, Nate?"

"Yes, we did. But I never forgot you. I loved Nola and she never knew about you. Did you forget me?"

Mabel laughed. "I can't believe we are discussing something that happened so many years past. No, I didn't forget you. However, my marriage was not a good marriage and there were times I could have socked you."

"I had my punishment for leaving you for Vivien," Nate replied. "She was carrying my son. She made Bill think he was responsible for the pregnancy. I lost and I've had to live with the consequence all these years." He turned to her. "When I realized you were the love of my life, I had already messed up with Vivien. Bill took her off my hands." He chuckled, "she was difficult, even in that day, but I lost all rights to my boy." Nate sighed. "I loved that boy from afar when he came to stay with me that year, I can't tell you, it was like I felt God had finally forgiven me."

Nates's sense of right would have faltered had he known at that moment, Britany was executing a new plan. He had no more than left the drive and she was driving through the metal arch, she had her own key. She knew Matt would have checked the fields and would shower before he rest the remaining part of the day. Climbing the stairs, she heard water running and a smile crossed her face. She would wait. He came out of the bathroom, head down, a towel wrapped around his mid-section. She knew when he saw her feet, by the gasp of surprise, and then he was towering over her. "What are you doing here?"

"I came to see you." She waited to hear the pleasure in his voice. Instead there was the rustle of jeans being hastily pulled over semi-wet skin, and then he was back standing over her.

"Britany. You cannot do this. I am a happily married man. You cannot come into someone's house unannounced and unwanted."

"This is Uncle Nate's house. Besides, I think you want me, Matt. We go a long ways back."

"Britany. This pursuing me has to stoop. We are not kids, anymore. I love Marigold and I'm not divorcing her to marry you." He was peering int her face, as though she were a child. "Do you understand? I am a happy man. I love my wife and son and soon we will have another child. This is not good." He blew out a hard breath of air. "Marigold and I are happy. Please, don't come to the fields when you know we are there. Count your blessings, Britany. Find someone you can love and appreciate."

She rose full height. "I appreciate you, Matt." She started to touch him, when she saw his eyes narrow.

"No. No. I said, I don't love you. There will never be a life for the two of us together." He was pointing to the door. "Go home. Now. Please Britany. Leave." He saw her defiant look as she started to unbutton her blouse. She saw him tower over her, his eyes smoldering, as she sank to the floor.

He reached down, picked her up and headed down the stairs, kicked open the door with one foot as one hand turned the knob, taking hurried steps down the brick steps to her car, where he pushed her under the steering wheel and slammed the door shut. "Don't you ever do this again. It may have worked once, I was a boy you toyed with but it's foolishness, now. Stop it." His eyebrows drew together and she saw the fury in his eyes. She pressed her body to the back of the seat; he looked more dangerous than she could ever have imagined. "No more fooling around. Do you hear me?"

He was no longer the kind gentle Matt she had known. "I could have had you once."

His eyes were stormy. "I was a kid. I am a married man, now, and I love my wife."

Something was gone from her heart, a huge gaping hole Matt once filled when he watched her enter a room. Maybe she had not loved him more than she had herself. She had never loved him as a lover, but his mother wanted her to have him and she'd made up her mind Matt was the best she would find around New Haven and she wasn't leaving. She would simply employ a different tactic. In the meantime, she would choose someone so low in character that Matt would be ashamed he had brought her to that station of life. Oh, yes, he would be sorry, it was his fault, but no more fooling around? She knew a man so ill equipped; he would never know what hit him when she moved in on him; he was already in line. And Matt? Matt would be sorry he caused the problem.

Chapter Sixteen

Ellen prepared the gift bags, adding the pocket nuggets last. Daniel sat watching. It was early morning hours, before the children stirred. He studied his wife. The cancer treatment had been harsh, but she was determined to go "full stream ahead," as she called it. Their three days at Misty Vale Church had not been without incident. It was Vivien Langley's home church, after all.

"Let's talk about this incident, months down the road," Ellen had said, practically crawling into the van that last night when it was time to go home. "I'm exhausted. How about you?"

It remained vivid in his mind. "There's a power struggle going on in that church. I'd feel sorry for the pastor, except he is in Vivien Langley's pocket, so, there's not much pity I can give him if he chooses to go there."

"That must be difficult, knowing what the Lord intends but confined to do what the highest paying contributor expects of you," Ellen sighed. "I'm certain, neither of them has joy in their heart under such an arrangement."

"It's so unnecessary," Daniel rose up and began to pace the room. "If a congregation calls a man to preach, then they all must trust each other and let him do the work God has set before him." He sit the empty coffee cup in the sink and turned to stare hard at Ellen. "I think we can understand, now, what Marigold is up against. If I were Matt, I'd keep my wife as far away from his mother, as possible."

Ellen chuckled. "Yes, you would. But your mother is gone now. However, your aunt and I love each other." She placed the last gift bag in the box. "It's sad, we know these people who are caught up in having their own way and what they do, they forget all about Jesus plan for their lives." She paused, "Mrs. Langley, Britany, and the poor minister…but, on a brighter note, you know what? Pastor Levi has stepped up to the plate, he is serving with strength and fortitude. Marigold told me about his church and its people, and Ruthie and I are going there today. May God go before us and prepare the way."

"Don't let them eat you alive," he muttered as he stepped up behind her, his arms encircling her waist. She laid her head back on his shoulder. "What are you speaking on, what subject?"

"The Peace that Passes Understanding. How does that sound?" He turned her slightly that he could kiss her lips.

"Sounds good. With Ruthie there to help you, you will come out swinging and they will be the winner." He chuckled. "They'll never know what hit them." Now he turned her completely, to face him. "Just remember, take care of yourself. We need you here, much more than Shining Light church does."

"I know." She smiled, her arms around his neck. "How did I ever get so lucky, all those years, back, to sell the most handsome man in the whole wide world, a pair of size twelve boots, and then, I married the ga-hoot?" Daniel was picking her up and carrying her to his favorite chair.

"Whatever, is a ga-hoot? Isn't this nice? Lay your head back and rest a minute, little wifey."

She and Ruthie arrived in time to join the ladies for lunch. They were making an effort to put the two at ease, when the door opened and Marigold's arch enemy stood there, head set at an angle, arms akimbo, she stood there, examining the attending speakers, her eyes lowered at half-mast. When she had seemingly accepted, they were there, she raised one hand and said, "Greeting, ladies, I come in peace." From that moment on, she ignored Ellen and Ruthie.

Ellen surmised, quickly, that Miss Britany was intent upon taking charge, but it wasn't going to happen. Nodding to her daughter, Ellen stepped behind the decorated podium, as Ruthie took Britany by the hand and led her to the last empty table with one name tag on it, Leah Merkal. Ellen knew the pastor and his wife would make entrance, as planned, at last minute and sit with Britany.

"Greetings. I am Ellen Gates, here with my daughter, Ruthie and I want to thank you for the invitation to share God's love with you. Today, I have seen your work and I commend your service to the community and the Lord. The lap pads you supply to Nursing Homes and individuals are not only a useful necessity but a wonderful testimony of your love for others." Displaying one of the lap pads, she said, "I had not noticed at first, but this is a very special item, it demonstrates consideration of the one who made it for the one receiving it. There, in the corner, almost unnoticed, but how could it be? Someone has embroidered the words, Peace, Hope and Victory."

"I find this a blessing from God, who always knows our plans and steps ahead of us in preparation. You see, when I was asked to come, I considered what to share with you today. I thought of your commitment as women in keeping peace. My husband asked what I planned to share, what topic. I replied, Peace that passes understanding and you see on this item, the words, Peace, Hope, Victory."

"Before we begin, I'm going to ask you to form a circle around the room. Take the hand of the person next to you and for a moment, close your eyes and think of a need in your life. Everyone thinking. Got it? Now, consider the person next to you. We are going to pray and I ask you to consider that person standing by your side and when we pray, ask God to bless the one whose hand you are holding and leave it up to him to supply their need. The last thing we will do, there's a song; the words desire peace, which says, let it begin in me." She glanced to where Ruthie was standing. "Ruthie will step into the circle and take the hands of the two on each side of her." Ellen saw Britany and another woman break hands to admit Ruthie. Now the circle was complete.

"Let us pray. Father God, our Creator, Healer, Sustainer, we come to you, Father, asking your blessing on our gathering. Here, Lord, are incredible women, who come regularly to bless others and in doing so, are blessed beyond measure. Lord, our combined prayers are to honor these women, the recipients of the gifts they make and give to others need. We ask, dear Father that you keep them in your care, and always Lord, that they form a love for each other, so tightly bound by your mercy and grace upon them that wherever they go, your people will know they are set apart, your hand is on them, they are important, special and loved. Strengthen them, where strength is needed, give health's elements into their lives, and help them to know they are part of your plan, what they do is important. Lord, we love you, we praise you and we thank you that we might stand in the circle of your love, together."

"Amen."

Strangely subdued, the ladies sat quietly, expectant, their attention holding as Ellen began to explain scripture. "To know the extent of peace in our heart, we first must understand there are times of trial. Those times we aren't sure where to turn. We know we have not been promised life will be an easy street. Think of the worst trial you have encountered. Did you rely on your faith? What is faith?"

"In our own words, faith is a confidence that what we hope for will happen. In scripture, faith is the evidence of things hoped for, but not seen. Hebrews chapter eleven tells us by faith we understand that the universe was formed at God's command, so that what we see was made out of what was invisible." Ellen laughed. "Aren't a lot of our problems made out of what is invisible to us at the time?"

"Have you ever wondered why, why is this happening to me? Jeremiah29:11 tells us, "I know the plans I have for you, plans to prosper you and not to harm you, plans to give you hope and a future." God gave these words to the people in exile. He has given them to us, today, to bring hope, peace and victory. There are people around us, in bonds of their own making. They are so miserable; they want to make others miserable. Have you heard the old adage; misery loves company?" A sigh of agreement swished around the room. Those people, lie to themselves to keep on practicing habits which are harmful. They are unwilling to let go of that which will destroy them. They accept second best in a world where our Savior, Jesus Christ bled and died for them; where they could receive blessing unnumbered." The ladies were nodding agreement.

"If we look at what the Bible teaches us, we realized God is calling us to have a relationship with Him. He wants to draw us close in time of trial. Under his wing, in Psalm 91:1, we read, He that dwelleth in the secret place of the Most High Shall abide under the shadow of the Almighty. Why do we want to be in the presence of the Lord? To receive Peace, Hope and Victory. Because of the Lord's great love, we are not consumed by those trials that we thought were going to knock us down. His compassion never fails, it is new every morning, and He is good to those whose hope is in Him. That word, again, Hope."

"We can know hope in the midst of turmoil, we can find peace and we will have victory. Philippians, chapter 4, verse 7 tells us, "The peace of God which passeth all understanding shall keep our hearts and minds through Christ Jesus." Think of that peace, as we look around at our sisters in Christ, let us claim that hope, that peace, offered to us, that we feel, even in the midst of trouble, a calm in our heart and mind."

The hour passed quickly and the ladies opened to the times their hearts were troubled and shared in despair they had turned to the Lord. Mabel was one who first expressed the despair she had known, "my whole life turned upside down, the one I loved was in terrible pain. I knew he was dying and while I hurt for his pain, I also had this feeling of emptiness knowing I would be going on alone. How was I to do that?" The hour turned into moments of hugs and understanding. There were tears, with smiles shining through those tears. Ellen brought the meeting back together as she begin to sing the song, Victory In Jesus, my Savior forever, he sought me and bought me with his undying love."

Pastor Levi, stood as one in a trance, watching the ladies of his congregation love each other through a nod of the head here, a hand reaching across to clasp another hand. They were enraptured to know, they had been there, suffered, walked through the valley of the shadow of death, and persevered while abiding under the Shadow of the Most High. There was where these marvelous women received the strength that helped them in time of sorrow. Yes, hope, faith, peace, victory, he found himself joining the women in song. It was some time later, Leah whispered, "Did you notice, little Ruthie held Britany's hand? Whether for support or other, I don't know, but Britany's expression lost that coldness we often experience in her, she actually seemed to loosen up. Even her body seemed to respond and I noticed her features softened. Praise the Lord."

"Let us hope it lasts," were Levi's words.

The ladies lingered, mingling with each other but drawn to Ellen to discuss more personal happenings in their lives. Ellen loved the feeling of openness and participation. Many were enraptured with Ruthie, feeling a specialness to the child, they could not describe. One lady phrased it best, "There's such a love in you two, that can only come from God. When your little girl took my hand, it was like a river of peace flooded my soul." Thank you," Ellen replied, pointing to heaven. "Remember God loves each of us."

She was prepared when Britany came to her. "I understand you are a friend of Matt Langley?"

"Yes, indeed, we are very good friends, Matt and Marigold and little M.J."

Britany gave a slight laugh. "I suppose, one day you and I will be friends, then. A friend of Matt's can only be my friend, too, minus Marigold, of course."

"That's a very hurtful thing to say, concerning one's friend." Ellen leaned against the podium behind her. "Why would you say such a thing? You are aware they have a son and a new baby on the way?"

"That is insignificant. I knew Matt when she was unaware, he existed. We are meant for each other."

"Have you talked with your heavenly father about this?" Ellen asked, as Leah joined them.

Britany's smile was coll. "I don't have to. I'll be a good mother to those children and wife to Matthew. I know their background. Our home will be perfect." Her yes fell on Ellen, "This is none of your business, anyway." Her glance slid sideways to Leah, "Back there, a few minutes ago, I was almost persuaded, but I believe you have something in your life that will disrupt any peace, you think you have. You would do well to come clean about your own digression to your husband. Did you think no one knows?" Britany moved on, gliding down the hallway as if she owned it.

Ellen glanced Leah's way. Laying a hand on Leah's arm, she said, "I honestly have no clue what she is talking about. What concerns me most is the fact she said, I was almost persuaded. Does almost mean she has not given her soul over to the Lord, that she knows Him, but she is straddling the fence?"

Unknown, to Leah and Ellen, Mabel and Suze were involved in clean up and overheard the conversation between the three. When Britany moved on down the hall, they found chance to glance each other's way. With silent agreement they walked away, and once they knew they were alone, standing by the broom closet, Suze said, "That sounded like a threat." Mabel appeared to be considering the whole picture. "She was warning Pastor's wife, or the speaker, not to interfere." Suze paused. "Why are you so quiet? You always grasp these situations, quickly? Was she telling our Leah to tell her husband about clandestine meetings with another man, thinking the forbidden had happened?"

Suze stared at Mabel, unsure why her friend remained silent. Now as they folded cloths from tables unused and gathered soiled ones for laundering. "What if it is what we overheard? We thought they were having an affair but we gave them benefit of doubt. Maybe someone else saw them and thinks the unforgivable happened."

Finally, Mabel spoke, "Or, perhaps it isn't true at all and we should mind our own business. Shining Light cannot stand another thing to happen. Already, the deacons are thinking of replacing our pastor. I overheard Herm on the phone and his words were, "it's a matter of time." I felt he referred to Pastor Levi. I've been praying Herm doesn't stir up anything else, but it is his nature. He never leaves well enough alone. And that one," she glanced down the hall where Britany had disappeared, "She is meddling in another woman's marriage and that means the sin is on her hand and she needs to accept what she is doing is wrong. I thought, once, when I glanced her way and the little girl was holding her hand that I saw a glimmer of hope, but within minutes she was wearing that hard body stare in her eye."

"I don't know how you hold it all in. It bothers me," Suze said. "I want everything right in our lives."

"Didn't we just have a lesson on that?" Mable headed toward the door. "Let's go. We've done our part." Suze knew Mabel meant she was leaving. She followed, mulling over Mabel's last words.

"Speaking of Herm. You know I get the Cape's newspaper, something Wade started, and, well, there's an article about our Herm and that cousin of his, the one used to visit here. The truth is, there's a man with a family who has been accused of killing the cousin we know and he will be going to prison for killing him, except he is not dead."

Mabel was tinkering with her phone, seeming aloof to Suze conversation. "I don't follow you."

"Herm's cousin. Remember? He visited when they were kids, when he was older, he left and we heard he had died but his name, the one we laughed about and he told us to remember for the day when he ran for office." Suze was becoming a bit irritated with Mable. "You, communicate with every one. Don't you recall? His name. What was it?" Mabel was holding back. "He came every weekend, especially Saturdays. The family shielded him. They said he had an unfair amount of sickness, but they never said the name of his illness." Suze wondered what was so important with Mabel and her phone?

"Walden? Finally, the name came to Suze. "Yes. That's it. He came up missing and we heard that higher ups, those with authority, were shielding him, just as the family did. He wasn't sick at all. He was in trouble and his Momma was covering for him. It was said he married some rich girl and got into more trouble. I can't believe you don't remember him. Tall, thin, with an attitude. You," Suze was at her wits end. "You didn't like him. He liked you."

Mabel was beginning to listen. Seldom did Suze go to such lengths to explain anything. "What are you talking about? Who liked me and how do you know all this stuff, I wasn't sure you knew what…"

Suze interrupted, "you thought I was just rattleing?" She felt insulted. "You know Herm comes by and talks and you said I should be nice to him, though I don't know why. I don't want my personal business familiar to someone like Herm. But Herm mentioned, this Walden person did not die. I could tell he was dying to tell me some piece of news he had, that he thought no one else knew. But, he was afraid I would connect the dots, that Walden is actually hiding from the law. If they find him, he goes back to prison and it would free that fellow being blamed for killing him. However," this was Suze exclamation point, "Someone must know, because Herm is receiving threatening letters."

"Why are the letters important? It appears to me; the authorities need this piece of information. If this cousin of Herm's is indeed alive. There's a man in jail, being charged for killing him." She paused, thinking. "I believe I did hear the man charged with killing is a family man with one child and another on the way? I don't know how true that is…maybe the baby has arrived by now. If you are talking about the tall blonde boy that chased after me and I couldn't stand him, Herm's cousin? I don't think he's alive."

"You finally understand? I often wonder if Herm is trying to take on his cousin's identity. You know as kids; we wondered if he had a split personality. When he speaks of politicians….he loses me. It is a depth of conversation I do not understand."

"Isn't that the way?" Mabel nodded. "Corrupt politicians help, only if it benefits them. Maybe, Herm is considering his cousin escaped jail, or maybe he knows something. How does this have anything to do with us, other than we don't want an innocent man going to jail for something he didn't do." She considered for a moment. "No, I'll stick to my first thought, I don't believe Herm's cousin is alive."

Exasperated, Suze seemed to be praying for strength. Mabel was usually the smart one. This was beyond her patience. "Yes, an innocent man will go to prison because Herm's cousin is not dead."

"Well, I do apologize for getting on your nerves." Mabel's eyes narrowed. You are telling me Herm acts strangely. What's new about that? He seems to have tied in with that Britany woman and we saw how she is, an hour ago. That's pretty fresh on the mind. What else? Now, you have my attention."

"Mabel. I don't know how he is doing it, but Herm sends things through the mail to those two men that are instrumental in telling the world that family man killed Walden, their boss, when Walden is very much alive. Herm can't resist telling me things and I'm scared he will turn on me. He gets this crazy look in his eye and I swear he becomes someone else." Suze was wringing her hands. "When he leaves he says, Suze you know I care about you. Deeply." Suze sighed heavily. "I just want to cry. I think he likes that woman, Britany."

"That bothers you?" Mabel sounded astonished. "Really, you care for Herm?"

"NO. I'm scared to death of him. I wish he never came by to talk to me again. I'm afraid of Herm."

Looking up to heaven, Mabel exclaimed, "Why didn't you say so?" She could see now, Suze was sincerely terrified and she felt unsettled, herself. "I thought you were just rattling on. I can't believe this. Our hands are tied and yet, someone needs our help." A flash of pastor and the deacons beating the fire out of her yard surfaced in Mabel's brain. "Lord, help us."

"May I ask? What were you doing that you found it so hard to listen when I began to tell you this?"

"If you must know, I was trying to learn to text back to Nate. He insisted I must have a phone for safety's sake, but truth is I don't understand the first thing about it. I have to concentrate to use it."

Once home, Mabel thought to text Nate. Finally, she dialed him. "That texting takes forever," she said in reply to his greeting. "I want to ask you something. Do you remember anyone named Walden?"

"After all these years? Let me think. How could I forget that tall rich boy that liked you. He was a snob." Nate grew quiet and then said, "You know our boyo, Matt stays with me while down here managing his parent's farm. I didn't make connection until now. He mentioned a friend of his was going to trial, picked up on bogus charges. He's in jail, waiting his court date. Is that what this is about?"

"Possibly. Nate, can you have a talk with Matt and see if there's any connection, if this is his friend?"

"Yes, I will. I wanted to ask, since you were going to attend the Women's meeting today, I was wondering if Britany was there. Would Britany relate to Herm or Walden?"

"I heard Walden died." Mabel had a flash back of Suze. "Suze was so seriously concerned for the young man. She is concerned whether Herm is trying to assume Walden's identity."

"I try not to think of Walden, at all. I guess that's why I dismissed similarity of name when Matt told me." Nate chuckled. "He was pretty hot for you. Caused me all kind of trouble. He was rich. I wasn't."

"I never liked him. He had an attitude that what he wanted was his already. I didn't settle for that."

"I'm glad you didn't settle for Walden it was difficult for me, that I let you get away. This is our second, chance, Mabel. How do you feel about that?" He became very quiet, waiting for her response. He could hear Mabel's movement toward the door.

She returned to the phone. "Oh, Nate, I must attend to a little girl from next door's school project."

"Quickly, before you go, was Britany at the meeting? I'm worried about her. She's pulled away, and she does that when she is burdened. You know with her parents gone, she's alone now."

"You look out for her, don't you, Nate?" She couldn't hurt Nate, even though she had seen how Britany treated the speaker and Leah. Britany had no right to judge Leah. "Yes, she was there."

"Thank goodness. After Nola died, Britany always invited me for family dinners. She's not part of the coup, with Herm or Walden, is she?" Nate coughed, to clear his emotions of caring for Britany.

Nate lingered, with the phone in his hand, staring at it. He had lost the moment, hoping for an answer from Mabel concerning their future. His mind had strayed to Britany, actually praying she did attend the meeting. Britany was always used to having her own way and she could be quite bold in getting it. The thought now entered his mind, had Mabel heard his question and ignored answering?

He would take a walk to clear his head and started out the metal arch over the driveway, taking a left to head into the cool of the Forrest he refused to cut down, not to farm the land, no, it was a pleasant place to walk and put a man's thoughts in place. Upon his return, he found Matt cleaning the mud off of his boots. Finished, he placed them outside the back door and swept up the mud and dumped it in the trash bin. Nate's eyes welled up, with tears. This was the child of his youth, when emotions surfaced and testosterone ran high, and the boyo didn't even know he was his father. He had chafed over Vivien passing his child off to another man but his own mother asked, "Nate, can you give him any more through the years, than your friend will? The man thinks the boy his own child. He will love and protect him. What more can you ask?"

When he and Nola bore no children, Nate often wished he had claimed Matt and Vivien be damned. Hindsight was always better than foresight. If only he could tell Matt; instead, he watched the boy grow into a good man, all the years enjoying the Christmas gifts Matt showed him, thankful Matt wanted to share with him. "You're my best friend, Nate," Matt would say and Nate would say a prayer, thankful for the blessing. Now, in greeting, he asked, "How'd you mess up your boots?" Taking a seat on the porch step, Nate waited for his heart to settle. The emotion of seeing his son always made it beat a little faster.

"It was while I was checking the North forty. Water was running across the lower end. I decided I could shovel it off." Matt grinned. "I almost bit off more than I could chew." He studied Nate. "You all right? Your color's a tad off." He sit on the porch, concerned for Nate. "Did you walk too far?"

"Maybe. It's this dad-burned Arthritis. Weather seems to play havoc with a man's bones."

"I'm going to the Cape for the weekend, if you are sure, you are all right. Are you?" Nate nodded. "I need to check on my friend. The one I told you about. His name's Andrew Graves." He waited for the light of recognition to dawn in Nate's eyes. "Andrew left home when he was fourteen. Taking jobs, he put himself through college. With a degree, he worked his way up the ladder, with a few politicians." Matt's eyes met Nate's. "Some of them were corrupt politicians and Andrew learned their ways. He said in order to keep his job he had to beat them at their own game, but the game pulled him in and long story short, he lost his marriage. Though he kept his son, I'd say he wrongly finagled against his wife, Anne. She's a good woman." Matt sighed heavily. "Andrew's boss ended up dead and guess who they blamed? Andrew. We thought he was cleared of the crime but this year the Feds showed up, said they'd reinvestigated and all fingers pointed to Andrew as the killer. Now he's up to his ears in trouble."

"This friend, doesn't seem your type, Boyo."

"No, I guess, not really. I met him when I was overseeing a construction crew. He needed a job." Matt laughed. "That first day, those soft hands were bleeding with blisters. We toughened him up, eventually. I tell you, he was worn out that first day when he left work and as luck had it, my boss and his wife had taken him in, by order of the court. If he didn't shape up, even then, he was going to jail."

"A different crime?" Nate asked. Matt nodded. "You think he's innocent of the present charges?"

"Yes, I do. My boss and his wife had a big hand in straightening up Andrew. It took a while, but they changed him. He began to see what a jewel his ex-wife was. He had to start attending church, before she would believe he changed, and go through counseling. Now he counsels young people caught in the court system. I worked with him, but I learned who he was even more when he started attending the church where Marigold and I go."

"Who did you say he killed?"

"Walden?" Matt scratched his head, thinking. "The man ran in last years election. He probably campaigned through here. You must have read about it in the newspaper, at the time?"

"He didn't happen to marry the heir to Lan King's estate, did he? The Kings could buy and sell anyone or anything. The young woman had a flair for handsome men, with money. Did Walden have money?"

Matt laughed. "As I understand, Walden had flair. She had the money and family to back it up." Rising, he said, "I've got to get going, Nate, if you are sure, you are all right." Nate nodded, again, as Matt extended his hand. "Thanks, Nate for everything. I'll be back to work Monday morning and see you that night." He smiled. "I like you, Nate, but I can't wait to see Marigold and M.J."

Nate watched him leave the drive. He decided to call Britany. "Girl, where you been, haven't seen you in a while." He listened. She had been busy. She would be by. "I hear you are keeping company with Herm Smith. He's a bad one, Hon. I don't want you getting in trouble." He was just someone she sit by in church, bad breath, loafers and no socks. "I miss you at Misty Vale." I'll be back, she said, don't give up on me. "No, I won't," he promised, and then he listened as she said, I think he's involved in something. "Don't get in trouble, Hon." I won't, she said, Uncle Nate, you and Matt love me, don't you? Soon, I'll prove to you what that means to me. She hung up. Nate pushed hard to rise from the porch step. Maybe he should call a few of his old friends, Representatives, Senators and a couple who plod along in the halls of justice. They would recall last year's election and give him a better view of what had happened to Walden. Did he remember Walden? Indeed, he did, otherwise he would've married Mabel.

For a moment his thoughts swung around to Vivien Langley. Thank God he hadn't married Vivien. To have Matt as his son would have brought endless joy, but Vivien was a pain where you didn't want it. Still, he couldn't stand to see his sweet Britany soiled, keeping company with Herm or Vivien.

Suze placed the hot cakes in the carrier. Surely Mabel wouldn't go out after the morning rain. Suze needed to clear the air; she and Mabel weren't on the best standing, yesterday. Mabel came to the door. "You've been baking. That means you're in trouble. What's on your mind, Suze?"

Glancing at the floor, she was aware Mabel took the carrier. "Could you tell Nate about Herm, Mabel? I don't understand him and it does worry me when he drops by. You remember the last time Herm lost reasoning; he nearly destroyed our church."

Mabel was a good friend but she was blunt. "Come on, sit down and relax … or go home. I'm tired, this morning. Hopefully, the treatment Herm received will last a lifetime. Now is there more to this?"

"I believe I'll just go home." Suze headed to the door. "I'm not good company, either, but I am afraid of Herm Smith." She walked across the street and hurried down the block. Once inside, she locked the door. ***"If I ever needed you, Wade, it's now. I don't know why you left me alone."*** Her mind was fairly screaming. Her nerves were on edge. She opened the window for air. She was sweating. And then she sit down at the computer. His photo popped up. She turned on audible.

"Where have you been? I worry when I don't hear from you."

"I worry all the time. It makes me sick when I worry.'

"Tell me why you worry, dear lady.'

"I don't know you. Whether you are the person in the picture or if I'm texting with more than one of you."

"I'm the man in the picture, dear. Why do you find that hard to believe?"

"Tell me something about yourself." She heard him chuckle. "Please, send me some form of identity."

Within seconds a photo appeared. The man in the picture was the same as on his profile. Except, this time he wore a hastily scratched name on white paper clipped to the front of his shirt. SUZE. She laughed in delight.

"You have a very nice laugh, my dear. You need to laugh more."

"You can't see me."

"No, but I heard you. I want to come see you. May I?"

Suddenly, she froze. No one knew about him. Her body shivered. She was unable to speak. She would be ostracized by the community. A disgrace talking to a man on line. They would hang a scarlet letter around her neck. “I can’t. I mean, you must not.” She closed down the computer.

Outside, someone stood listening at the opened window. He had come to visit. So, she talked with another man. He was not the only one in her life. He was wasting his time. Fury pounded through his veins. His face turned red. He clenched his fist. Without a thought, he slammed the window shut and ran to the other side of the house. He would get even with her. He hurried home, considering how to make her pay. The other person inside his body was more cunning. He allowed him to come through and before he knew it, he was laughing.

Levi and Leah were taking an early morning walk, while the air was pleasant, after the rain. They were passing Herm Smith’s home. “What is that sound?” Leah stopped, glancing each direction, settling finally toward the front room of Smith’s house. “Levi, is that laughter? It sounds delirious.” Levi was grabbing her hand, pulling her along.

“Maniacal,” he whispered, glancing back, furtively. “Perhaps, it is true. Leah, it is whispered, Herm Smith is a man of two personalities. I was not sure that actually happens, but that laugh raised the hair on back of my neck.”

Chapter Seventeen

Marigold closed the shop, picked up M.J. from Harriet's and headed home. She was tired; tired from the trip in the rain. The road block she had encountered on the way home had made her appreciate good roads, but she wondered what they were looking for. Most of all, she was lonely. Matt hadn't called today. She glanced at the house. It was dark, except for that one light, the one that said, I'm here and soon there will be other lights flooding this house. A chuckle bubbled up, "Yeah, sure, the lights talk." The thought made her giggle. She was that tired. She helped M.J. out of his seat. "Here we go, Bud. You can walk and Mommie will bring your bag."

Headlights flooded their path to the house, as a door to a vehicle slammed and someone came running from behind them. Marigold felt a moment of alarm and then Matt's arms were closing around her, as somehow, he managed to bring M.J. up with them. They were a mass of arms, hugging each other and the night was filled with M.J.'s giggles and Marigold's joy in laughter.

"Man. It was worth battling that rain all the way to get to you two." Matt lift M.J. high, on to his shoulders. "You got a key, Mrs. Langley?"

"You called me that, the night we were married." Her voice was soft, remembering. "I needed you, desperately, tonight, Matt."

Matt sit M.J. down. His eyes on her, one finger beneath her chin, he leaned n to kiss her lips, soft and searching, becoming butterfly kisses as it seemed he couldn't turn loose of her and she melt in his arms. "You could never need me more than I need you, my love. I've nearly drowned in sorrow this week waiting to come home."

He felt tears fall on his wrists. "Babe, what's wrong? Don't cry." But her tears flowed down her cheeks dripping onto his arms. "Is the baby all right?" He pulled her close. "Tell me." But she had to finish the crying. Finally, he led her to the chair, settling in with her on his lap. "What's wrong?"

"I don't know." The tears came in sobs, now, her face hidden in the hollow of his neck. "It's everything." She tried to quieten, so as not to disturb M.j., "I need you here. Everyone has problems. I pray for everyone. We all do, but you are away and I need you. I'm tired of you being away. We need you and it's not fair, you not being here. I'm sorry I sound selfish, but we are having a baby…you should be here." Her cry almost became a wail.

She felt little in his arms, her body swollen with child, he mused and still she felt small. The baby moved beneath his hand and he was thankful. There, life stirred and this was but a temporary set back. "I'm torn," he said. "My heart is here with you, but Sis's husband has no idea how to run the farm and right now, Dad can't." He heard the clang of toys as M.J. played in his room. This was what they came home to every night, the two of them facing a house without him, while he slept at Nates, weary and worn, not from the farm work, only, but his mother's shenanigans, Britany's intent to destroy his marriage and his heart aching with missing Marigold and M.J.

"I can't leave the farm unattended, Marigold. There's no one to see to the crops or to tell the employees what to do. It's not their responsibility." How many times, that week had he considered the farm owned its people, not the other way around, he was merely the tool that operated the acreage. Land controlled a man's life, if it was his choice to make a living from it, dictating every step taken, expecting care and consideration. It wasn't fair. He needed to be with his wife and child, especially now with another baby on the way. "We have the weekend," he said.

"It's not enough." Marigold's hand tightened on his arm. "Two days?"

They yawned in sync. "I hope to see Andrew while I'm here."

"And church," she said, snuggling closer to his body. "This feels so good. I've missed you every night."

He chuckled, "I've missed you every hour, Mrs. Langley. We need to attend church, too."

"Okay," she was so warm and protected, her body was going numb while her mind was trying to find something. There it was. "Matt, we have a problem. Britany…she's…I…need…I can't handle her anymore. She's demon psss…"

Matt sit there, listening to M.J. playing in the next room, his wife asleep in his arms. If she only knew. Perhaps, that was the word. Britany was possessed, always, with having something that belonged to another person. He wanted to tell Marigold about Britany's visit, but leaving again in two days wasn't enough time to cement their lives so she wouldn't worry.

Sunday at Christ Church

Many were the phone calls, prior to Sunday church. The group of friends, Daniel thought, needed to gather. "We need to find time," he told each family, "to visit and listen and share what's going on in our lives. Come over, after church. We'll catch up." Leaving for church on Sunday, he reached across to take Ellen's hand. "Was it too much setting up? Are you all right, my darling?"

"I'm fine." She squeezed his hand. "Haley being home at her parents, made the difference. She knew what to do and together the two of you whipped everything in place. Thank you for catering our lunch, though."

From the backseat, Ruthie asked, "Is everyone coming, even Uncle Matt?"

"Yes, everyone has been invited." Ellen's voice dropped, as in pain. One they loved would not be with them.

"It's okay, Momma." Ruthie felt her mother's pain. "Bitty's happy in heaven. We'll see her again, one day."

Christ Church schedule rolled along, study groups, songs of praise and finally Brother Joe stood before his congregation. His smile could not contain the joy he felt seeing on the first three pews, sit his closest friends. They would break bread together after church. "Let us stand for the reading of the word."

For a short while, God's people listened to the reading of his word and then they were on the way to Dan and Ellen's home. There was such joy in the group coming together, hugs abound. Matthew and Daniel shared the usual bear hug. Matt's expression was priceless, as he said, "Thanks, Friend, for having us over." Serious, he scanned Dan's face. "I know I'm jumping in pretty quick, but I may not have another opportunity to ask you how's Andrew? Is he holding up?"

"Harriet hired a detective," Dan said, quietly. We've all tried to come up with a clue to Andrew being taken to jail, but we fail to find a motive, other than it seems set up. The detective said it's a dead-end road. Someone has wiped the records clean. It is as though Walden never existed, and yet, Andrew's going to trial for murdering him."

"I don't understand any of this. Is it true a package came in the mail, anonymous, of course, that contained a set of clothes believed to belong to Walden?"

"That's was kept quiet, but when Harriet's detective checked it out, they were Walden's. D.N.A. proved it, but how could you know?"

"It's almost as though Walden had contact with the New Haven community," Matt replied. "I often wonder if there is a family connection. Walden and Herm Smith were boyhood friends, some say cousins and it is said they delved into a lot of pranks together." He didn't mention Nate said he would look into any possible connection. "It seems to me if this is adults playing pranks, things got seriously out of hand."

"Andrew is going to face serious time in the big house if something doesn't come to light, soon." Daniel turned toward the door as voices from outside filtered into the room. "Annie just arrived. Let's all gather around and pray together for Andrew and everyone else's needs."

Matt and Andrew exchanged a glance of understanding, having seen Anne enter. She was showing the strain. "We have to remember, what Harriet and Ellen often tell us, "not to give up, because often the Lord does work in mysterious ways, his wonders to behold." As Daniel tapped a spoon against a glass, the group settled to a quiet expectation of answered prayer.

"Does anyone have a specific need or prayer you want us to join in?" He waited and when no one spoke he continued, "Matthew 6:34 reminds us, "sufficient to the day is the evil, thereof." Which means, each day has enough trouble, we are not to borrow more by looking ahead and speculating and making ourselves sad. Instead, we come together now, according to scripture that reminds us we are to pray, believing. What we ask in the Lord's name is honored… That gives us hope. Remember the song that says, our God is an awesome God? He is bigger than any problem we might have and when things seem to go astray, there's a lesson in there to grow us into better people for God's kingdom." He glanced at Ellen. "Do you need to tell us anything, my love?"

"Only, this, as we are together, as Daniel was speaking, I thought of the time Ruthie was taken, I was at the end of my rope in despair, fearful something terrible was about to happen. All of you came together, as we are now, and I want to thank you that we do this, God answers prayer but we do see each other through the ordeal. I'm very thankful for friendship and bearing each other's burdens."

It was then in silent agreement, every head bowed and no doubt, every tongue confessed, Jesus Christ is Lord.

Harriet had only arrived home when the phone rang. "Yes, this is Harriet Becker." She listened. "Matthew Langley's friend, Nate? Yes, I'm Marigold's mother. I'm glad to meet you, Nate. Yes, I did hire a detective, trying to help Andrew." She listened. "It would be helpful to put our heads together, to try to find a solution, yes."

"Yes, I'll go first. What we know for certain, is Walden has ties with someone in New Haven, whether it is a relative or not, I don't know. Someone sends out packages. Either they are paying the Postmaster a piece of the prize, or, it is someone the Postmaster knows and trusts completely and doesn't question what is in the package. It is rumored those packages hold the missing drugs, which has upset the drug lords and when they suspected Walden for trying to cut in on the product that brought in heavy revenue, they are the ones that killed Walden and set it up to look Andrew was the killer. Yes, I know, drugs are in every community."

"I have a friend," Nate replied, "That believes the fellow that controls the purse strings to the drug lenders, is having an emotional problem, and if that is true, innocent people could be hurt, children playing without supervision might be in that line of innocents. That's why I called. We can't let little children be the receiver of such an atrocity. They are God's little innocents."

"Who are you implying that relative to be?" Harriet was making notes.

"My friend reminded me that Herm Smith once went off the deep end and tried to destroy the church. She wonders if he is a relative to Walden and perhaps covering for him. But there's another relative, a cousin, she tells me that stirs about in the community though people pay little attention to him. He comes into town by way of the woods, purchases supplies and returns to his own private lair. She thinks, Walden, Smith and this Woods dweller are possibly all three cousins and shared the same grandmother, who kept them hidden when they were in trouble."

"Interesting," Harriet murmured.

"It is her opinion that someone needs to start paying attention to who frequents the wooded area around the community, perhaps pushing farther into the density of that line that rises in the ridge above the town. She said as children, they were afraid to venture far and even now women caution their children to not go farther than the tree line." He gave a tired laugh. "As adults, you and I know, even we must be cautious where we walk. That old adage, where there's smoke there's fire, may very well mean, if Smith frequents the woods, he knows who lives beyond. Haven't we seen those little huts, in our lifetime, that didn't just appear, without reason?"

"I've never heard the story you are telling, me, Nate. That is a community different than mine. With the school of Nursing and the College located here, it is possible there's more of a stirring than in a smaller village type setting which I believe the only thing I'm really familiar with is Shining Light Church, because my daughter is instrumental in the renovation and I believe Smith does attend that church."

"Maybe someone can at least look into the possibility of another connection to Walden and those selling drugs in the community. But we are intrigued, are we not, with the possibility of a lead, or any clue, to save an innocent man's life, is certainly worth the effort?"

Nate hung up the phone, thinking, often it was the work of women that settled a case. Perhaps, Harriet and Mabel did not know each other, but it seemed the heart of a woman was willing to become involved to find answers to questions, when it seemed harm was upon an innocent person, be it man, woman or child. He chuckled, thinking of Mabel describing her friend, Suze's despair. "God bless them, all," he said, aloud, softly.

Harriet glanced at the phone and then the notes she had taken. "The woods guy? That's a new thought. Possibly another cousin. I'll give these to the detective. It seems the plot thickens. Maybe there's hope."

Chapter Eighteen

Levi was feeling God's wonderful love. Leal was sitting on the front pew and she was smiling. Laurie Hutchens left the new piano for a moment, going to sit beside Leah. No doubt they were talking about Laurie's pregnancy. Jake was a happy man. Levi didn't know the details, except what Jake told him. "I thought our marriage was over, Pastor. Then Laurie attends that Women's Day study, whatever it was, and the lady in charge…" Jake's eyes filled with tears. "You probably know all about it, what with Leah being there, and the two of them are friends and we are expecting our baby. I'm a happy man, Pastor."

He had gripped Levi's hand with a strength that hurt. When Levi winced, Jake turned loose and apologized. "It's going to happen for you and Leah, too, Pastor. Wait and see. God is visiting favors on Shining Light Church. Here we are in our newly renovated building, someone gave us a new piano." He saw Levi's worried glance toward the piano. "Oh, that little spiff from Britany? It'll pass. Churches go through that kind of thing and come out stronger.

By the time the hands on the clock rolled around, it was time to begin Worship hour. The pews were full. Hallelujah, what a Savior, the singers were lifting hearts and hands to heaven. Levi had almost given up on his own marriage but Leah's return from her sister had pumped new blood into him and their marriage. He could almost believe Jak when he said it would happen for him and Leah to have a baby, too. God willing that was what Leah wanted. What they lost, returned with a newness for their marriage. Old things were put away, new meant they each were trying and life was good.

The first note of the doxology rang out. Everyone stood. Praise God from whom all blessing flow, Praise him all creatures here below…Miss Britany came down the aisle to take her new seating arrangement beside Herm Smith. Levi noted, Miss Britany appeared serene this morning. He prayed it was so. The song service finished. An offering was taken. It was time to present the scripture and the morning's sermon. Levis took his place behind the podium.

"May we stand for the reading of God's word. If you will, turn in your bibles to Isaiah 53:5-6. As we read verse five, let us substitute the word he with Christ. Verse five. "Christ was wounded for our transgressions. Christ was bruised for our iniquities; the chastisement of our peace was upon him; and with stripes we are healed. Verse six. All we like sheep have gone astray, we have turned everyone to his own way, and the Lord hath laid on him the iniquity of us all."

"You may be seated." He waited for the settling of bodies on the pews. "This is not the Easter story, nor the scripture we associate with Jesus dying, and yet it is. It is the prophecy of Isaiah, comparable to Jesus ministry in Jerusalem and the surrounding country side, the week before he died. Do we understand from the scripture, Christ was wounded for us, bruised before he arrived at the cross by hecklers who condemned him to death…how do we abuse him, today?"

Levi noticed Herm was busy whispering to Britany. "With wonder and disbelief and perhaps amazement, the prophet declared Christ would be rejected by the Jews. These were God's chosen people. How could God's chosen people show content to the Son of the one who made them His chosen people? We are told through scripture, he was wounded for our transgressions, chastised for our sins, his facial features were beaten to a pulp, and yet by his stripes we are healed." Levi took a moment to steady his focus. It was difficult,

Herm and Britany were now in audible dialogue. People were listening to them. "The Bible tells us, Jesus wept." Levi could see Herm was becoming agitated. Britany's hand was on his arm, restraining him.

Glancing Leah's way, it hit him, Levi was experiencing Shining Light's newest problem. Hadn't he heard, Herm Smith had a history of losing control of his mind and when that happened, he was dangerous. It seemed the congregation tolerated Smith, when anything was needed for the church, he managed to supply the money. As a minister, Levi felt that was at odds with how Christ's work was performed; but he was a pastor to the flock, not the Judge of their sins. Leave that to God. If he was supposed to go out into the world to preach the word, he hoped he wasn't faced with a room full of heathens. That thought coming to mind at the moment, startled Levi. Worse, Herm Smith was standing now, a menacing scowl on his face.

He pointed a hand of warning at Britany. "Woman," he shouted, loud and clear, "don't you understand? This is what Pastor is talking about. Rejection. Neglect. Secrets." He turned to face the congregation seated behind. "There's a secret in every heart in this room." He stepped out into the aisle and stood in line with the pulpit. "This sermon, we are hearing has the meaning of saying how neglectful we are. We don't understand just like those who abused Jesus and needed to be punished, we got a whole roomful of the same right here."

Levi stepped down, and offered his hand to Herm. "Don't you think it would be better, we discuss this behind closed doors, in the privacy of the office, not before the congregation of innocent…"

Herm interrupted. "You don't even know? And you are our Pastor? Secrets and hidden sins."

"Herm, we will dismiss the service, and then we will speak of the problems you see within us."

"No," Herm's voice raised another pitch. "Everyone stay put. You need to know what's going on." Herm walked to where the

Hutchen's were sitting. "Take this man. He's a doctor. Supposed to be a Christian, yet, I saw him with another man's wife."

"He's a doctor, Herm. He takes care of people. He has a wife, a great marriage, he's a family man."

Herm gave a scornful laugh. "You don't know that." He stepped over to where Leah sit. "This is your wife. This is the woman I saw meeting another man, one of your friends."

Levi was sweating profusely. "Jake's a friend, Herm. Leah and I trust him."

"Foolish. Foolish." Herm stared out at the people, then cut his eyes around to Suze. He pointed. "Her name's Suze. I wanted to marry her, but she thinks she's better than me. Why is that? Because she in carrying on with a man on the Internet. In my book, that's a sin."

Levi heard the quick intake of breath from the congregation. "Herm? You are out of control."

"I'm never wrong. Take this little gal right here," He reached for Britany's hand. "She knows. I can tell you the sin of every person in this room."

Levi waited for the intake of breath, but the room was silent.

"Larry. Jake." Levi called to the two largest men sitting in the congregation. "I need you up front." They came reluctantly. "Please. Walk Herm out and take him to the nearest hospital for treatment." He turned, to where Herm had left Britany standing. "Miss Britany, you may take your seat or follow the men as they escort Mr. Smith out the door."

The room came alive with whispered remarks. Levi wished not to hear one of them, as a rustle of personal items being collected followed. "All we like sheep, have gone astray, and the Lord hath laid on him the iniquity of us all. Let us bow our heads and be dismissed by prayer."

Heads bowed, eyes closed, Levi, gripped the table set before the altar with room for him to stand behind to administer the Lord's Supper. "Heavenly Father. We are at this moment in a state of disbelief. The Sabbath you set aside for worship, that we might honor you with a magnitude of holiness, has been disrupted, possibly by illness, possibly for the furthering of your word. We pray restoration to the one who is concerned for our congregation, in an unusual state of mind. Come into our hearts, Lord, that we realize moments of distrust and judging others comes to each of us, at different times, and only your Holy spirit can cleanse us of such turmoil. We are not to judge our fellow man, that is your position in our life, to judge us at the end of our days, to recognize we have asked forgiveness for our private sins, to know, you love us beyond our human function. Lord, our hearts cry out for understanding. Give us wisdom, how to handle this situation, that will spread beyond our congregation. Give us forgiving hearts and loving attitudes…."

Finished praying, Levi walked to the front pew and sank onto the cushioned seat before he fell on his face, in weakness and despair. He felt Leah's hand on his shoulder and thanked God she was there. He could not make it, immediately to stand in the foyer to shake hands with his people as they left, until Leah leaned forward and whispered, "Darling, come. I will stand with you. We must."

There were many hugs of encouragement and vigorous pumping of his hand, a number of kisses on the cheek, for Leah. When the last parishioner had left, Levi sank on the last pew to the door and Leah sit beside him. "Is there no end to this?" He lay his head back, his eyes heavenward, "The people are confused. Now they don't know if you and Jake are having an affair, if Suze is in sin on the internet, poor Suze. I doubt she ever hurt a soul in her life. She has no need for Herm in her life, so he gets even."

"I always thought I would go where the Lord called me and I wouldn't leave until he showed me, he had a next place for me…

but this, maybe when I was privately told there was a member who created chaos…."

"Let's go home, Levi." Leah gripped his hand, her eyes on the door as if Herm might return.

"I don't know, what we can do about this, Leah." He had run his fingers through his hair until it was standing straight up. Tears filled his eyes, overflowed and ran down his cheeks. "What am I doing wrong, Leah? God brought me to Shining Light Church…where will He send me?"

"You love these people, that much, Levi?"

For a moment, shock ran through his expression. "Don't you?" He reached for her hand. "I love you more than life. When it seemed, you were not coming back, I thought I'd die. But this, is my calling. Have I failed God? Like I failed you, Leah?"

Tears spilled from her eyes. She saw his torment. Her heart ached in a way; she'd never experienced before. His love for the church people was understandable, her love for him had become profound. How would Levi react to the secret she and Jake kept? Nothing happened between them but they had kept their meeting secret. She took a deep breath. "You never failed me, Darling. You have been faithful to my need."

What was she to do? Tell Levi, or let the secret simmer until it burst into flame? Laurie had come to her in friendship. The devil must be smiling, his evil countenance rearing up in her mind, as strong as the goodness that exist in her husband. Nausea, not unlike that of the morning hours, rose up, rolling in her stomach making its way up to her throat. She needed to hurry, to leave the sanctuary of Shining Light Church. Not knowing, Levi took her outstretched hand, turning back to lock the door, normally left open for one wanting to pray; one who found comfort when they settled to ask forgiveness at the Altar.

Levi seemed on an even keel, but as they approached the Altar, he sank to his knees, a violent sob wracking his body and Leah dropped down beside him, her arm across his back. They prayed silently, waiting for the Lord to come and if it took all night, both knew, they would stay.

Chapter Nineteen

Suze stood at the window. The lights had grown dim when the last person left the church, but she could see a glow through the stained-glass window near the altar. The thought crossed her mind, to go there and throw herself, prostrate on the floor beneath the altar; There, where saint and sinner were allowed to bend their knee.

Herm had cast angry eyes, his finger pointing wickedly her direction as he called out her name. "She's carrying on with a man on Internet." His accusation was loud. All in the building could hear. How would he know? Was he savant? It had been said when he was a child, his mother offered, "Herm had not the blessing of other children. He roamed the woods as though they were his friends. His need for affection from friends, was never met." Through the years, incidents, large and small were laid to blame at her son's feet. Suze, had seen him in the woods, when his mother died, leaning into a tree, sobbing terrible painful cries of one who had lost precious treasure. She had stayed away from him, but Mabel said he was a lost soul and they must be nice to Herm. Nice, was not as Mabel meant. Suze never asked him inside, some personal feeling, said she must not. They stood outside and talked when he dropped by.

In comparison, she was not afraid of the stranger who came each day to talk or text with her. His, were nice words, honoring her request that nothing intimate be said. Now, she made up her mind, following Herm's accusation, she must end their communication.

She could not know, if he was the man behind the photo he sent. She had no proof, such a person existed, how could she trust him? He had asked nothing of her, yet there was a secrecy about him, whether of her doing or his, she didn't know.

She sat at the desk, staring at the computer. 'I am no longer available. Our discussion of poetry and listening to music together, have been enjoyable. Thank you for the hours we have shared. Goodbye.' It did not seem enough. He had been kind. 'Something has happened," she typed, I feel this association must end. Thank you for the hours of acquaintance. I pray you find someone who appreciates your time.' Suze

Nothing eloquent, she thought, pressing enter and then she deleted his name and blocked further contact. Dressing for bed, she realized all ready she missed him. She picked up the bible and read a number of verses, before turning off the light and praying God heard her prayers. Her heart was heavy.

Mabel saw the light go out in Suze's bedroom. She knew Herm's accusation hurt her friend. Now as she spoke with Nate on the phone, she gripped the instrument listening as he brought up Britany's name. "I'm worried about my little friend, Mabel," he said. "Something doesn't seem just right with her, presently. What should I do?"

Who was she to bring up Britany's obvious involvement with Herm's scene at church? "I don't' know, Nate," she replied. Hesitant, she knew he needed to know some part of it, but which part? "Your girl was in attendance, with us in Shining Light service. Tonight was a bit of confusing. Herm came unglued."

They spoke for an hour and nothing was conclusive of what anyone could do. Shining Light Church appeared to be coming loose at the seams.

Levi pulled Leah into his arms. Daylight was breaking and he had seen her stir. "I've been waiting for you. I think our time with the Lord, last night, was what we needed. Don't you?"

She smiled through a yawn. "We left our burden with the Lord, didn't we?" Her voice held a hint of awe, "Like the song says, Our God is an awesome God. We don't always realize it."

Levi traced one finger, the line of her cheek, down to her lips and raised up to kiss her. "How do you feel?"

"Good," She snuggled close, "But Levi, I have to tell you..." Rising, he pulled her tighter to his body.

"Shh," he said, "We left it all at the altar; our failures, our hopes and our dreams. It's in God's hands."

"But..." He silenced her with another kiss. "We can't go there, Leah. God spoke to my heart. He asked me what's most important? I know what is. Can we live with that? When you returned to me, I became taller," he chuckled, "it felt that way, and I became stronger. But last night nearly took me down. I faltered, but when you laid your hand on my shoulder, I knew you loved me. Whatever lies ahead, we'll make it."

She reached up to clasp her arms around his neck. "Oh, Levi. I was so miserable. How did I get there?" She sighed. "I can answer that, myself. I was so sad, wanting to have our baby when all around us everyone else was having their own. But somewhere, along the way of my misery, maybe it was your prayers, I found my way back. Sometimes you feel your prayers go no farther than the ceiling and then one day, you know, just know, they do. God was listening all the time." Her voice went wistful, "but I am still waiting."

Suddenly, Levi was bouncing out of bed. "You know what, answers come with rejoicing. That's it. We haven't had a Rejoice Fest. That's what we are going to do and we're going to invite others. Is it too early to call Father Joe?"

"It's barely six in the morning." This news was unsettling. "What does Joe have to do with anything?"

He glanced at the clock. "Really?" Disappointment showed on his face like a little boy. He sank back on the bed, pulling the sheet up, tucking it around Leah's body as though she were a child. "Well," He let his breath release onto his chest. "Go back to sleep." He lay down to comfort her, but his eyes closed.

They overslept. Levi showed up at the office with a sheepish grin on his face. He was not infallible. Tully studied him, as one would a two-year-old. He had that look she had come to know. "Well, I must say you don't look much worse for the wear. That was some service, we had last night." She lay aside the paper she was working on. "Why don't you just tell me, what you have up your sleeve? I can see, you are antsy and need to let off some steam before you explode." He went into his office, leaving the door open. She saw him dial and then, "Joe, how ya doing? Yeah, Levi, here."

He listened to Joe's gentle ribbing, and then asked, "What's my chance, of you and the Gates, and any of your church people joining us the next weekend for a Rejoice Fest?" He laughed. "I know, it's upon us but if the Lord laid it upon me, surely he has his people who need it ready, doesn't he?" They discussed the event a few minutes "And ask that Gates lady if she can do a brief speech, too. Yeah, let me know, will ya?"

A short time later, Joe called back. "I'm amazed. Completely in shock. They all jumped on it. Anyway, the ones that would lead from this end, the Gates, Anne, Marigold and my faithful choir leader and his saints." Joe was laughing. "Friday and Saturday? They are all in."

"We need a banner, Tully." Levi's countenance was exuberant. "We are having a Rejoice Fest, except, Joe thinks we should call it a Praise Fest so, lets call it a Praise and Rejoice Fest. Friday and Saturday." He was laughing. "We will do Friday night here at the church and Saturday we are going to the park. Praise the Lord." He extended a hand to Tully. "Come on, let's you and I check the storage closet. If there's anything left from other projects, we'll use them." Tully was rising. Her arthritic bones were groaning within her body but she was smiling. "You feel it, too, Tully?" Levi patted her shoulder. "Man! God spoke to my heart and I can hardly handle it."

"For awhile there," Tully replied, "I was afraid we were getting a message from the devil with Herm Smith prophesying. You know I watch all those Walking Dead episodes, and it didn't look good here."

Levi was so happy he was laughing. "If you had heard what Leah and I heard the other night…"

"You watch The Walking Dead?" For a moment, Levi turned to see if she was serious. She was. He stared at Tully's sparse frame. She was angular, wearing a blue three-piece business suit, her hair piled on top of her head. She was old, anyway sixty-five, he thought, but her business aptitude set right with him, but this? This was different. "Hmmm," he said, noticing how her three silver bracelets clanked together, "I never would have thought Herm part of that scene." Maybe she was right.

"What else am I going to do, to get the blood flowing through these veins?" Her brown eyes snapped as she waited for his answer. "I can't do those silly exercise down at the New Vibe Spa."

"So, you sit home and watch the Living Dead on television from the comfort of your home?"

"You got that right," she replied, observing now the mess of the storage room and wondering what in the world Levi would find there to advertise his newest brain storm. "Praise Rejoice Fest?"

"You got that right," he said, turning to face her with a big smile and waving a flag that bore the word, Peace. He grinned, "If, Peace is here, maybe Hope and Joy and Praise or even Rejoice is, too."

"Are." She corrected, remembering once she taught English Literature in a Public School.

"Can you call Mable about refreshments?" Levi was high-fiving the hat rack. She shook her head. Maybe she was getting old for this job, but miss the excitement? Nah. "I'll call St. Peter, too," she said, "and Jake."

Chapter Twenty

Ellen sent out an e-mail, to the many friends she and Ruthie had met along the way. With both friends fed and bathed and in the sitter's care, she and Ruthie met with the men and women ready to do business for the Lord. Most were from Christ's Church, answering Brother Joe's request that they exercise willingness to serve the Lord when the need presented.

"Where we going, Ellen?" She answered the question. "It's a country church, New Haven's bests. On Friday night, we will worship together and prepare for Saturday, a day we will witness in the park with our testimony and good music to back us up. Thank you, for your willingness to serve. Scripture tells us the effectual honest prayers of God's people are honored and the pastor of that church tells Pastor Joe that they are going through a rough spot, he needs our prayers and for us to put feet to those prayers."

Helen Curry was new to the church, but she was a willing server for the Lord. Already she had recognized, the woman named Ellen, that was speaking had a gifted little daughter. "Will Ruthie go with us? She's not with us, tonight, so I was wondering."

"Yes, she will." Ellen smiled and touched the woman's hand. "Thank you for asking."

Helen felt a blessing fall on herself. She couldn't understand why, at the exact moment Ellen touched her, it came to her mind, that she loved the Lord and this woman leading the group certainly loved him.

"Jake will lead us in prayer, before we dismiss," Ellen was saying. "Let us pray the Lord goes before us."

"Well," Mabel said as the Sewing Group was in place. "We have a great number attending, today." She suspected, in light of Herm Smith's antics, everyone came to hear the latest on his treatment and too, the church would be co-sponsoring A Praise and Rejoice Festival in the neighboring town.

"What's happening with Herm Smith?" Of course it would be Hannah asking. "I heard he asked the Police Department to investigate the people whose names he mentioned, according to him, living in sin."

Mabel huffed a breath of air, muttering, "of course, you would ask, Hannah."

"Well, I heard Herm went off on everyone, glad I wasn't here." There was a tiff of giggles to her remark.

"We have never understood why our church ca-toes to his ridiculous way, other than he donates well. But if our memory serves us, Herm was related to Walden. You all remember Walden?" She glanced around to heads nodding. "Yeah, the tall skinny boy that was nuts for Mabel." Everyone laughed. "They say he is dead. His family said that, but we don't believe it. Herm covers for Walden and sometimes he acts like he's his cousin, but we know by now, when Herm acts the part, he believes he's that part."

Turing to Suze, she said, "I bet that got you when he made his foolish statement you were fooling around. Everyone knows you still live in Wade's shadow, you'd never go for another man, especially not on Internet." Heads wagged in agreement. Suze was studying the floor. "Makes you wonder if Herm's taken up peeping through people's windows. Did you ever see him at yours, Suze?"

"No, not that I knew of, Hannah." She was uncomfortable being center of attention. "Mabel, why are we here?" She squirmed, "I mean, other than to make lap pads for the community Nursing homes."

Christ Church

It was the meeting before the Praise and Rejoice Fest. Laurie Hutchens was at the new piano. Levi stood in the Foyer greeting the congregational members. Larry came bustling through the throng of people, arriving at Levi's side. "Hey, brother. He gave his pastor a bear hug, nearly lifting him off the floor. "Did they call you? The Police Department? They said they were going to."

Levi took out his cell. "No. Why would they call me?" At that moment the praise team from Christ Church arrived. "Excuse me, Larry. I'll get back to you. That's our other worship team."

"Man, you bless us," he said, shaking Daniel's hand. "How many do you have with you?" He was looking for Daniel's wife. "I've heard a lot about your prayer group, never knew I'd be calling you, though."

"We have five car loads," Daniel replied. "How did you hear about the group?"

"Joe and I attended Seminary together. We keep in touch, and you know your wife led our women's group. Now we are in need of all the prayer we can get. You've heard we had a man lose his senses?" He turned as Larry joined them. "Larry was starting to tell me the latest when I came to greet you."

Larry handed them each a paper, with the Police Department's logo topping the page. Daniel and Levi were scanning the page. "How could one man do all that?" Daniel shook his head, "That's time consuming." Levi noticed it had Walden's name and mentioned the fact, it was said Walden was dead.

"Maybe Walden didn't do that," Larry replied. "Herm loses his mind and goes off, as usual, but we don't know what he's doing in the meantime. He's always been a loner and one to sneak around."

"That's a strong accusation, Larry." Levi fell into his job, as Pastor. "I admit you have connection with the Police Department, but you need evidence to back up such an accusation."

"Take for instance, someone mails out those drug samples. Mailing when Herm's away. He said he went to Chicago, but that was a lie. He was tracked to St. Louis."

"I don't follow."

"Where does our mail go after it leaves here? To St. Louis. Wouldn't that be convenient? The drug packages came out of our main office, St. Louis. That's close enough, Herm could drive back home and be here when they arrive." Levi didn't understand. "Alibi, brother. Alibi," Larry sought understanding.

The first strains of the Hymn, To God Be The Glory rang out. That was Levi's cue, the Friday night meeting was about to begin. He was glad. Larry's discussion was getting too deep. Levi shook Daniel's hand again. "Glad you are here, Brother." Levi reached the podium to see Britany arrive. She came to the second pew as usual and sit down, not noticing until too late, she was sitting by Ellen and Daniel's daughter. He watched Ruthie smile as Britany's face took on a surprised expression. Iron-will against friendliness, he thought, followed by strange words in his mind. Ruthie's happiness met Britany's hostility. Lord, he said silently, must we always have a chWadege present in Shining Light Church?

Suze saw this, sitting across the aisle by Mabel on the end of the pew by the aisle. Nate came in and slid in, by Mabel. They seemed comfortable. In her mind, as quickly as that thought arrived, she remembered the man she had lost contact with on Internet but still thought of each day. Oh, Lord, deliver me, she prayed.

The Friday night preparation for The Praise and Rejoice Fest was a time of expectation. There was singing to one's content and testimony to praise the Lord for the good things in life. They were nearing the end of service when James Green stood. "Pastor, I don't know if you are aware, we are to meet in the park tomorrow and well," he paused, "how do I explain this? Well, our school, one of the clubs is having a meet, to raise money for some activity they support and well, they say there's even a dance off."

"What's a dance-off?" Helen Curry believed in getting to the bottom of what seemed a problem.

Outside, Suze stopped a minute. "Are you waiting for Nate?"

Mabel nodded. "He said he needed to speak with someone. I suspect he meant Britany." The two stood watching Christ Church people loading into cars to return home. "They don't even seem tired, do they?"

"No, it was a good meeting. I guess the Lord spoke to Pastor Levi to do this because everyone seemed in agreement and the Lord knows after Herm, we all need some kind of restitution." Suze saw Nate returning to Mable's side as the doors to Shining Light closed and the foyer light went off.

"I couldn't find her," he said. "I thought she'd come to me, but she got away quick." He sighed. "Something is a little off kilter with that girl. I feel it."

Levi and Leah shut the door behind the last person and walked out the back. In the shadow of the church, Levi stared up at the star-lit-sky. "Thank you, Lord," he said. "It was a good meeting."

Yawning, Leah asked, "How are you going to feel tomorrow night if the school dance off takes precedence over the Praise and Rejoice Festival." She smiled, tiredly. "Do you know, if Shining Light' Church's people dance and what about Brother Joe and his Christ Church people? He wasn't here."

Levi took her hand. "He had a death in the family and had to go out of town tonight. Didn't I tell you?"

"I tell you one thing, I'm too tired to dance. Whatever that bug, or virus I had it zapped me pretty good."

Driving home, Daniel was quiet. The two who had ridden with them to Shining Light, had family pick them up after the meeting. Now, he, Ellen and Ruthie were alone. He considered the news of Walden, that Larry had supplied. Something was being used by the Police Department concerning the vehicle Walden drove. He knew when Chester Mayfield left to live near his daughter, the man had access to information few in the surrounding areas were privy too.

"Are you worrying about something, Daniel?" Ellen glanced to see if Ruthie was asleep in the back seat. She wasn't.

"Thinking things over. Every place we go, there's speculation as to Smith's identity." He glanced her way. "Andrew knows nothing about what his friends are doing, searching endlessly for information to clear his name. If he did, he wouldn't want us involved. I'm afraid Andrew is giving up."

"Why would Andrew stop his friends from trying to help him? Afraid someone would get hurt?"

"That, and the fact he has false pride." Dan sighed. "He has told me; in the past he did do a few things wrong. It's as if he thinks he should be punished for things of the past. I tried to tell him, when God forgave his sins he gave him opportunity to turn his life around, a complete change. I ask him, did you break God's commandments. Did you steal? Did you dishonor your parents? We ran the whole gamut. You know what he said? He said, I was a young boy, Daniel, trying to make it. My Dad left us. My mother remarried a man that was mean to both of us and when I left, she had told me not to tell her I was going because Rufus would kill her thinking she had a part in it. Rufus was his stepdad. Not a good person, I gather."

"Young people in that situation often do things to live that the rest of us know nothing about."

"Yes, and Andrew said he was on his own from age fourteen and did whatever it took to exist."

"I don't know how to call that one," Ellen replied, "but as a mother, I would move heaven and earth to see my child cleared. "Where is Andrew's mother. And if you were accused, I would do what Anne is doing, I would do all I could to clear you.'

"Well, Mrs. Gates, I do appreciate that." He tapped the steering wheel three times. "I can't imagine Anne's strife. They went through so much. The divorce and then he straightened up and now this. If it hadn't been for the Gipson's in his life, I don't know what would've happened."

"And you," Ellen pat his arm. "You've been a good friend. How could he give up?"

"He's not given up," Ruthie said from the back seat. "But Miss Britany has decided to do something about that other stuff. I just don't know what."

Daniel looked heavenward. "Maybe she's going to dance at the Praise and Rejoice Festival." He tried to lighten the atmosphere. "Maybe, your mother and I will join the dance-off. We might win. What do you think?" By way of the visor mirror he glanced back to Ruthie. She was grinning.

"I think you will be busy doing other things, but it won't hurt you to brush up."

"Practice? Is that all you're giving me?"

Ellen's cell clicked. "I have a message from Helen Curry." She read, "two clubs are raising funds for trips to Washington, D.C. They were originally scheduled to hold their fund raiser in the Cape, but the Veterans of Foreign War are meeting there to honor their oldest living member. Out of respect the school teams moved to New Haven."

"Hmmm," Daniel quipped, "A Praise and Rejoice Fest and a high school dance off. Interesting."

"God does work in mysterious ways," Ellen replied, quietly, "His wonders to perform."

Chapter Twenty-One

He made up his mind. He was breaking out. Who did they think they were dealing with? He was tired of masquerading as his rotten cousin, that country hick. Silently, his inner laughter bubbled up, lit up his eyes and pounded through his veins. He heard the Jailer say there was a big to-do in the park; a high school fund raiser and some pious religious group meeting to sing praises. The streets would be crowded, this little hick town had little else to offer. Well, he hadn't paid this one, giving him information, like the last, but he would. The guy strut his stuff, more brawn than brain, but he had that look, he would take money any day.

So, he made mistakes; he would live with those mistakes, by not making the same one again. It was a waste of time, attending that little church with it's know it all preacher, all the while he sat there, head down as if in deep prayer. He scorned them, while he did know there was a fear to the man's creator, hadn't his grandmother drilled it into their heads, "as a man sows, so shall he reap."

He hadn't figured on that poor little rich girl messing them both up. Oh, no, she was caught up in her own selfish affair, wanting another woman's husband and willing to do whatever it takes to win him over. What about that preacher's wife? Friends with the wife of the one who she was trysting with. The silent laughter ripped through his mind again; she wasn't counting on anyone finding out, so neither she nor her husband's deacon were telling the truth to their own mate or making confession. Now, this spoiled little rich girl wanting a married man wasn't aware he knew of her past transgression. There was another knew, the man from the other church; why he felt it his duty to see after her, he could not understand. Nate, they called him. Nate. Watching over the poor little rich girl who went after another man in another setting and the man's wife came after her with a ball bat. Two black eyes later, she was home to Momma and Daddy. Except it was not her momma and daddy, it was Matt's parents. Clarity was regaining control of his mind.

People and places became clearer. He decided, at two o'clock he would escape while music in the park was playing and everyone's attention was on the young people trying to make sales. He could sponsor them in a minute, pay all their way to Washington, D.C. The Jailer came back to question him. Are you related to the rich guy that lives in the woods? Are you him? Are you Herm Smith, or, are you that Walden fellow? Tell me about your life. Just sit here and fill me in. We got all the time in the world.

He listened to the idiot trying to find answers. So, they didn't know if he was Herm or Walden? The laughter nearly escaped his body. He knew who he was. He had spent years away from New Haven after Grandmama died, became educated on the money she set aside for him; climbed the ladder, married for money, that one was a strong-minded woman. Still, he established his own business but he took on that young cub, as wicked and evil as himself. That was the beginning of his down fall, but he regained his power. Dead, they said he was dead. He was as alive as one could live. Sometimes his brain did shift and for a while he seemed to lose control. He wasn't always able to remember what he did during those times, when his head hurt terrible, Grandmama said he was dangerous to himself and others, only then, other times, she said he was smart and powerful and could bend people to his way of thinking.

Through the open window he heard the day progress. The band played. The Holy Rollers sang. A praise song. Goodness and mercy, shall follow me, he heard the words and he writhed in anxiety. "Shut the window," he screamed to the jailer and heard vile laughter. He had to think. The singing continued, "Peace like a river," his head pounded in agony. He tried to put that behind him, he had made a pact with the devil and still Grandmama's words filtered through his agony. "You must make peace with God and get this anger and ill will toward others out of your system. No one has hurt you anymore than the next person, get over it and try to live a life of peace and calm." At that moment, he could have snuffed out her life but a part of him loved her. She was all he'd ever known. She had flaws. He saw them, but in her own way, she loved him and as she lay dying, she wanted him to have peace in his soul. Maybe she needed that peace for herself. Words to the song, came through the window, "I was sinking deep in sin, far…." He glanced at the clock on the wall. Five minutes til two. Would they sing all day?

Walking Main Street, Levi nodded and acknowledged people's greeting. "Beautiful Day." Yes, it was. "It's been a successful day for the young people," a man from Christ Church, smiled at New Haven's pastor. "My nephew is in the group. He thinks they will all go to Washington, D.C."

"Good news," Levi replied. He saw a lone figure sitting across the street in the Park's gazebo. "Isn't that Britany?" Leah saw the question in his eyes.

"You said you have to speak with Daniel. Go find him. I'll test the waters and visit her while you do." She left him and crossed the street, stepping onto the wooden floor of the gazebo.

"Mind if I join you?"

"Why would you want to?" Britany stared beyond Leah. In the distance she saw the pastor join a man from the Cape.

Leah extended a hand. "I thought we could get acquainted. I'm Levi Merkel's wife, He's pastor of…."

"I know who you are." Britany raised her sunglasses, momentarily. "Put your hand down, I don't need it." Britany ignored Leah. "I often attend your husband's church. I don't need you."

"You don't need a friend?" Leah sat, opposite her. "That's all I was offering."

"Friendship never works."

"What would make it work?"

"To be left alone. I don't need your fake concern, just leave."

Leah winced. "Are you that miserable? It's a beautiful day. Look at these beautiful young people needing encouragement."

Britany was rising from the seat. "Are you leaving, or am I?' Leah stood and looked into Britany's face, studying her.

"Are you well?"

"That's unexpected." Britany's head dropped. "Please, don't insult me with fake kindness. Don't pretend…"

"I'm not pretending." Leah sit back down and stared up into Britany's face. "I've been there, where I suspect you are, miserable, maybe for different reasons, but I've been there." She sighed. "It's not easy being a pastor's wife. You don't always know who you can trust. Not that I refer to anything wrong in life, but sometimes you just need someone you can share with…things that trouble you."

"Isn't that what husbands are for?" As though the strength left her to defy anyone in her way, Britany spoke in a low voice. "Since the day my parents died, I've had no one. No one believes in me." Defiance returned as she stared hard at Leah. "I answer to no one. Do you understand? My parent saw to my material needs."

"You need more than your parents' material care for you, in their absence," Leah replied, softly.

"You have caught me at a vulnerable moment. I don't like that, it robs me of my determination to make it on my own....I," Britany faltered, "I realize you do mean kindness, but I'm unused to that and I need to leave." She started to walk away.

"Are you on medication?" Leah, faltered. "I don't know why that came to me."

"I am. I needed something to buoy me up, but whatever I was given isn't working."

Leah felt her breath catch in her own body. How had God slipped that information into her mind. "I know there's a story circulates, that New Haven is suspected of being a drug underworld, here where the charm of the city spills over into our lives and seems impossible." She saw Britany's hesitance. "If you are taking drugs, be careful who your supplier is. Go to a doctor for medical assistance."

Britany's laugh was resentful and full of scorn. "Are you implying I would help such low life?"

Leah took a deep breath, a prayer to God for his help, before she replied. "I only meant, there's word circulates, here, even through Shining Light Church congregation, whoever is behind the impact of drugs on this little community is dangerous, cares for no one and would kill to protect how he makes his money."

"That sounds very cladistic," Britany, smirked, "not becoming knowledge for a Pastor's wife." She leaned toward Leah. "I'll repay your obvious display of kindness, whether genuine, or not. I am aware of what you are hesitant to mention. Here is my kindness in return. Be careful on the street." She stepped away and was outside the gazebo. "There, I have repaid your kindness. I owe you nothing."

"Britany, wait. Put my number in your phone. If you ever need me, trust me and call me." Leah had her hand out. Instead of touching her, Britany handed over her cell. Understanding, Leah entered her own number and gave the phone back.

Pocketing the phone, Britany started away, as she said, "Remember, be careful on the streets."

Levi returned with Daniel and family in tow. His glance to Leah, seemed to infer the visit had not gone well. Leah was stooping to hug Ruthie. "You are a welcome sight," she said. "Come sit, tell me what's going on."

Levi could not pass the moment, as he turned to Daniel. "Do you, by chance recognize the young woman we just met that did not speak? Britany?" He glanced to Leah for the last name, but Daniel was letting the question pass over to Ellen.

"Ellen knows who you speak of because she is friends with the woman who oversaw the renovation of your church." Ellen rolled her eyes, that Daniel was handing the conversation over to her.

"Britany grew up as neighbor to Matthew, Marigold's husband, and she had tried to reenter his life, but the problem is, he has a wife and child and another on the way, so it's not a good situation."

"Something strange, came out of our conversation, just now, she said we are to be careful on the street."

Ellen and Leah's eyes held, and then slid to Ruthie, a child in their midst.

"She's not well, today," Ruthie spoke up. Daniel realized Ruthie had picked up on something. "Is she stable, Ruthie?" Ruthie was shaking her head. "I don't know, Daddy Daniel. I didn't get to touch her. I just saw her face as we walked by. She is troubled."

Levi gave a deep sigh, outwardly concerned. "If she gave warning, that means something will happen. She's new to our congregation and I'd say she is different than when I first met her. Not long after she came into our fellowship, she," he searched for a word to describe Britany. "She seems, almost brain washed. I first thought she was one of those self-centered people wanting their own way, but now it seems almost as though, someone else is instructing her what to do." He glanced to Leah…for support.

"Like, one on mind bending drugs…?" Ellen asked. "This is getting to be a deep subject." She glanced to Ruthie, realizing had Ruthie touched Britany, she would have an insight into the woman's thought. "Has there been anything strange happening to your congregation. I mean, other than the destroyed paintings?"

"Oh, my word," Leah replied. "If you only knew." At that moment, Mabel passed by, Nate close behind her.

"Better get a move on," Mabel called out. "They're getting ready for the Dance-off. What a perfect day."

"Leah and I might not make the grade," Levi called back. "We'll leave it to our visitors." He grinned. "Do you two dance?"

"Number seven here, we have to pin the numbers on our back. You ready, Sweetheart?" Daniel gave Ellen a funny mocking expression of Groucho Marx, his eyebrows raising up and down. "Come on, Ruthie, girl, let's see what your Dad-o can do."

Ellen bent down and looked into Ruthie's eyes. "Keep watch, Darling, and keep an eye on that lady we just met. Don't go after her, if she leaves, but always keep her in your line of vision. You understand?"

Chapter Twenty-Two

Inside the Municipal Jail, the lone prisoner heard the song they had rehearsed all week long. He had his two in readiness, but would they carry through? Had they practiced, as promised? His blood seemed to quell in anxiety. He found his shoes, where the hick jailer had placed them, slipped open the lining and dipped below into the hollowed heel. Here, was what he needed, today most of all, saved to give him strength. Without fluid, he swallowed down the drug that made him more powerful than any other.

"Number Seven take the floor." The Grand Master, called out as the band struck up a new song. Daniel and Ellen stepped out as Marigold and Ruthie dipped and swayed on the side line. It was a kaleidoscope of color, a stream of humanity feeling the surge of music in their bones with happiness on faces. The music was loud, the drums prevalent. It was a wonder the gun shot was heard. The bullet flew through the air, over their heads, into the Cypress trees beyond. Ellen saw Ruthie's expression, her eyes wide in fear.

"Daniel. Ruthie." Ellen's voice cried out in the din of those who heard, but did not understand what was happening. Ellen tried to point to her child. Daniel was trying to take in the melee of activity. They were lost in the throng of bodies trying to escape as gun shots sound in the air and no one knew where to hide.

Everything felt in slow motion. Ellen saw her child, Marigold's hand reaching out to Ruthie, the pastor and his wife from Shining

Light trying to get out of the sidelines as the street became a scrambled mass of humanity and she prayed to God, take care of us, Father, we do not know what to do.

Marigold reached for Ruthie, finally grasping her hand, "run, Ruthe, run." She was practically dragging the child. But Ruthie's eyes were searching beyond.

"She's by herself," Ruthie was crying as they ran. "I'm supposed to be watching her, Momma said."

"Who? Ruthie. Who?" Marigold was pulling Ruthie toward a stand of trees.

"She needs my help. She's sick."

"How do you know, Ruthie. How do you know she is sick?" Marigold pushed Ruthie down. A hedge of shrubbery beneath a row of Crepe Myrtles, was there only shelter from the chaos of people fleeing for their lives and the rash of gun shots over their heads. Band students had thrown down instruments, metal chairs were obstacles in the way of those running for their lives. Some one screamed, "Sniper."

From beneath Marigold, thrown across her body, she saw Britany was no longer in the chair. She lay huddled on the ground. "She's not moving," Ruthie moaned as someone removed Marigold. She heard Marigold explaining Britany was down the street, lying on the ground, not moving. At that moment, Ruthie went into action. She heard Matt's voice, comforting Marigold. He would take care of her. She must get to Britany.

Matt pulled Marigold into his arms. "It was on the news; I was almost home when I heard it and I came to New Haven. Babe. Babe. What are you saying, Ruthie is not with you. Are you sure?" Together, they scanned the turmoil of the street. "Down there," he pointed. Matt set their course to arrive at Ruthie holding on to Britany. He pulled Britany from the street. Together, Marigold, Ruthie and Matt carrying Bethany made their way back to the security of the trees.

In the distance they could hear the siren of an ambulance arriving. Within minutes, the ambulance attendees were seeing to Britany's needs.

Marigold could hardly bear to turn loose of Ruthie. A local News station had arrived to film the chaos. "You, Sir." The man tried to make contact with Ruthie's parents, along with Pastor Levi and Leah. He was taking in Daniel, gripping a woman he suspected was his wife, and a little girl, his daughter. "Sir," he smiled, "I hope that woman you are kissing is your wife. Since we have you on camera," he finished lamely.

Levi had his arm around Leah. "Thank you, Jesus." He couldn't describe his feelings. "Praise, God. It seems no one else is hurt."

"The bullets were flying overhead, but one mis-fire and someone could have died." The Cameraman was aiming toward Daniel, as the reporter ask Daniel, "are you a minister?"

"No, he is." Daniel pointed to Levi.

"Why are you here, Pastor?"

"I live here. We were having a Praise Festival." In the background Daniel gave Matt a bearhug. "This is my wife, back there," Something seemed to make his knees almost buckle, realization, he supposed of what they had just experienced. "Back there, people from the neighboring community." Daniel was introducing Matt. It was all just too crazy. "Glad to meet you, brother," he was saying to Matt," his eyes taking in the woman Matt was holding by the hand, "and I'm assuming our renovation expert is your wife?"

"You got that right." Matt was grinning ear to ear as a second cameraman appeared and whispered to the reporter. No one cared the reporter moved on, but they overheard the discussion of the two.

The Cameraman was filming the strewn instruments on the lawn. "Looks like a storm hit, folks," the reporter was saying. "There's another story here, we're told, during this melee of destruction, the local Jail report a prisoner escaped. Turns out, there's a theory the jailer may be instrumental in his escape."

"If we have to endure such as this," Marigold was saying, "wouldn't you wish this was the beginning of clearing Andrew? It was rumored, Herm was Walden that was supposed to have died, though there was no proof, unless they dig up the man they buried, supposedly not Walden. Now, whoever was put in jail is gone."

"Babe, where do you get this information?" Matt gave her an intent look. "And what about you are you all right? Ruthie said you were running?"

"Was I running?" Marigold began to laugh. "I didn't know I could still run…but I do listen to the locals talk about Walden. It seems they have more stories to tell about him than Andrew ever shared."

The evening news was rife with stories of gun shots, high school students and a few people from the local church, celebrating a Praise Fest. No one had answers of how the prisoner obtained a gun. It was speculated the prisoner had help in escaping. The reporter ended the evening news, "let us understand, the bystanders in today's event are glad it is over, with good reason."

The group had convened to the church. Mabel had instructed the ladies of the church to deliver remaining food to the church kitchen. Dan noticed Ruthie staring off into the distance. "You are awfully quiet. I know you are tired but I also know that look. What are you seeing, Honey?"

"Daddy, I keep seeing an old house, I've never seen it before, so I don't know why it stays with me."

"Levi," Daniel explained, "We need to let you in on something, you may not know. Our Ruthie has a gift." He reached for Ruthie's hand. "She never uses it, except for the glory of God to help someone in need." The Pastor was listening to Daniel as the group grew silent. "Ruthie, can you tell us anything, else?"

"I think it's a cornfield that has a road leading through it. The house is very old at the end of the road. The windows have only broken glass in them and there used to be a porch, but the posts are setting on the ground, now, and the floor has rotted away. There's a mailbox out front, but there's someone needs help."

Levi stared at the people. "Does this mean any thing to anyone?" No one made connection but Larie and Jake Hutchens were joining the group and Levi called them up front. "We don't know this community as you do. Listen to this little girl's description of a place that might be around here, and see if you know it." Everyone listened again, as Ruthie concluded, "And there's an old horn on the mailbox."

Laurie nodded. "Why are you interested in the old Horn Place?"

Jake offered, "I don't think anyone goes back there, except maybe the farmer who plants corn on it."

Dan and Matt made eye contact. Levi stood up to join the two who were leaving. "Jake, I believe these men will need you to lead the way. Fellows, I'd say this is a good time to kiss your wife, before you leave."

"Now, why would he say that?" Laurie was confused. "I mean, I know we've been through a lot today, and I was scared to death, but no one got hurt. I checked and Britany had taken the wrong meds, but the old Horn place?" She was perplexed. "One of the girls was my friend, but Mr. and Mrs. Horn died a few years back. The place is falling down and you can't see it when the corn grows all around it."

Ruthie sat smiling at Laurie. "I think we met, didn't we, Ruthie?" Laurie asked. "And you gave me the most precious smile. You knew, didn't you, that I was expecting a baby, way before Jake or I knew."

"I saw you in my mind but I hadn't met you. Marigold asked me if Miss Leah was going to have a baby? I couldn't tell her. God is responsible for everything but sometimes he uses me as his person. I cannot explain how it feels."

"And you don't have to," Leah replied. "You are an instrument of God's peace and we are most thankful God allows you in our lives. I know your parents guard your privacy that your gift never gets into wrong hands."

Two hours passed and the women were becoming anxious over the men not returning. "I'm exhausted," Marigold asked, "What do you think, Ellen, should we go home and let the men ride home together?"

"Why don't we wait just a few, and then we will feel better about leaving."

"I have a question, then. Laurie, there's something I don't understand, the lady that bought the piano for your church, how did she get mixed up with Herm Smith, or whoever he is, the Walden person?"

"First, Leah can explain that better than me, Laurie replied, "You seem to know her."

"I do," Marigold replied. "She and my husband, Matt grew up next door to each other. His mother chose Britany to be her son's wife, but Matt chose me, and it is a thorn in Britany's side, although she left him and married another." She gave a weary sigh. "How is she connected to the man named Walden?"

"I'm trying to be a Minister's wife, here," Leah explained. "I'm not sure. And if you mean, does Levi know? I don't think so." She giggled. "I must be tired, I just thought of Levi's secretary, Tully. Now, I believe he's scared of her, but he doesn't let on, except sometimes to say, "boy, she's tough."

Laurie was standing. "This baby is tightening up in me, I'm going to have to walk to settle it down."

"It?" Marigold asked. "You know, by now. Don't you?"

"We decided to wait for our baby's arrival, but oh, my goodness, I'm going outside and walk the block."

"We'll all go," the group chorused.

They had only walked a short distance when Dan's suburban came into sight. The men were soon piling out. Laurie called out, "Did you find the old Horn Place?"

"You won't believe it." Jake came to meet his wife. "Remember Ruthie said someone needed help?" He scratched his head. "Someone did need help. We found Herm Smith tied to the only standing front porch post."

"What do you mean?" Laurie gave Jake a worried look. "You mean he was…"

"It's a wonder he's alive. He was practically incoherent. We don't know how long he'd been there, I mean, today's happening couldn't have made him that thin, this quick, like I mean really thin. Starved."

"We took him to the facility down town that's associated with Cape hospital," Daniel explained to Ellen. "As a Nurse, you would have known what to do, we didn't, but now they're transferring him to the Cape."

"He looks bad," Matt added. "Skin and bones, I'd describe him. No telling how long he's been there."

"Then," Marigold said, "It couldn't have been him in the jail that escaped." She shuddered. "Why do I get the feeling you aren't telling us everything?"

"You were hoping something from today would clear Andrew, but so far, we have nothing."

Dan could see his two were tired. "Let's go home. Everyone's had a longer day than they imagined." They were all thanking each other for sharing a stressful time. Ruthie kissed Laurie and Leah on the cheek, but it was Marigold she clasped arms around her neck and said, I love you. Everyone heard Marigold reply, I love you, too. Daniel had a sickening thought. Walden had threatened to go after

Andrew's family. He wondered, would Walden know to look for them at Harriet's house, when they weren't at home?

"You are quiet, Daniel. What are you keeping to yourself?" She glanced to the back seat. "She's asleep. You can tell me."

Pulling on to the Interstate, Dan set the cruise control above the speed limit. But that wasn't enough. He pressed his foot to the gas pedal and the Suburban shot forward. Sixty miles to the Cape and he needed to be there now.

Chapter Twenty-Three

Weren't they the devious ones? He saw the signs, front and backyard, protected by. He laughed. No security system in the world was good enough to keep out. If he wanted in, there were ways. He leaned against the screen door to the porch. No noise came from the house. The garage door was down. No windows. He couldn't tell if there was a vehicle inside or not. Returning to the front, he stepped onto the porch and rang the doorbell. No one answered.

A kid in the next yard was watching him. Storing the bag, he carried, back in the Van, he walked over to the kid. "Don't suppose you know if the Graves are home?"

"They're at Miss Harriet's." He saw the man needed more information. "Miss Harriet Becker."

"How would you know?"

"Andy told me." The boy was wary, his eyes appeared a bit scared. "Andy's five. I'm four."

"You shouldn't be out here, alone, especially close to the road. You could get hurt."

"I didn't do anything wrong. Who would hurt me."

"You never know. I might. Get back inside. Now. Before I leave." The kid was off and running. He stood behind the screened door watching as Walden laughed, looking down at the toy the boy dropped. He picked it up and put it in his pocket. Taking the guard's cell phone from the shirt he'd taken off the guard, too, he found a residence and phone number for a Harriet Becker. The name had a familiar ring and it came to him. "The old rich dame who wouldn't contribute when I was running for office." He threw back his head and laughed, noticing the little boy slammed the door as he went inside the house. His body shook with victory. He'd give the old bag a visit and settle a score at the same time. He was in charge, again. His blood veins tingled with anticipation. Harriet Becker, here I come.

His stomach rumbled. He didn't have time, but then why not? He had all the time in the world. He was in charge. "She's old money, as I recall." He always talked to himself, when he was making plans. "Old house, Old brick street where all the rich live, as I recall. They wouldn't let us in. Didn't like us. Now, look at what they got? Hippies buying up old wealth houses, but not hers, you can bet. Pristine and guarded."

"Stomach issue, settled," he said. "Check one." He pulled away from the fast-food diner. He'd stayed longer than intended. "Phone. Check two. Gun." He took it from the console. "Check three." His head was hurting, but that would end once he reached his destination. Andrew's wife would be with the old dame, Harriet Becker. I'm coming for you, Harriet Becker and you too, Anna." It troubled him, for a minute. Was her name Anna, or Anne? "Such a fine line," he giggled. "I wonder how old Herm's doing. He should be dead by now, if the guys did their work right."

Within ten minutes he had cased the house from the brick street. Pristine, all right. He reached down for the gun, placed in the back band of his trousers. Here he was. Clint Eastwood and Roy Rogers, all in one. Ready for action.

Harriet saw the throw of light cross the sheers at the window and stepped across the floor from kitchen to gathering room to peer through the filmy material out on to the street. A man was getting out of a van. He wasn't dressed the best, and appeared a bit bedraggled. Most who came to her door, were clean if nothing else, even in the shadows of the street lamp, this man was on his last leg. Something didn't set right.

Hattie had stayed late. Something in her gut, said, don't hurry home tonight. Gut feeling, she surmised, looking out at the man heading toward Miss Harriet's door. Miss Harriet was inside. Hattie had been with Miss Anne watching the children. But the boys needed a drink. She'd gone inside to the little refrigerator Miss Harriet installed for the purpose of taking care of the children's needs. Hattie saw the gun in the man's hand. Her mind went into action. Mr. Becker had a gun when he was alive. Where had she seen that gun, away from small children's hands, but where?

She slipped into Mr. Becker's office. She'd dust those books for years. One after another, she slipped the books from the top shelf. And there it was. Was it loaded? She thought Mr. Becker said, why have a gun in the house, and up-high, unloaded? Shuddering, she took the gun. Where could she hide it? Her pocket wasn't deep enough. Could she do it? She couldn't place it between her breast, but maybe.... yes, she stuck under her arm, there in the band of her woman garment. It stayed. She let her arm down, covering the cold metal. If she made a mistake, she prayed she'd done the job intended, first.

Anne was completely engrossed in the children. Hattie saw Harriet hurrying through the house and out the door. She couldn't know the man was coming around the side of the house. Hattie hurried to the phone. He was moving slow, not to alert Anne, but Miss Harriet must know, there was alarm in her voice, when she called, "Anne, children, hurry in, quickly." The children never hurry, Hattie was thinking.

Again, Hattie tried the phone. There was no sound. Outside, she heard the man's voice. "Harriet Becker. Long time, no see. Remember me? You wouldn't donate to my campaign; said we needed no more riff-raff in our county." He gave his diabolical laugh. "Hurd those little children into my view, mighty one. Let me see what you've got here." Harriet Becker eyed him, arms akimbo, as though she protected the children. His laugh deepened. "You didn't believe in me then, but you will this time, after I collect what I've come for." He watched the young woman pull the children together, in a huddle.

"What do you want? Who are you? If it's money you want, I'll pay. These children haven't done anything to you."

"But you did, you old bag." He circled her. "Thought you were too good for the likes of me."

"I'm sorry, I don't remember you. Perhaps, at the time, I made a mistake. I apologize."

"Get down on the ground and we'll see how sorry you are." She seemed ready to resist, but he brandished the gun. Menacing, Walden waved the gun toward the children as Becker fell to her knees.

Anne saw his face, for the first time, realizing it was the man from the picture Andrew had shown her. "You're him," her voice was more a sob, "the man my husband is accused of murdering, aren't you?"

"Aren't you the smart one? I'm the one your husband stole from. He took half the contraband. But that's beside the point. When he dies in my place, he will have earned it. When I kill you, I will settle our debt." His eyes strayed to the children, "but before I relieve you of your pain, you and the little boys need to come with us to your house to retrieve the rest."

"My house?" Anne's expression was troubled. "I don't have anything."

"You don't know?" Walden cackled. "Of course, you don't know. My goons hid it, beneath your house. Don't worry, it won't be harmed, it's in an air tight container. I knew if the law found it, they'd blame dear sweet Andrew, your beloved. The one who left my step daughter at the altar, disgraced her, but to my liking. I'll remember to thank him. Just think, if he'd found it and sold it, he would be a rich man."

Anne pulled the boys tighter against her body. Her body was shaking, to the point she could hardly stand, but for them. Her eyes were on Harriet. Harriet spoke up. "Don't take the children. What kind of man would do that?" Walden's laughter sliced through the air. Walking to Harriet he placed the gun against her head. Dodging his arm, Harriet saw Hattie on the side of the house behind Walden. She was motioning. Harriet shuddered; Hattie was holding something but was it enough?

"Move out," Walden said. Anne held a hand of each kid to march them to the van on the street."

He never knew what hit him. They had begun the trek to the van, cleared the first corner and approached the second where the tall Arborvitae grew. Anne was holding the boys hands so tight, they began to cry. The crying seemed to agitate Walden. It was then, Hattie came flying from behind the spread of the tree and swung hard, hitting Walden on the side of the head with the flat side of a twelve-inch black iron skillet. He stumbled, dropping the gun. Harriet was close enough to grab it. Walden was trying to reach whoever owned the skillet. He grabbed for an apron string. Hattie swung again. Fearing Harriet would stumble, now, Anne was holding the gun.

Hattie had Walden on the ground when he decided to make a move. Upsetting Hattie, he reached for the skillet, prepared to swing, when a bullet hit the ground in front of his feet. Walden fell, face down. Daniel eased up, behind Hattie and reached the length of her arm to retrieve the gun.

Daniel heaved a heartfelt sigh. Thank you, God, he whispered. Now that he had Walden face down, he wrapped the torn strings of Hattie's apron around the man's hands. Walden a bit addled, laid his face on the ground and closed his eyes. Anne walked a distance, picked up the second gun and laid them away from the children. Ellen and Ruthie came from the side of the house and folded her into their arms. Daniel registered it all, as in a bad dream. He knew, without a doubt, Walden would have killed them all.

Chapter Twenty-Four

Andrew would be released, "as soon as proper test are run," the Chief of Police told the reporter from Cape's number one newspaper. "Statistics say our man is Walden, but we have to be certain. His personal records will prove his identity." He uncuffed Graves. "A special unit is at your home, Graves, to retrieve stolen goods Walden says he personally hired two thugs to store, unknown to you. Are you certain you have no knowledge of the supply of drugs being beneath your home?" He waited, a courteous gesture for Andrew's reply. "Stay, close. You understand? Don't think to leave town, we will be on you." The Chief was working on a stack of papers. "Give me a few to complete these, and you can go."

Walden's laughter rang throughout the facility. "That pretty boy? Chief, are you crazy? He knows nothing of what I'm capable of, nor do you. You think this is over?" His laughter seemed diabolical, even to the hardened Chief of Police. He realized Graves wanted to face his opponent. He nodded, permission and watched as the one he was releasing walked the hall to face Walden.

"You're so smart?" Andrew gave Walden a stone eyed stare. "You messed with my life, you tried to kidnap my family. Will I testify against you and all the demonic worthless situations I recall? When you threatened my life and those I love and I got so deep into your world it's a wonder I could crawl out?"

Walden knew an enemy when he faced one. "I raised, you, boy. You think you own your soul? I do."

Turning back, Andrew pointed toward Heaven. "You have never owned my soul. While I was with you, I wasn't even aware I had one, but thank God, He saw worth in the life he created in me and gave me another chance. God placed me in the home of a man and woman that knew Him. Do you understand? They know God and they offered His salvation to me, through love and caring for a man that had nearly lost his life to burn in hell, just as you will, if you don't change your ways."

Walden smirked. "You think God wants me? After I sold out to the devil? Look what I achieved. Riches."

"What good will riches do you if you burn in hell?" Andrew looked on Walden in pity. "Think about it."

Walden could stand anything but pity. He beat his hand against his chest. "You have no idea what I can do. You think this is finished? It's not over. Guard your little family, Graves, my men are still out there."

The Chief of Police was listening. As he thought, there would be repercussion. Walden was a danger to society but first he would call on his henchmen to settle the score with Graves. He sighed, wearily, he would put a detail on the man's home, but how could he follow every step of Graves and his family?

"Your ride's here," he said, handing Andrew a sheaf of papers. Andrew saw Matthew's truck parked on the curb. "I told him I'd send you right out. Be safe." The Chief offered his hand and Andrew took it.

Matt was on the phone, speaking with Daniel. "Yeah, the Chief called me, said Andrew ask I pick him up. They got Walden, shortly after he made it to the Cape." Matt laughed. "I didn't know you were instrumental in the capture. When the chief filled me in, I laughed like crazy. It was joy, brother. Joy." He listened to Dan's reply. "No need being so humble. Chief said they'll put him away for life, if they can't prove he killed, he still has so much against him he can't be turned loose on society."

Hattie was in her element, serving iced tea, canapes and cucumber sandwiches by the dozen to the group that had gathered at Miss Harriet's home. She was taking it all in stride, enjoying their teasing of her expertise with an iron skillet. "He done tore the strings off my apron," she replied. "Miss Harriet done had to find me another apron. No ma'am, we still got the skillet."

Before leaving, Daniel asked, "Matt, could you lead us in a moment of prayer as we are thankful no one was hurt?"

"Well, Herm Smith was hurt, if it hadn't been for our Ruthie seeing him on the old Horn homestead, he might have died. I admit, it is a bit far out that the story goes, he and Britany are on the same floor in the hospital and have become somewhat of a couple." Ellen relayed the information to the group.

Marigold sighed. "I'm telling you; Britany made my life miserable but I wish her no harm. I pray she finds happiness." Impishly, Marigold looked into Matt's face, "but never with my husband."

Everyone bowed heads as Matt led. "Heavenly Father, you have watched over us and brought us through another time of conflict, as our lives have joined with our sister church family and friends, Lord, we come to you thanking you for being with us, for giving protection where needed, and for looking into our lives that are joined by faith and your guidance as we live out our lives as your children. Dear God, it is times like these we realize our cup does run over because of your mercy and grace. We thank you, Father, in your Holy name.

Amen." Marigold stood on tiptoe to kiss Matt, and then wiped the tears from his cheeks. She was almost ready to time to deliver the new baby and today she had been under gun fire.

On Monday, Levi called Joe. "Just wanted to thank you again, for joining us in the Praise and Rejoice Fest that turned into a scene like a fight at the last corral." He listened to Joe's description and then laughed. "I guess we are back to normal, whatever that is." Tully interrupted with information he was to pass on to Joe. "Word here, is Britany is being released today, but not allowed to go home alone. It seems she will be staying with one of our own, Mabel Hisaw." Levi and Joe closed their conversation and Levi turned to Tully.

"What's on your mind? You have that look."

"Well," Tully began, still shuffling papers as she spoke. "Laurie Hutchens will be taking leave of absence, to have a baby and we are going to need someone to play piano and as I understand the woman who bought the piano for our church is an accomplished pianist, you might look into her taking Laurie's place."

Levi scratched his head, waiting, "What else?"

"We aren't supposed to judge people, are we? It seems when she purchased the piano, someone knew she had a rather colorful past and they didn't want her sitting in front of the congregation, you know as though she wore a scarlet letter, or something?"

"Just give me the regular talk, so I can understand." Levi, said, "I'm no good at figurine out woman talk."

Tully came to stand at his desk. "Pastor, people take sides, they judge each other as easily as they take comfort from one another. Must I elaborate on this? A church holds many secrets, things we keep in a safe place of our heart for years, is it that difficult to grasp? We aren't supposed to judge each other, that's God's work."

"Tully, if I had the experience you have, with this congregation, I might be a better Pastor."

"You are doing all right. We need you to lead. Be our shepherd, care about us, forgive us as Jesus said, when we do wrong, and let God's mercy and grace spread through our midst in a way we will love each other and grow into the people He wants us to be."

"Thank you, Tully. With you to remind and keep me in line, I'd love to grown right along with the rest."

When the phone rang, Tully said, "Jake Hutchens wants you and Leah in his office at five this afternoon."

Levi found Leah down the hall, in the ladies sewing room, talking with Mabel. "I'm not good with a needle," she was saying.

"What we decide," Mabel glanced up to acknowledge Levi's presence. "We decided after the Gates lady met with us; a short devotional set us on the right path to work together in the spirit of love and friendship." She waited for her words to soak in on Leah. "We'd like for our Pastor's wife to give us that blessing. What do you say?"

Levi filled Leah in on the appointment and picked her up from home when the time drew near.

Jake's last appointment was running late. "I wanted to tell you something," Leah said, as she and Levi sit alone, in the waiting room. "It's about when I was away. We have never taken time to discuss what I did."

"Whatever you did, is all right by me," Levi replied. "I'm so happy you returned to me. I hope it was a time that we both realized our life together is Christ blessed and no one or any situation could ever cause us to doubt each other." He took her hand into his own. "Is that good enough for you?"

She sighed. "Yes, but Levi, I…"

"I love you." He said, and kissed her on the lips. "That's all we need." Leah smiled at him through tears.

Jake came to the door and welcomed them into his office as his last patient left the office. "You two, are incredible. I've left you several messages and I have seen you a few times but always in the presence of others. Why didn't you return my calls?"

"We've been busy, Jake and Leah had her hands full with trying to recover that virus thing."

"Suddenly, I'm feeling a bit scared, Jake." Leah, reached for Levi's hand. "Did something come back wrong with my test?"

"Different," Jake replied, "not wrong, just different. You both need to know." Levi and Leah leaned forward; their expressions concerned. "You are going to have a baby."

"What?"

There was a knock at the door, before it opened a crack. "Come on in," Jake waved Laurie into the room. She saw the wide eyed expression on Levi and Leah's faces.

"Is everything all right?"

"Leah has something to tell you," Jake said, a smile beginning to slide across his face lighting his eyes.

"Oh, my goodness, you two look like you've seen a ghost. Is it that bad." She had her eyes on the couple and completely missed her husband's smiling face.

Tears were running down Leah's cheeks. "I'm pregnant. I had almost given up." Laurie was hugging her until she thought the breath was being squeezed out of her. Jake was reaching over to check Levi's pulse.

"I couldn't keep this to myself much longer. I was beginning to think we'd have to call a business meeting at the church." Jake was laughing and proud for everyone concerned. "God is so good."

"When?" Laurie was asking.

Jake glanced out the window, "I'd say about the time tulips bloom, next Spring."

Shining Light church took on a new glow. Babies were being born in to the congregation. Forgiveness was in play as the new lady in the congregation played the piano in Laurie's three month leave, sitting on the front pew so she could slip out quickly if her and Jake's new baby made a sound. The pastor's wife was with child and seemed happier than ever. Mabel Hisaw had a man come most Sundays for worship service, slipping into the seat beside her, smiling first to Mabel and then at Miss Britany, playing the piano. It seemed Shining Light had become a beacon to the neighborhood. Attendance was growing, fellowship was good.

Suze Norman sat quietly, listening to Pastor Levi. "Secret things belong unto the Lord, our God," he was saying. "Those beautiful times we commune with him on things no one else would understand, whether private or shared, we find He blesses us in the utmost way and allows us to commune with him on situations we find difficult to explain to others." Her secret was safe. Herm had not mentioned it again. She wondered, had he guessed she communicated on Internet with a man? For a minute a twinge of sadness worked its way through her heart. She had loved Wade, and would never forget her husband. But the man who called her my lady and seemed to enjoy conversation with her was not forgotten, either. "I'm coming to meet you, My Lady," he said. Sometimes she had regrets and wished out of the state of her own loneliness, they could have met. He seemed to be a gentleman and one of God's own.

THE END

Follow

The continuing story of Suze Norman

SERENDIPITY ON ANGELS WINGS

BY

BETTY LOWREY

www.ingramcontent.com/pod-product-compliance
Lightning Source LLC
Chambersburg PA
CBHW061430150726
47987CB00001B/164
* 9 7 9 8 9 9 0 6 8 1 8 5 9 *